VENOMOUS

WOMAN

Recent Titles in
Contributions in Women's Studies

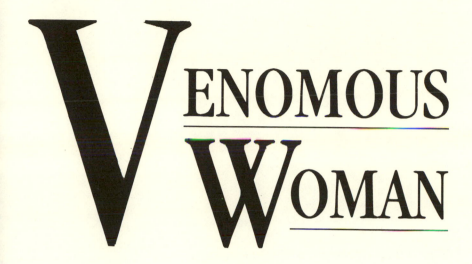

VENOMOUS WOMAN

Fear of the Female in Literature

MARGARET HALLISSY

Contributions in Women's Studies, Number 87

GREENWOOD PRESS

New York
Westport, Connecticut
London

Library of Congress Cataloging-in-Publication Data

Hallissy, Margaret.
  Venomous woman.

  (Contributions in women's studies, ISSN 0147-104X ;
no. 87)
  Bibliography: p.
  Includes index.
    1. Women in literature.   2. Poisoning in literature.
I. Title.   II. Series.
PN56.5.W64H35   1987   809'.93352042   87-10711
ISBN 0-313-25919-4 (lib. bdg. : alk. paper)

British Library Cataloguing in Publication Data is available

Library of Congress Catalog Card Number: 87-10711
ISBN: 0-313-25919-4
ISSN: 0147-104X

First published in 1987

Greenwood Press, Inc.
88 Post Road West, Westport, Connecticut 06881

Printed in the United States of America

The paper used in this book complies with the
Permanent Paper Standard issued by the National
Information Standards Organization (Z39.48-1984).

10 9 8 7 6 5 4 3 2 1

To my daughters

And if any woman becomes so proficient as to be able to write down her thoughts, let her do so and not despise the honor but rather flaunt it instead of fine clothes, necklaces, and rings. For these may be considered ours only by use, whereas the honor of being educated is ours entirely.

Louise Labé (c. 1520–1566)

Contents

Preface: Secret Weapon

> Trust none of the dishes at dinner:
> Those pies are steaming-black with the poison Mummy put there.
> Whatever she offers you, make sure another person
> Tries it out first....
> What I can't stand is the calculating woman
> Who plans her crimes in cold blood.
>
> JUVENAL[1]

If all philosophy is a footnote to Plato, then all misogyny is a footnote to Juvenal. When connected with women, the image of poison in literature is an image of fear: fear of female power to deceive and destroy men.

In Agatha Christie's early Hercule Poirot novel *The Mysterious Affair at Styles*, several characters discuss the problem of undiscovered crimes.[2] Miss Howard observes that " 'murder's a violent crime. Associate it more with a man.' " Swiftly Mrs. Cavendish disagrees: " ' Not in a case of poisoning.' " Poison is also a secret weapon; as Mrs. Cavendish continues, " 'owing to the general ignorance of the more uncommon poisons among the medical profession, there were probably countless cases of poisoning quite unsuspected' " (7–8). Agatha Christie follows a common pattern here: in detective fiction, "traditionally poison is a woman's weapon."[3]

In criminal justice studies as well, the elements of the murder by poison mentioned in the Christie dialogue are considered seriously. The idea of secrecy seems to provide a natural connection between women and poison. The prestigious criminologist Otto Pollak, tackling the problem of women's underrepresentation in the ranks of murderers, postulates that women's crimes are more likely to be hidden. Because women usually function in private, domestic, nurturing roles (like Juvenal's "Mummy" baking her black pies), Pollak sees them as in " 'circumstances favorable to committing crimes which are difficult to detect [and] which are often not reported.' "[4] Pollak thinks women are particularly prone to such hidden crimes because their anatomically determined ability to hide or feign sexual feelings leads to a " 'greater lack of sincerity' " in their characters.[5] This accounts for the tendency to use a secret weapon and to conceal the results.

The place in which such crimes are hidden is the home. Murders by women are usually a domestic affair. While arguments that women commit unde-tected crime, arguments that proceed from the absence of evidence, bespeak a deep irrational fear, actual evidence is frightening too. Women do indeed murder very little, but when they do, the victim is almost always a loved one. It is a paradox, but also a truism, of criminal justice that women are unlikely to kill anyone but loved ones—women kill parents, children, lovers, husbands, or themselves, but almost never do they kill strangers. As Ann Jones points out in *Women Who Kill*, "unlike men, who are apt to stab a total stranger in a drunken brawl or run amok with a high-powered rifle, we women usually kill our intimates."[6] Acting as if determined to illustrate these theories, Velma Margie Barfield, the first woman executed for murder in the United States in twenty-two years, poisoned her lover, her parents, and two elderly people she was nursing. The newspapers delighted in re-porting that she died, feminine to the last, in pink pajamas; but no one commented on the traditionally "feminine" nature of her crime.

Finally, women's proneness to poison is (again paradoxically) related to their well-known distaste for violence. As Christie's character points out, and criminologist Miriam Hirsch corroborates, women "commit murder with a minimum of violence."[7] Thus the composite portrait of the female murderer is of a gentle, deceptive person who is a danger to no one but those she loves. She has access to the food they eat and the medicines they take. She has no need to claim credit for her crime, so she will conceal it and will probably escape punishment. These are strong motives for the fear of domestic poisoning that Juvenal expressed so long ago.

To analyze the idea of poison as a woman's weapon is to examine a variety of misogynistic notions that find a locus and a focus in an image of primitive fear of the secret enemy, the serpent in one's very bosom; it is the purpose of this book to explore this fear as it appears in Western literature. Of course, men who poison are frightening too, but when men poison, it is not seen as an action expressing malign qualities peculiar to masculinity. The notion of the venomous woman is misogynistic in the sense in which Andrée Kahn Blumstein uses the term in *Misogyny and Idealization in the Courtly Romance* in that from the "shortcomings of an individual woman" is drawn a generalization applying to all women.[8] Because the image of poison as moral metaphor is so frequent in literature, the investigation must be restricted to those cases in which poison is not only metaphor but also plot element—that is, where the behavior of characters and the outcome of the plot is determined by the use of an actual physical substance perceived as poisonous.

Murder by poison, while the most obvious, is only one of the ways in which the image is used. Even more important is the character of the *venefica* ("potion-maker") and the woman whose association with the venomous animal gives her preternatural power. Potion-makers use their secret knowledge to manipulate a man's behavior and keep him in their special domain. Seductive women, already powerful through their sexuality, use the potion to increase that power. Envenomed women come in two basic varieties: women who metamorphose into venomous animals and women whose very flesh is contaminated. All of these use whatever power they have on a man, rarely on children or other women. There are exceptions: for example, in the fairy tale called "Little Snow-White" in the Grimm version, the wicked stepmother's poisoned comb and poisoned apple are directed at a girl child; and Euripedes' Medea makes an envenomed dress and tiara for Jason's new bride. But most commonly, the image of poison is an image of an attempt to control male-female relationships through the use of an insidious equalizer. Murderers, potion-makers, and serpent-women: all these belong to the tradition of the venomous woman.

The tradition gains significance from its endurance over time. Juvenal says, and so does Hemingway's Robert Wilson in "The Short Happy Life of Francis Macomber," that women use poison.[9] But in the twentieth century, the impact of the image changes because of extraliterary developments. As Peter Gwilt and John Gwilt point out in their article "The Use of Poison in Detective Fiction," such use involves "expertise in the fields of pharmaceutics, pharmacology and toxicology."[10] Such expertise is mainly a development of the twentieth century; before that, the image of poison is surrounded by magic and mystery, enshrouded in medical ignorance, therefore all the more feared. So although the tradition continues to the present day, this study will concentrate on periods during which the medical ignorance essential to the image's power prevailed. Interest in the venomous woman, while continuous, peaks in the literature of the Middle Ages in England, France, and Germany; in the Elizabethan and Jacobean drama in England; and in the nineteenth century in England and the United States. It is on these three periods in Western literature that the study will focus, with a brief excursion into the twentieth century for illustrative purposes in the introduction. In the first of the three periods, the venomous woman is a murderer; a potion-maker, a *venefica* or practitioner of witchcraft; or a woman who metamorphoses into a serpent. In the latest period, interest focuses on the woman who is serpentine in nature or whose flesh is envenomed. The tradition culminates in Nathaniel Hawthorne's "Rappaccini's Daughter," the most sophisticated use of the theme in Western literature.

Writers using the image are allusive, highly conscious of their antecedents in mythology and earlier literature, so no work can be seen in isolation from what has gone before. While creating their own character, writers in the tradition are anxious to remind the reader of all the past poison ladies. Lurking in the background are Medea, Circe, Deianira, Lamia, Arachne, and especially that arch-temptress Eve, who by her affinity with the serpent invented sin. The tradition, then, is allusive, overlapping, and repetitive. While reading any work involving a venomous woman, the reader is assumed to be remembering all the rest of them. Every seductress is, in some way, Circe; every potion-maker, Medea; every serpent-woman, Lamia. In addition, each character has elements of all the rest; for example, the potion-maker is also serpentine, and the seductress is a spider spinning her web.

Poison in this study will be defined as it was until the present century, as a generic. In the periods under discussion, literature followed medicine in regarding the term poison as including potions, medicines, mind-altering drugs, in fact, in A. T. Hatto's definition, "any draught that is drunk, whether for good or ill."[11] Venom, on the other hand, is customarily seen as a quality inherent in the character rather than acquired from an external source, as the poison/potion is. Poisons, potions, medicines, and drugs are voluntarily made or acquired, whereas venom is an involuntary malefic influence of which the woman herself is often victim too. Poison involves free choice, but the envenomed woman does not choose to be the way she is, and this makes her story more complex.

The image of the woman who uses poison or is venomous is, above all, an image of female power and male fear of that power. The power comes in three forms: power derived from a woman's special secret knowledge of the poison/potion, power derived from her special relationship with a venomous animal, and power derived involuntarily from an external source. All of these are perceived by men as evil. In my research I have discovered only one case of a poison-lady story written by a woman, a comic tale from Marguerite de Navarre's *Heptameron*, published in 1558. Women do not see themselves as poison ladies; men see them that way. All the misogynistic notions related to the image are manifestations of male fear of domination by a woman. The envenomed or serpentine woman in particular becomes a strong metaphor for the woman who is too unusual for the ordinary man to handle. The male protagonist in such stories cannot cope with the extraordinary demands placed on him, and he retreats in fear, thus failing not only her but himself as well.

Because this book's purpose is to examine the image in the context of male-female relationships where man is the receiver and woman the doer of the action, the equally interesting subject of suicide by poison will have to be set aside. The woman who poisons herself (and, in life as well as literature, poison or its contemporary manifestation, drugs, is far and away the suicide weapon of choice for women)[12] is often punishing herself for failure in a sexual relationship, as do Emma Bovary and Thérèse Raquin. But since her victim is herself, she strikes fear into no man, and this study is about fear.

An undercurrent of the tradition is also the incompetent poison- or potion-maker. The misdirected or misconcocted potion is often a plot element.

Because the ineffective female poisoner is seldom seen as threatening, a further modification of the thesis can be made: poison, or a relationship with the venomous, is not only female power but also female intellectual power. Therefore the most threatening combination of all is the woman who combines the morally venomous power of female sexuality with the asexual power of the mind. In this literature, the smart and sexy woman is the most terrifying of all. The male protagonist's task is at least to survive her, at most to subdue her—in other words, by showing his power to control her, to become a hero.

*   *

Any project as long and complex as writing a book requires participation of many people in addition to the author. I wish to thank the Humanities Council of New York University for allowing me to participate in the Humanities Seminar for Visiting Scholars, funded by the Andrew W. Mellon Foundation; this seminar gave me the impetus to continue with research and writing. The administration and the board of trustees of Long Island University granted me the sabbatical year 1984–1985 during which the greater part of this book was written, and the Research Committee of the C. W. Post Campus provided released time for its completion. The chairmen of the English Department, S. C. V. Stetner and Arthur Coleman, supplied encouragement and, more concrete, a teaching schedule that gave me time to write. For helpful suggestions, I thank my colleagues, Joan Digby, Richard Griffith, Katherine Hill-Miller, Norbert Krapf, Edmund Miller, and Jean Welcher.

My parents, Grace and Raymond Duggan, taught me to read and write and have encouraged my preoccupation with these two activities ever since. To them, and to my extended family, Sister Marion Duggan, Sister Thomasina Doran, and Frances Hallissy, much gratitude is due for their practical assistance to me, especially in my graduate student and early teaching days. As I studied or taught, my loyal family provided child care and moral support. The Wife of Bath calls her woman friend her "gossyb"; my gossip, Jean E. Fisher, has ceaselessly feigned enthusiasm for a field of study far from any of her own. I thank my daughters, Maria and Jennifer, for, in Jennifer's words, loving me when I was "only an unpublished Mom," and for their confidence in my ability to complete this book, which shamed me into doing so. In addition to doing many of the things for which I have already thanked all my other helpers, my husband, Gerald J. Hallissy, has endured much teasing about the book's subject and his possible vulnerability as the main victim of my cooking. I hereby inform the reader that, of the males mentioned hereafter, he resembles only Odysseus.

VENOMOUS

WOMAN

1

Introduction: Archetypes and Stereotypes

One sometimes wonders that so few women, with the thing so facile and so safe, poison their husbands.

H. L. MENCKEN[1]

Every poison lady in literature owes her full significance to archetypes and stereotypes—characters from the literature of the past summoned like shades from Hades to add greater dimension to her characterization and notions about women in general upon which men base judgments of individual women. These archetypes and stereotypes influence the reader's responses to the venomous-woman character, including whether we take her seriously. Consider, for example, Joseph Kesselring's well-known comedy *Arsenic and Old Lace*, in which two old ladies poison eleven men and bury their bodies in the basement of their Brooklyn home.[2] Why are these murderers funny? The answer clarifies the definition of the true poison ladies, which the sisters are not. Abby and Martha Brewster are two sweet little old ladies, helping and serving everyone. Their comfortable home serves as an occasional boarding house for homeless old men and also for their mad nephew Teddy, who fancies himself President Roosevelt. Another nephew is a conventional murderer, and yet a third, the protagonist Mortimer, is the one who discovers the aunties' crimes.

The old men who board at the Brewster house are alone in the world, without family or friends. When one of these unfortunates collapses and dies in the Brewsters' living room, the ladies are favorably impressed: "When his heart attack came, and he sat dead in that chair, so peaceful . . . we decided then and there that if we could help other lonely old men to find that same peace, we would" (46–47). Once inside the womblike Brewster home, these men spend eternity there in the ultimate place of refuge, buried by the Brewster sisters with religious ritual appropriate to their beliefs (the Brewsters are, after all, good church women). In death, these gentlemen find permanent stability and plenty of company. Abby and Martha see their actions as "a mercy" (131), one of the charities for which they are famous, akin to sending soup to the ailing Mrs. Brophy. Their screwy mission— providing a home for homeless men—becomes their life work.

Poison is their weapon. As soon as it becomes apparent that a new house guest is indeed homeless and friendless, they give him a glass of their delicious elderberry wine—spiked with arsenic. Like their soup and the wine itself, their poison is made according to a careful recipe that preserves the wine's delicious flavor. In poison lore, as far back as Avicenna (980–1037), poisons are often said to be served in wine so that the strong flavor of the wine (presumably a hearty red) will conceal the poison's flavor. In fact, this mixture often stands as a convenient symbol of deception, its administration an action "coloured with an outward shew of an honest intent," as an anonymous Elizabethan pamphleteer put it.[3] The Brewster sisters continue a long tradition when they offer a man a poisoned glass of wine as if to refresh him after a long, hard day. They do it kindly, thoughtfully, and much in keeping with the domestic ritual. They certainly appear brimming with "kindness, generosity, human sympathy" (109). To them there is no contradiction between act and motive; their murders are a continuation of their customary loving and nurturing behavior.

No one ever suspects the sisters of eleven murders because they are blinded by the sweet-little-old-lady stereotype. Indeed the play is populated with stereotypes: a black-sheep nephew; dim-witted Irish cops; a suitably Germanic mad scientist; a sweet, young ingenue; a paranoid schizophrenic with delusions of grandeur. When Jonathan, their nephew the murderer, finds out that his aunts share his vocation, he says to Officer Brophy, "You think my aunts are charming, sweet old ladies, don't you? Well, there are thirteen bodies buried in their cellar" (161). But of course Officer Brophy refuses to believe this: "You'd better be careful what you say about your aunts— they happen to be friends of ours" (162). In spite of a peculiar family history that should make them suspicious, even when Miss Abby admits to the murders, townspeople do not believe her. The Brewster sisters have inherited a laboratory and plenty of information from their father, a patent medicine maker who "used the house...as a sort of clinic" and "used to make mistakes occasionally" (14). Although the local police found him "pretty useful on autopsies sometimes, especially poison cases" (14), they never suspect that this interest in and knowledge of poisons might be passed along to his daughters.

The protagonist is a stereotype too, a young journalist, Mortimer, also a Brewster nephew, who must (as roving reporter) unravel the mystery and stop the murderous aunties—a difficult task in the face of the general skepticism. The romance subplot between him and the sweet young thing is the stock situation of unmasking the hero's origins: he is in fact not a blood relative but an orphan child, adopted by the family and raised as their own.

So, uncontaminated by the Brewsters' lunatic genes, he may indeed marry and confidently procreate with the lovely Emily.

All ends happily. The thirteen bodies in the basement (counting the first gentleman, who died of natural causes, plus Jonathan's contribution) rest in peace forever because the aunts decide to join Teddy in the Happy Dale Sanitarium. Not that *they* are crazy, of course; they just cannot bear to be separated from their beloved nephew. Poetic justice is served, and the murders ended by their incarceration; nobody knows the truth except Mortimer, and he is not telling. Exit the old ladies, loved and respected by all. Not only are they never punished, they are regarded as saints of devoted femininity.

Why? Because they use their poison within the limits of acceptable feminine behavior, reinforcing rather than subverting the traditional feminine role. From their unusual viewpoint, they are serving men, caring for their mad nephew, doting upon the abandoned Mortimer whom they have nurtured from babyhood, acting for the ultimate benefit of their roomers. Above all, the Brewster sisters are not true poison ladies because no sex is involved. They are maiden ladies beyond the age of pulchritude. Their use of poison does not emanate from their sexuality, because, of course, they have none—they are everybody's old-maid aunts. The association of women with poison is sexual; in those rare instances where the venomous woman retains her virginity, her story is centered on her attempt to get rid of it. For the Brewster sisters, permanent virgins, poison is innocent because it is not an instrument of power, especially sexual power, but of subservience. They can kill eleven men without being much of a threat at all because they are operating within the patriarchal order.

The use of poisons as a feminine weapon is related to stereotypes involving men's and women's different relationships to inner and outer space. Throughout literature we find the notion of male motion and female stasis: Odysseus wanders and Penelope stays home; the woman is the steady foot, man the wandering foot, of the compass. The woman in fact is the home and draws the man back to it. But she must do so gently, allowing him freedom to withdraw, else she is perceived as enmeshing him, the net being a frequent image for the fear of entrapment. If she has long hair, which men consider alluring, the symbolism is even stronger; her combing it is like the activity of the spinning spider, and a man can get caught in its coils.[4] When a man goes into a house, seen as a woman's domain, he is in need of relief and refuge. What happens in the house is an indication of the balance of power between male and female. In the patriarchal order, he is supposed to be able to take from her what he needs and leave again, his powers restored. She meets his various needs: food, warmth, shelter, rest, sex. If she is not content to follow this role, her intent can be to keep him there, in her place. Seduction is one way to keep him there; poison is another. To keep the man inside is the triumph of the female; to go away again, having taken what he needs from the female but remaining free of her domination, is the triumph of the male.

A striking similarity exists between the comic treatment of this old plot pattern in *Arsenic and Old Lace* and William Faulkner's short story "A Rose for Emily."[5] In both, a murder is hidden within the recesses of the house; the victim is a man; an ancient "maiden" lady is the perpetrator; poison is the weapon; a family heritage of insanity, particularly that of a father, influences the crime; and observers are deceived by their own stereotyped thinking. Why, then, is Miss Emily's story a horror, while the Brewster sisters' is a burlesque? The difference lies in the use of poison as an instrument of sexual power. The spider, a venomous insect that also weaves a web, is often connected with women through the domestic responsibility delegated to the distaff side. In a medieval painting entitled *Women Weaving*, two pleasant-looking women share the chore.[6] But dominating the scene is an oversized spider, black and deadly. The spider and its web serve as a negative commentary on the apparently peaceful domestic scene, implying that even these two docile-looking women are threatening. The spider's weaving is a metaphor of both domestic duplicity and the fear of entrapment; the women who lures man into her home/web with intentions of keeping him there against his will is a fearful figure. Poison becomes the primitive fear of sexual entrapment: if I go in, will I get out? Miss Emily has poisoned only one man, but she has done it to exert control over him.

As the townspeople reconstruct the story after Miss Emily's death, her Yankee lover was her last chance at the ultimate fulfillment for a woman, marriage. When it becomes obvious that he is about to leave her, she poisons him to keep him in her house; in the necrophiliac final scene, it becomes obvious that Miss Emily has been sleeping with a corpse for thirty years. Leaving aside the level of meaning in the Faulkner story on which Faulkner criticizes the South's clinging to old, dead ways too long, we can see that Miss Emily's crime lies in her desperate defiance of sexual mores. She refuses to accept the role of spinster that would have been hers if her lover left her. Instead, preferring a dead lover to no lover at all, she creates a permanent wedding night. Her goal is achieved: she keeps the appropriately named Homer in the house. The evil of her action is increased by the distortion of the idea of the house, a place of refuge for the man who takes what he needs and then leaves. Here poison is connected not only with sexuality but with the deviant sexuality of necrophilia, stressing Miss Emily's corruption and rendered even more disgusting by her age and unattractiveness. Devoid of the connection with sexuality, as in *Arsenic*, poison is less threatening. Although the Brewster sisters have killed eleven men and Miss Emily only one, Emily is the more evil because she did it to serve not men's needs but her own.

The woman's proper role is to render service to others, to be nurturant and sexual, in the house. The house (sometimes a garden) is a refuge—in

Christopher Lasch's phrase, a "haven in a heartless world."[7] Woman's job is to restore the man and send him forth again. She may not keep him. But since he comes to the house in a weakened state (as in the romance and epic, disarming himself, expressing the vulnerability that brings him there in the first place), he places himself in her power, in the place of that power. If she chooses to take advantage, the ideal pattern can be distorted: he comes to the house in need; a powerful woman uses a potion as a way of exploiting his need and keeping him there: engulfed, enmeshed, entrapped by house and woman, he can never leave again.

Thus the poison image is about the balance of power in a sexual relationship. If a man is not strong enough, he will succumb to the drug he is given, as do the Brewsters' victims and Miss Emily's lover. If he is strong enough, he will be able to dominate. Few such men exist; Odysseus is one of them. The proper outcome of the plot sequence involving man/woman/house is seen in the Circe episode of Homer's *Odyssey*.[8] Odysseus makes landfall in Aiaia; he and his crew are "worn out and sick at heart" (169). To his relief, he sees Circe's hall. He is attracted to it but considers carefully whether he should go in. As if to remind him of his masculinity, which might be threatened there, a "big buck" crosses his path. He kills the buck and brings it back to his crewmen; "And all that day until the sun went down / we had our fill of venison and wine" (170). Through this demonstration of prowess in hunting, his un-threatened masculinity, which will enable him to cope with Circe, is prefigured. Also, he approaches Circe's hall fed by his own powers, not hungry and dependent on hers, so less in need. Like an early draft for the Hemingway hero, Odysseus expresses his maleness by killing animals and controlling women.

At Circe's hall, Odysseus and his men hesitate at the entrance way, still able to escape if necessary and behold the beauteous lady within:

> Low she sang
> in her beguiling voice, while on her loom
> she wove ambrosial fabric sheer and bright,
> by that craft known to the goddesses of heaven.

(171)

Because of its connection with the spider, weaving, the main job of the distaff side, is seen as a deceptive and dangerous act; even Penelope, faithful to Odysseus, is deceiving her importunate swains. The idea of the deceptiveness of women is essential to understanding the image of poison. Poison can never be used as an honorable weapon in a fair duel between worthy opponents, as the sword or gun, male weapons, can. A man who uses such a secret weapon is beneath contempt. Publicly acknowledged rivalry is a kind of bonding in which each worthy opponent gives the other the opportunity to demonstrate prowess. Such heroic rivalries must be between equals, between the same kinds of creatures; an earl does not duel with a churl. But women, inferior creatures, cannot participate in this male bonding ritual. In fact, a woman cannot openly and honestly declare herself a man's enemy at all; there are no rituals to express male-female rivalry. Unlike the duel, or its larger equivalent, war, male-female enmity creates a situation in which no one gains glory. Men cannot demonstrate prowess by fighting an opponent so weak; women have no hope of winning in hand-to-hand combat. Therefore they use poison.

The dueler is open, honest, and strong; the poisoner, fraudulent, scheming, and weak. A man with a gun or a sword is a threat, but he declares himself to be so, and his intended victim can arm himself: may the best man win and have the public glory of being acknowledged the best man. But poison must always be used deceptively; the poisoner must be a person with no psychological need for public recognition of a conquest. Poisoning can never be an impulsive, passionate crime, with the romantic overtones and lessened legal and moral responsibility such crimes have; it must always be plotted, premeditated. Poison is an insidious equalizer of strength in the battle of the sexes. The poisoner uses superior secret knowledge to compensate for physical inferiority. A weak woman planning a poison is as deadly as a man with a gun, but because she plots in secret, the victim is the more disarmed.

Circe the weaver, concocting potion and plot, is singing in a "beguiling" voice. A main facet of the tradition involves the untrustworthiness of women's speech. In every age, customs surround binding words exchanged by men: the Anglo-Saxon warrior's boast, the medieval knight's pledge of fealty, the contemporary businessman's handshake. But these have been primarily male rituals, and, except for wedding vows, there seem to be no corresponding male-female "truth" rituals. This exclusion from rituals of the binding word is either cause or effect of male suspicion that women's words are written on the wind. Probably deception is a feature of the slavelike behavior adopted by chronic subordinates; probably it is attributed to women because of their anatomically determined ability fo feign or hide their sexual feelings; perhaps, too, men and women differ in the way they use words to communicate. In *The Laws*, Plato says that "the female sex ... is generally predisposed by its weakness to undue secrecy and craft."[9] Certainly Plato was not last to notice that women have always had a reputation for mysterious concealment. Mencken sees this as women's only hope: "Women, in the last analysis, can prevail against men in the great struggle for power and security only by keeping them disarmed, and, in the main, unwarned."[10]

Like everything else about Circe, the "pretty song" she sings disarms the hearers. The potion-maker, of whom Circe is the archetype, is often part of the appearance/reality motif: she seems innocent (" 'Goddess she is, or lady' " [172]), yet appearances are deceiving and so is she. Polites and his followers go in and are apparently well treated:

On thrones she seated them, and lounging chairs,
while she prepared a meal of cheese and barley
and amber honey mixed with Pramnian wine,
adding her own vile pinch, to make them lose
desire or thought of our dear father land.
Scarce had they drunk when she flew after them
with her long stick and shut them in a pigsty—
bodies, voices, heads, and bristles, all
swinish now, though minds were still unchanged.
So, squealing, in they went. And Kirke tossed them
acorns, mast, and cornel berries—fodder
for hogs who rut and slumber in the earth.

(172)

At first she seems to be the ideal hostess, everyman's perfect wife. She exalts their manhood, seating them on thrones and behaving with the utmost subservience, apparently aware of her proper place. She prepares and serves food and wine. As a good housewife, she must be sensitive to the guests' food and drink preferences, which also helps to ensure successful administration of the potion. The wine is seasoned with "her own vile pinch," her love potion, which reduces the men to a form of life below hers, to animality. The mixture she serves, poison concealed in a sweet substance, will recur in literature, and even in theology, as an image for deceptive evil. Now Circe has power over them, and they cannot leave. The menu and the service abruptly deteriorate. Now the men are weak and contemptible; her former subservience was pretense. The role playing was only a means to an end; Circe's real nature is dominant.

Odysseus, unlike his men, is strong and wary. Part of his strength lies in the fact that he knows what happened. Eurylokhos reports back and warns him, which allows him to arm himself with his broadsword and long bow so he is not powerless against the enchantress. Also, Odysseus has divine assistance, a counterpotion in an amulet provided by Hermes. If Circe's cup represents female power, Odysseus's amulet represents male power, and the amulet is stronger than the cup. Its purpose is clearly to restore the correct balance of power:

"Your cup with numbing drops of night
and evil, stilled of all remorse,
she will infuse to charm your sight;
but this great herb with holy force
will keep your mind and senses clear:
when she turns cruel, coming near
with her long stick to whip you out of doors,
then let your cunning blade appear,

Let instant death upon it shine,
and she will cower and yield her bed—

a pleasure you must not decline,
so may her lust and fear bestead
you and your friends, and break her spell;
but make her swear by heaven and hell
no witches' tricks, or else, your harness shed,
you'll be unmanned by her as well."

(174)

Circe's cup and its " 'drops of night' " are " 'witches' tricks' "; this connection between the potion-maker and the witch will persist. Hermes' " 'great herb' " will keep Odysseus's rational control intact. Protected by the amulet, Odysseus can drink Circe's " 'unholy drug' " without fear. He can touch poison and not be harmed. She, ignorant of his superior power, attempts to assert control, wielding the " 'long stick.' " But Odysseus is ready to restore the right balance of power. He draws his sword, asserts his masculinity, makes clear to Circe that he is not influenced by the poison at all and is the boss. He has a " 'cunning blade,' " superior knowledge and superior force. The powerful sexual woman is often feared as the *vagina dentata*, a threat to a man's masculinity. Only the bravest man can risk the loss of his vital spirits, his masculinity, or even life itself in the confrontation with her. But Odysseus is such a man. He, and only he, can reduce the powerful Circe to her proper behavior, cowering and yielding up her bed. He is a real man, not " 'a boy . . . soft and doting.' " If he goes into the smaller chamber, to Circe's " 'dangerous bed,' " he will not lose his manhood because she has acknowledged his superiority and sworn to " 'work no more enchantment' " (175). Then and only then will he go to her bed, which he must do, because this is part of the restoration of the correct balance of power, which will result in the liberating of his men. Odysseus apparently performs satisfactorily, since upon the morn he gets all the good things of domestic life without the threatening parts: busy serving maids, richly colored throw rugs, tables laden with golden baskets, wine in golden cups (without potions this time), a bath in warm water, a soothing balm "warming the soreness of [his] joints away," a clean tunic and cloak, a "silver-studded chair," "many savory slices" of bread served on a polished table (176).

In this episode of *The Odyssey*, food and drink are mentioned repeatedly. Odysseus slays the buck, providing food and drink for his men and reassuring them that they will not starve; they dine all day. During the first feasting scene at Circe's hall, Odysseus is plied with lavish food and with the potion with which Circe tries to establish dominance. During the second feasting scene, Odysseus dominates, but when Circe realizes that he is dissatisfied, she phrases her insight in terms of food and drink:

"Why sit at table mute, Odysseus?
Are you mistrustful of my food and drink?

Can it be treachery that you fear again,
after the gods' great oath I swore for you?"

(176)

The man of action does not stop to analyze this remark, but Circe's comment focuses attention on several elements crucial to the comprehension of the poison-lady character. The preparation and serving of food and drink constitute a symbolic ritual central to male-female relationships, as the "bed and board" expression for conjugal life acknowledges. The man approaches the woman for satisfaction of hunger and thirst. The mealtime ritual, how- ever, can be an opportunity for her to exert secret power through poison. She may be pretending to serve him when her real intentions are evil. It is essential that he be able to trust the person who cooks and serves the food he eats. Each meal is an act of faith in the trustworthiness of the food-giver. For the same centuries during which inaccurate medical science made cause of death impossible to determine, cooking was a mysterious task requiring obscure ingredients and specialized knowledge accessible to women only. The food-giver had the prime weapon and opportunity; and what love relationship lacks a motive? The fear engendered by the possibility of being poisoned by the food-giver on whom men are so dependent permeates the tradition of the venomous woman. The second element of Circe's remarks addresses this question of trust. Circe knows that men have little confidence in women's oaths. Circe wants to reassure Odysseus that now her appear- ance and her reality are identical, her transformation is real. He can trust her and her food as well.

When Circe invites Odysseus to remain with her, she phrases the invitation in terms of food: " 'Remain with me, and share my meat and wine' " (179). She offers to fatten up Odysseus's men, to restore their gallant hearts behind their ribs, nurturing them in body and spirit. When Odysseus agrees to do this, it is clear that correct order is restored. He and his men "lingered, feasting long / on roasts and wine, until a year grew fat"(179). Another ritual meal precedes Odysseus's announcement of his departure and his request for Circe's aid. The significance of the food rituals in this episode, then, is to indicate conformity to or deviance from a correct balance of power between the sexes.

During the second feasting scene, after Odysseus has tamed Circe but before he has freed his men, he is still "oppressed" because he has not done the task for which he came to Circe's hall. The hero who becomes obsessed with the pleasures of the lady's bower and loses track of his main goal is a recurrent figure in literature, but Odysseus is no such sluggard. Domestic comfort does not weaken Odysseus at all, for he can still negotiate for his men's release; the chastened Circe reanoints them, which breaks the spell. They stay for a year, but this is Odysseus's choice; he is in control of the situation. When he does tell Circe that it is time to go, she is all duty and accommodation: " 'you shall not stay here longer against your will' " (180). She warns him of the dangerous journey ahead but makes no attempt to stop him. Like a dutiful wife dispatching her husband to work in the morning, she "dressed [Odysseus] in [his] shirt and cloak" (181). And off he and his men go, to more adventures, having escaped the fate of those other men for whom entry into the house is entry into the tomb as well. Male power is, then, being able to leave when a man wants to; female power is the reverse, keeping him when he wants to go.

POISON AND POWER

Because they are so widely separated in time, these three works illustrate the endurance of the image of the venomous woman. In both *Arsenic* and "A Rose for Emily," several continuing elements of the theme are present. The administrator of the poison is a woman, the victim a man. The poison is administered secretly and deceptively. In *Arsenic* definitely, and in *"Emily"* presumably, it is mixed in a drink that usually connotes love and service. The man has come to the woman's place to have a specific need fulfilled. At the Brewsters,' he seeks food, shelter, and companionship; at Emily's, he seeks sex. Because of his need, he is vulnerable—disarmed—yet he fully intends to leave when his need is fulfilled. His secret manipulator, the woman using the poison, intends to keep him in her place forever.

In the Circe story, however, we have a striking difference in the relative power of the characters. The hero is forewarned and ready. He has his own strength—both the inner strength of his manhood and the amulet that represents it. These can counteract the evil of the poison lady. Like her, he has supernatural assistance. In this situation, too, he is also smarter than she is, since he knows more about her baleful powers than she thinks he does. So unlike the victims in the other two works, he is not taken by surprise, nor is he disarmed. Odysseus also has a degree of self-control that enables him to use his attraction to Circe as a way to tame rather than be tamed by her. Not only is Odysseus stronger and smarter than Circe, he is stronger and smarter than his men, and by extension the rest of mankind. In Odysseus we see the real man who need not fear the poison lady. He is stronger and smarter than most other men perceive themselves to be, only a dream to which they might aspire, which perhaps accounts in part for the endurance of his story over thousands of years. Most men—in life as in literature—are more like the typical victim of the poison lady: they can be seduced, or deceived, or both.

The image of the venomous woman depends on a combination of misogynistic notions and traditional role expectations; in other words, evil women stand as representatives for all women. In the literature of misogyny, women are seen as weak reeds, lacking physical strength and dependent on men in all things. Because they fear open confrontation with a stronger opponent, they try to get their way through deception and manipulation. Added to this, even leaving aside the diseases of Venus, is the long-held belief that sex debilitates men and is metaphorically poisonous is being physically harmful. Making the potion becomes a metaphor for being seductive, and women in general, not only poisoners, are harmful. In a 1480 painting from the lower Rhineland entitled *The Love Spell*, a young, long-haired woman, naked but for a fetchingly draped gauzy scarf, is in a small room. Next to her is a small box from which a mysterious smoke emanates. At the door lurks a young man, apparently trying to decide whether to come in.[11] The painting's iconography crystallizes the sexual implications of the potion image. As the title indicates, the young woman has, in addition to her physical allure, a special substance in a small container. The young man will surely come in. We see him at the door, in his last instant of freedom, before coming into the seductive woman's space, the realm of her destructive power.

Like this young woman, the potion-maker may intend not to kill but rather to control; entrapment or confinement in a woman's sphere of influence, or shaping his behavior to meet her needs, is often the goal. Knowledge of potions and other supernatural aids is attributed to witches and their *maleficium*, evil-doing; but even if a woman operates within her proper role, she is still suspect. Since she takes care of men at times when they are weak and vulnerable and tends to their basic needs at all times, she can also be a silent enemy who uses those needs to her advantage. If she cooks or medicates, perhaps she poisons. If she weaves, perhaps she has envenomed the clothing. If she provides shelter and sex, perhaps the man who seeks such relief may be destroyed in the process. When a woman in literature does any of these things, she is doing what men fear all other women may do: waging a secret battle for domination.

The fear of the female is nowhere more powerfully embodied than in the image of a woman whose flesh is envenomed. No matter how virtuous she may seem (or indeed be), contact with her is deadly. She needs no love potion; her physical nature, combining preternatural allure with the attraction of the forbidden, is dangerous. No force can overcome this aphrodisiac come to life. At the outset, the hero is deceived as to her true nature until he is already in love with her, and often he needs the help of another, more rational, stronger male if he is to free himself. An added complication involving women who are envenomed is that they are never so of their own choice; their predicament is always caused by someone else. Their situation and that of the man who loves them invite analysis of the complex factors affecting attribution of moral guilt in sexual matters. In the religious traditions that influence Western literature, the female body is viewed as an enticement into sin. Even if she is *virgo intacta*, virtuous as can be, she is never really innocent; she is always sin incarnate. If women are temptresses and relations with them are dangerous, this raises the question: whose fault is it? Women do not perceive themselves as either evil or dangerous. Yet paradoxically, without this aura of danger surrounding them, women are virtually powerless.

Poison, then, is an instrument of female power. If Susan Brownmiller is right and crimes of force, like rape, maintain male power, then, at least in literature, crimes of secrecy, like poisoning, maintain female power.[12] Poison is an insidious equalizer. A woman who poisons or is poisonous is strong. If this strength is also evil, then so be it. Better to be venomous, as Dr. Rappaccini advises his daughter, than to be " 'a weak woman, exposed to all evil and capable of none' " (127).[13] Since a woman this strong arouses male fears, only the man who is not afraid can deal with her effectively. Thus we return to Odysseus, the archetypal man of courage in the patriarchal mode. Odysseus stands virtually alone in literature in his ability to dominate the venomous woman. Only the manliest of men, an extraordinary man, will be able to confront and master the fears within himself of which she is a convenient symbol.

Over and over, the venomous woman is seen as dealing with no Odysseus but rather with an ordinary man who cannot handle the challenge she represents. That famous curmudgeon H. L. Mencken saw the matter this way:

To be the wife of an ordinary man, indeed, is an experience that must be very hard to bear. . . . Women survive the tragi-comedy only by dint of their great capacity for play-acting. They are able to act so realistically that often they deceive even themselves; the average woman's contentment, indeed, is no more than a tribute to her histrionism. But there must be innumerable revolts in secret, even so, and one sometimes wonders that so few women, with the thing so facile and so safe, poison their husbands. Perhaps it is not quite as rare as vital statistics make it out; the death rate among husbands is very much higher than among wives. More than once, indeed, I have gone to the funeral of an acquaintance who died suddenly, and observed a curious glitter in the eyes of the inconsolable widow.[14]

The fault is not in the presumed deceptiveness of women, then, but in the nature of an institution that requires histrionism rather than honesty. Suspicion of women's proneness to crimes involving secrecy and conceal-ment is a tacit acknowledgment that pretense and deception are an ordinary feature of the relationship between the sexes. If all were well, there would be no need to fear revolts in secret. Conditions for secret rebellion exist when power is unevenly distributed and honesty impossible, so the would-be rebel resorts to deception.

In the portrayals of the venomous woman in literature, the domestic battleground is the scene of shifting power relationships engineered by var-ious degrees of deception. The holder of power might well fear that he is not capable of maintaining control, particularly when the rebellion is never openly declared and the weapons used are not those to which he is accustomed; so his fear of the dominant woman is an acknowledgment of his own weakness. In bed and at board, he may be at risk. The average man, no Odysseus, fears encountering a Circe and being reduced to powerlessness. Over a long period of time, across national boundaries, in well-known literature and in obscure, long-neglected works, the image of the poisoner, the potion-maker, and the envenomed woman are images of power: lust for its gain, fear of its loss.

2

Mother Eve and Other Death-Dealers

Tell me, what kind of people inspire the most horror? Whom do judges and magistrates strike down? Those who drink the fatal poisons, or those who prepare the draught and concoct the envenomed potions?
ST. JOHN CHRYSOSTOM[1]

By vigilancie and industrie meanes may be had to resist, or evite the most violent beast that ever nature bred, but from false and treacherous hartes, from poysoning murtherers what wit or wisedome can defend?
GEORGE EGLISHAM (1626)[2]

The ultimate primal scene is this one: a woman giving a man something dangerous to eat. Blaming Eve for the entrance of sin and death into the world is a tradition as old as the Genesis story, as is the proclivity of Eve's daughters to cause the Fall to be repeated in the life of the individual man. The essential selfishness of Eve's sin is stressed in the iconographic tradition, which depicts the serpent tempting Eve as having a woman's face, often Eve's own face, as in Raphael's *The Fall*.[3] This tradition, which began in the twelfth century[4] and flourished in the fourteenth through sixteenth centuries,[5] is related to the serpent-woman motif, which we will examine later. Eve's selfish motive in eating the fruit is the specific achievement of gaining special knowledge, which she immediately uses in a devious and manipulative way to gain power over Adam, who in consequence suffers a loss. Underlying the image of every venomous woman is the image of her mother, Eve. As the woman who brought death into the world, she is a symbolic murderess. Since murder is the most obvious use of poison, it must be explored in some detail because the conceptions surrounding it influence every other use of a poison or potion.

The rebelliousness of Eve, her desire to achieve superiority over Adam, is undoubtedly a carryover from the tradition of Lilith, Adam's insubordinate first wife, cast out from Paradise in a leadership dispute. Lilith was created the same way Adam was, and therefore, so the story goes, she saw no reason to subject herself to his rule. In some accounts, her rebellion took the specifically sexual form of refusal to submit to the male-superior position in intercourse.[6] Lilith, "protomartyr of female independence," was displaced by Eve, specially created out of Adam's side to stress her inferiority.[7] Lilith's fate is to wander the night, snatching newborn children and causing erotic dreams in men.[8] Her influence lingers. She is said to have persuaded the devil to tempt Eve using Lilith's characteristic themes: dominance and independence.[9] Lilith knows her successor well. According to St. John Chrysostom, a significant component of Eve's sin is "acting on her own," Lilith's behavior repeated.[10]

Once Eve falls, her only opportunity to bring Adam down with her is through deception. The words she uses to tempt Adam, as well as the dangerous food itself, are visualized as a poison in various accounts of the primal crime. Augustine's rationale for the necessity of Mary, the second Eve, to undo what Eve had done is expressed in terms of poison: "The poison to deceive man was presented him by a woman, through woman let salvation for man's recovery be presented."[11] Iconographically Mary's restoration of order has been expressed in her common statuary pose, foot upon serpent, symbolizing the conquest of the evil introduced when Eve addressed the serpent as an equal. In Anglo-Saxon poetry, sin is "the brew ... which Eve prepared for Adam at the beginning of the world ... later poured for Adam, her dear husband."[12] Lydgate's *Examples against Women* says Eve "first began / Death to devise and poison to man."[13] In *Concerning Famous Women*, Boccaccio suggests that Eve "brought her pliant husband to her way of thinking with enticing suggestions, foolishly thinking that she was about to rise to greater heights" (2).[14] Her attempt to use special knowledge to improve her station in life brings loss of Paradise not only to Adam but to us all.

This manipulative and deceptive behavior is not peculiar to Eve but characteristic of her daughters as well. As Tertullian points out in the famous phrase, all women are "the devil's gateway" through whom evil enters the life of the individual as well as the species.[15] Gratian, in his *Decretum* (c. 1140), warns all men to be careful lest they "fall a second time through female levity."[16] All men are in the situation of the ignorant Adam when it comes to the nature of the poisonous fruit being offered to them.

WOMEN AND POISONING IN CLASSICAL LITERATURE

The belief in the propensity of women to kill by poison is not peculiar to the Christian tradition. Ovid and Juvenal believed firmly in it, and their stories are repeated over and over in the poison lore, as if to increase guilt by association. In his first satire, Juvenal uses the unpleasant portrait of a woman who poisons her husband as an illustration of the decline of his society:

> Do you see that distinguished lady? She has the perfect dose
> For her husband—old wine with a dash of parching toad's blood.

The idea of concealed crime certainly applies to her:

> She trains her untutored neighbors
> To ignore all unkind rumours, to stalk through angry crowds
> With their black and bloated husbands before them on the hearse.
>
> (Satire I, p. 67)

Juvenal's attribution to women of a tendency toward concealed crime becomes a commonplace but also a pole of a catch-22 situation regarding women's speech. If a woman is as quiet as she ought to be, she might be scheming. If she voices her opinions, she is a shrew. Commentators on this subject never noticed that in terms of the danger of poisoning, men are safer with a shrew. Women who vent their spleen in speech never kill. Sweet wives do.

Juvenal also sets the pattern for all later writers on the venomous-woman theme by his allusiveness to stories from the past: Claudius poisoned by his wife, Agrippina Pontia poisoning her children. In general, Juvenal sees poisoning much as medieval writers do, moralisé, as an indication of inner corruption in women, particularly associated with their desire to control their husbands:

> Here comes a peddler of magic spells and Thessalian
> Philtres. With these any wife can so befuddle
> Her husband's wits that he'll let her slipper his backside.
>
> (Satire VI, p. 150)

The association of poisoning and potion-making with Thessaly, Medea's home town, will recur, as will Juvenal's fear of and hatred for the dominant woman.

Occasionally this special knowledge attributed to women falls short. One of the problems of using poison as a murder weapon, or indeed any other potion for any other purpose, is the potential for mishap. In addition to Eve, classical examples of women who poison their husbands or lovers include Livia, whose story, combined with that of her alliterative analogue Lucia, becomes a staple of poison lore. The former poisoned her husband intentionally because she hated him; the latter poisoned her husband accidentally with an overdose of aphrodisiac. Lucia becomes another stock figure: the incompetent, whose potion goes astray or is misconcocted. Another character in this thread of the tradition is Hercules' wife, Deianira, whose story is told in Ovid's Metamorphoses[17] and in Sophocles' Trachinian Women.[18] In Ovid, Deianira's story is a simple parable of deception turning on the perpetrator. She is also loved by the centaur Nessus, whom Hercules kills with an arrow when Nessus tries to rape Deianira. The dying Nessus gives Deianira the shirt off his back, drenched with his own blood and with "Hydra's venom," telling her that "all who wear it are possessed, / Seized by the magic of reviving love" (248). Deianira, believing the centaur (Boccaccio calls Deianira "credulous" [48]), stows it away for future use.

Later, Deianira hears of Hercules' love for Iole, "captive daughter of a king." Jealous and threatened, she remembers the magic shirt:

> Still thick with blood and virulent as ever—
> The perfect gift for Hercules to wear
> To make his love (grown pale for her) show life.
>
> (249)

Thinking to gain greater control over Hercules' affections, she gives him the shirt, and, "undoubting Hercules / Was glad to wear the Hydra-poisoned shirt" (249).

Of course, this is Nessus's post-mortem revenge on his killer and on the woman he died for. The envenomed shirt poisons Hercules' flesh, so that "as he tried to strip the shirt away, / His flesh came with it. . . . His blood steamed with the heat of Hydra's venom" (250). Unable to die because of his great strength, he finally brings surcease of his pain by throwing himself on a bed of flames. Deianira, whose naiveté led her to believe that Nessus meant only good in his parting gift, is the accidental murderer whose name and story become an *exemplum* of the danger of getting involved with women. Like the potion-users who try to influence rather than kill, Deianira tries to be certain, to maintain total control over the outcome of events. By trying to exert too much power over Hercules, she loses him entirely and, in the Sophocles play, her own life as well. Like Lucia, another accidental murderer, Deianira uses her potion because she cannot let nature take its course. She uses artifice to control men and events. Even a strong man is brought low; deviousness, incompetence, and sexual insecurity combine to make Deianira a threat disproportionate to her physical or even moral strength.

In Sophocles' *Trachinian Women*, Deianira's character is more complex than in Ovid's story. Her motivation, ironically, is to keep Hercules' love so as "to live thenceforth an untroubled life" (153). Because the happiness of women is so bound up with the approbation of their men, the potion-user's goal is restoration of marital order. The plot of this play is very much like a combination of *Medea* and *Agamemnon*. A more thoroughly developed character than in Ovid, Deianira has been "guardian of [Hercules'] home throughout all that weary time" (162) of foreign travel and adventure. He brings home with him a younger woman as concubine, and Deianira is understandably upset: "the flower of her age is blossoming while mine is fading" (162). The shirt, "a charm for the soul of Heracles, so that he shall never look upon any woman to love her more" than Deianira (163), will offset the effects of her decreasing physical attractiveness. Deianira is a bit hesitant, worrying that in using "love-spells and charms" to "prevail against this girl" she may be "acting rashly," and she asks the chorus of Trachinian maidens for advice (163). They encourage her, universalizing Deianira's wish to manage her man (162–63). Although she has her doubts about the safety of her gift (a tuft of wool used to anoint the robe with the magic salve left her by Nessus has disappeared, "self-devoured and self destroyed"[165]), she is so determined to achieve her goal that she ignores the warning signals. She sends the robe to Hercules as if it were a gift woven by her own hand. The venom is activated by heat, so when Hercules offers sacrifice to Zeus, the flames heat up the robe and begin Hercules' painful dying. The centaur's promise is ironically fulfilled: Hercules indeed shall never love another woman, but neither shall he do anything else.

The play concludes with an analysis of Deianira's action. The chorus of maidens understands that she used the potion to protect herself through ensuring the love of Hercules, on which she is completely dependent. Because "she saw a great mischief swiftly coming on her home from the new marriage," she "applied the remedy" (169). Since she is in the grip of sexual jealousy herself, she should have understood that of the centaur, but instead she unwittingly becomes its instrument. Internalizing her anger and guilt (and abandoning her feminine weapon), she kills herself with a sword.

Like Eve's guilt, Deianira's is questionable in that she "acted without knowledge, by the prompting of the Centaur" (171). Nevertheless, her thoughtless reaction is destructive of the proper order of things: no man could overcome Hercules, so his death is ironic in being meted out at the hand of "a woman, a weak woman, not born to the strength of a man" (174). What would become a typical *de casibus* theme—men brought low by the deception and/or incompetence of a woman—unites the classical hero and the first man.

POISON LORE AND LITERATURE IN THE MIDDLE AGES AND THE RENAISSANCE

For much of recorded history, the situation just described—ignorance by the supposedly more rational male, knowledge by the supposedly more intuitive female—was characteristic of poison lore. For the European Middle Ages and the Elizabethan and Jacobean periods in England, the lack of knowledge of the action of poisons on the living body was paralleled by a belief that women were likely to know how to make them. Fear of poisoners, male as well as female, was widespread. In the Middle Ages, the figure of Eve in the Christian tradition combines with the poisoners found in the classics to form a backdrop for the female murderer by poison. In Elizabethan and

Jacobean England, the same influences remain, and added to them is the stress on poison as metaphor for widespread sexual and financial corruption.

Murder by poison was greatly feared at the time. Before analyzing the influence of the idea of poison on the depiction of women in literature, it is necessary to take an excursion into poison lore. Lest the people of the Middle Ages and Renaissance appear paranoid on this subject, it is necessary to remember that for them, the term *poison* also included the concepts of infection and contagion—in fact, any illness for which the cause was unclear. Poisoning, infection, and contagion were not distinguished in the medical literature, and surely not in the popular mind, until well into the sixteenth century. At a time when medical remedies were largely ineffective and when disease could halve a population, the fear of sudden illness is far from inexplicable. Add to this the time's rough justice, with the ever-present possibility, especially among the great, of murder for political reasons. An illustration of this fear is the medieval custom of proving by mouth or giving credence.[19] A thoroughly staffed medieval household would include a servant who tasted the lord's food to detect poison. This unsavory duty gives us an insight into the fear of poison in an age long before the first real medical advances were made in understanding either poison or antidotes.

Let us look at the assumptions behind the practice of giving credence because they reveal the extent of ignorance about the operations of poisons on the human body. First, it shows fear of a sly and secret enemy, one who could not or would not confront an opponent in open battle. Death in such a battle, while undesirable, could nevertheless redound to one's lasting glory, but death by poison could not. The lord employing a taster naively hopes that this ignominious fate could be avoided. The practice also assumes that all poisons can be detected by taste and would act quickly; for the servant to provide an effective early-warning system, he would have to sicken immediately for the lord to be forewarned in time. But even if he did just that, it would still be unclear as to whether poison was indeed the cause, much less who was the perpetrator. No one would know for sure; poison was indistinguishable from contagion, from infection, from bacterial contamination, not detectable in life or post mortem. Conversely, any sudden and inexplicable death could be attributed to poisoning, any real or suspected enemy accused of it. So the act of giving credence was itself a sort of credo, an act of faith and expression of hope that the life-giving meal would not be death-dealing. In the fourteenth and fifteenth centuries, evidence that the fear of poison still haunted the minds of powerful men is seen in the frequency with which treatises on poisons and antidotes were dedicated to popes and princes.[20]

The idea of poison was a source of fear and bafflement. No progress in understanding poisons was to be made for hundreds of years. A consequence for literature is that poison and potions could be used as plot elements in ways that strike the modern reader as farfetched. Medical treatises discuss the symptoms and treatment of poisoning; animal lore reflects popular belief about the venomous animal; witchcraft lore attributes knowledge of poisons and potions to these wise women; exegetes and homilists examine the phenomenon of poison and the venomous animal for spiritual and moral significance; and all of these form a common stock of beliefs incorporated into literature. But the first of these, medical theory, on which all the rest depended as links in a chain, was weak.

Like all other medical and particularly anatomical knowledge, knowledge of the actions of poison was severely limited until the very recent past. Several factors contributed to this medical ignorance. In the Middle Ages, reverence for authority precluded contradiction of the ancient medical writers. The medieval writer on medicine, who may or may not have been a medical practitioner, saw his role as compiling, collating, and commenting on the writings of the ancients. These procedures, originally not only a didactic tool but also a mode of information preservation and transmission in ages when books and manuscripts were scarce, became ends in themselves. The sources upon which the compilations were based were flawed by lack of direct experimentation. For example, although the writings of Galen (A.D. 129–199) were an encyclopedia of medical knowledge and "provided the basis of medical practice for the next 1500 years," his writings marked the end of practical anatomy for hundreds of years also.[21] Galen was an authority who by definition could not be contradicted. So although he derived his physiological data from animals (human dissection was not carried on in his time), his data, which were really arguments from analogy, were considered irrefutable.

Another factor that impeded medical progress was the medieval love of the organized system. A body of ideas logically connected was congenial to the medieval mind. If an authority was beloved, a systematic authority was the more beloved, and the kind of empirical skepticism required to check the individual "facts" that were the system's components was a habit of mind foreign to the Middle Ages. The same tendency of mind that appreciated the philosophical system Thomas Aquinas constructed in his *Summa Theologica* appreciated the appearance of structure in a scientific work like the *Canon Medicinae* of Avicenna (980–1037). The deductive approach characteristic of scholastic philosophy took precedence over observation. Scholastic dialectics influenced medicine by making the structure of the syllogism more important than the accuracy of the conclusion. Combine respect for authority with a love of system, and the result is medical works that transmit the great man's work, or deductions derived from it, much as exegetes gloss Scripture, rather than additions to the body of knowledge derived from experimentation. Empiricism was heresy; transmission of received wisdom was orthodoxy: "He was the best doctor who could quote the most authorities."[22]

Medical education was mainly theoretical, stressing memorization. Practical medicine was impeded by various customs and beliefs. Progress in surgery in particular suffered from the belief that mucking about in the unclean recesses of the human body was a lowly task best left to barbers and other underlings. Since doing surgery was not considered an appropriate task for a doctor, there was little need for the study of anatomy. Its progress was further impeded by prohibitions against dissection of corpses—a matter of great significance in the study of poison lore because an allegation of death by poison was unprovable by autopsy.

Because of these attitudes, the kind of knowledge that would have contradicted the system of an authority, based on actual observation of the human body living and dead, was not forthcoming. Interest in the isolated physical phenomenon without reference to spiritual realities lying beneath could be construed as idle *curiositas*, a sin. Even the great Galen explained organic function in teleological terms. Like many other phenomena, disease was explained as a moral metaphor, sin's symbol and punishment. As sin permeates the soul, so disease and poison—not really distinct entities—suffuse the body. Girolamo Frascatoro, in *De Contagione et Contagiosus Morbis* (1546), was the first to assert that "persons who have been poisoned do not infect others" and to distinguish between poison and infection.[23] The first book on the action of poisons on the living body that we might regard as scientific was written much later, by Thomas Addison (1798–1866) and John Morgan (1797–1847). Until then, Avicenna's *Canon Medicinae* remained the authoritative source for the Middle Ages on vegetable and animal poisons, the bites of venomous animals and mad dogs.

The action of poison was generally regarded not so much as a medical problem as a reflection of evil in the spiritual world. Poison was seen as a demonic force, venomous animals as manifestations of the devil, and either religious or magical remedies, depending on the proclivities of the prescriber, were sought. Plato, Pliny, and Celsius attributed comprehension of the action of poisons to sorcerers and magicians.[24] "Poisoning and bewitching seemed very similar processes, especially at a time when men believed in the existence of poisons which could act at a distance or after a long interval of time,"[25] and through any one of the five senses.[26] In the study of antidotes, that the criterion of efficacy must have been almost irrelevant is apparent from many of the prescribed antidotes. "Not one drug in a hundred had the physiological action attributed to it."[27] Poison was considered the manifestation of an evil spirit, so more or less distasteful remedies were employed to drive it out. This, combined with the apparently obvious idea that the body's vital spirits transmitted the poison, led to remedies such as administering vomitives and performing venesections. The homeopathic principle postulated that a poison could cure its own results: the leaves of a poisoned tree, for example, crushed and drunk in water, cure the effects of the tree's own poison;[28] the flesh of a beast that lives on poisonous herbs is an antidote to the poison of those herbs;[29] the flesh of a poisonous animal, applied to the wound of its bite, cures it.[30] Obviously medieval people did not have a clue as to the diagnosis and treatment of poisoning.

Perhaps because they realized the hopelessness of their situation, medieval people greatly feared what Chaucer calls "pryvee empoysonyng" (I.A. 2460).[31] It was "an age when the poisoning of rivals and enemies was common," or at least commonly feared.[32] In a letter to Margaret, countess of Foix, Pope John XXII (reigned 1316–1334) thanks her for a knife made of serpent's horn, a substance said to possess the property of detecting poison.[33] In a 1609 *novelle* most noteworthy as a source for Thomas Middleton's *Women Beware Women*, a cardinal wears a "ring whose stone had the property of changing its colour when any poisoned food appeared on the table. And so he directed the stone of this ring at every dish that was brought to table."[34] There is little doubt that poison as a murder weapon could be used with impunity since medical knowledge was so scanty that its employment could not have been reliably detected, although autopsies for this purpose were being employed with increasing frequency.[35] On the other hand, since it was not known what substances were indeed poisonous or what effects a poison would have if ingested, charges of poisoning, especially by magical means, could be brought indiscriminately. An alleged episode involving the family of Philip IV (reigned 1285–1314) shows the contemporary intermingling of the ideas of poisoning and magic, plus the apparent belief that *poisonous* was synonymous with *disgusting*: "Guichard, bishop of Troyes . . . was accused of poisoning or trying to bewitch members of the French royal family . . . an apothecary was said to have poisoned Jeanne de Navarre, the wife of Philip the Fair, for the bishop by a mixture of diamonds and blood after a previous preparation of scorpions, toads, spiders and plums had been eaten by a knight who had died during the night."[36]

The idea of poison in the Middle Ages and Renaissance was thus enveloped in magic and mystery. It was the source of all contagious disease and the instrument of divine vengeance. It could not be detected in use or treated effectively. The deadly connotations were all the more fearful in that it could not be known what substances were actually poisonous; thus all substances were potentially so, and the idea gained the dimension of a universal malign force.

When the poisoner is a woman, all the misogynistic notions concerning her wiliness, deceptiveness, and seductiveness are reinforced. Throughout medieval literature, men are reminded of the ancient archetypes—of Hercules and Deianira, of Lucia and Livia. Of murder stories new to the Middle Ages, the best-known expression of the theme of woman as poisoner is the folk ballad "Lord Randal," which contains in microcosm all the themes connected with the venomous woman.[37]

The handsome young man has moved from the genuine shelter of his mother's house to the false shelter of his lover's. Although a normal part of maturation, this movement is fraught with risk. The tension of the poem is built on the new, and sinister, experience he has gained in the place belonging to his lover. Lord Randal returns to his mother's house a changed man, poisoned in both body and spirit. He has gone to his true love's house innocent and returned experienced. When he returns, his mother knows this. The function of the ballad's repetition is to elicit from her the "knowledgeability about the ways of the world which her son lacks."[38]

In the true love's house, he has accepted a meal, an act that symbolizes trust in the food-giver. The dinner consisted of " 'eels boild in broo.' " Although eels were a typical dish on the medieval menu,[39] it is also a sinister dish given the phallic connotations of the eel: the poisoner slyly seeks the power and dominance usually reserved to men. (In a French version, the meal consisted of fish, a less obviously symbolic meal but one allowing word play on *poisson/poison*.[40] Whatever the menu, the secretion of poison in a meal is a particularly sharp image of betrayal, since hostility "masks its aggressive intent behind the traditional trappings of love."[41] The treachery of the lady is stressed by the loyalty of the hounds, who trustingly share their master's meal and fate. The hounds presumably ate the leavings of the eels after Lord Randal; if they had eaten before, they would be like the loyal servants giving credence. Lord Randal has placed his credence in the wrong person; therefore he might well be " 'sick at the heart,' " psychologically poisoned by the realization of the "faithlessness confronting man in his quest for love."[42] He wearies of the hunt of love for the same reason. The motivelessness of the crime—neither son nor mother raises the question of why his true love poisoned him—stresses the theme of the wickedness of women and the general evil of sexual relationships often implied in the poison image. Lord Randal's murderous lover could be any woman; she needs no motive other than her feminine evil, source of spiritual and physical destruction.

This theme is comically echoed in Chaucer's "Nun's Priest's Tale," when Chaunticleer, completely without evidence, suspects his wife, Pertelote, of trying to poison him. Chaunticleer is devoted to the pleasures of his patron saint, Venus, and to "replecciouns" in food and drink. At the same time, he has dreams in which danger threatens. He sees himself in heroic mold, like those biblical characters with whom God communicated in dreams. His wife, on the other hand, attributes the dreams to digestive disturbances, not prophecy. As a remedy, she prescribes laxatives, preceded by "digestyves of wormes." Women in the Middle Ages were often in charge of minor illnesses such as this, physicians being inaccessible or too expensive to be concerned with such trivia. Like the contemporary derivative of this role, the concerned wife in a commercial for head cold medication, Pertelote takes charge of her husband's illness; she knows it all, including the theory that medical remedies for poison must include both vomitives and cathartics, to "purge . . . bynethe and eek above" (VII, 2953). Chaunticleer fears this, given the ominous reputation of women as poisoners. His fear has a scientific as well as a misogynistic basis. The similarity between the action of medicines and that of poisons was a medical commonplace. In preparing medicines, according to Roger Bacon's *De Erroribus Medicorum*, it is a common error to omit the requisite separation of harmful and helpful elements as in the viper the poisonous principle is separated from the medicinal flesh.[43] Whether through malice or incompetence, Pertelote might be a poisoner. Chaunticleer believes that he has only narrowly escaped being poisoned by his wife, although the story supplies no motive other than the misogynistic notion of women's unsavory connection with the venomous.

In Malory, the one truly insidious poisoning, one that encompasses all the significant ideas about the venomous woman, is the one of which Queen Guenevere is accused—and acquitted. The queen is holding a dinner for a large number of knights, among them Sir Gawain and other lesser lights, including Pinel and Patrise. Pinel had a score to settle with Gawain since Gawain had killed his kinsman. It was well known to all that Gawain "loved well all manner of fruyte, and in especiall appyls and pearys" (XVIII, 3, 613),[44] so Gawain's supper host always provided them. Knowing this, Pinel "enpoysonde sertayn appylls for to enpoyson sir Gawayne" (XVIII, 3, 613). As so often happens in literary poisonings, the poison is misdirected and results in the death of Sir Patrise, who eats the apple intended for Gawain. All "evidence" points to Guenevere as *venefica*: "Considerynge quene Guenyvere made the feste and dyner they had all suspeccion unto hir" (XVIII, 3, 614).

Why she is immediately suspected need not be made explicit because the assumptions about women and poisoning are operating under the surface of the narrative. Although Guenevere is not preparing the food herself with her own hands, she is responsible for the dinner because she authorized it. Because she is a woman, she is more likely to be attuned to the food preferences of her guests and to cater to them. Although everybody knows Gawain likes fruit, Guenevere "lette purvey" the particular fruit served at this dinner (XVIII, 3, 613), so she is responsible for it. In addition, Gawain's preference for fruit now in this context becomes a weakness, and women are well known for taking advantage of the weaknesses of men at the same time as they appear to fulfill them. Woman as food-provider has the perfect opportunity to rid herself of anyone she feeds.

Stereotypes notwithstanding, however, Guenevere has not poisoned Patrise. Pinel's using poison rather than settling a score in open battle marks him as at best unchivalrous, at worst a craven coward and traitor, well deserving of banishment from the society of worthy knights. When a woman poisons, she is seen as evil but not specifically as cowardly, because courage is not a quality expected of her; and of course she cannot really be banished from a society, the Knights of the Round Table, to which she is already ancillary. Moreover, if Pinel had defeated Gawain in open battle and had

Gawain been killed, it would have been less shameful than the death of Patrise. An additional evil of poison in the chivalric code is that, like accidents, it brings death without honor. Thus the murderer who uses poison is guilty of treason, "for the custom was such that tyme that all maner of [s]hamefull deth was called treson" (XVIII, 4, 614). But notice that Guenevere, though a queen, is to be burned at the stake for the crime, whereas Pinel, a mere knight, is only banished: a commentary on the greater seriousness of the crime when perpetrated by a woman, in acknowledgment of the absolute necessity of trusting the food-giver.

One striking feature of these medieval woman poisoners is their motivelessness. Lord Randal's lady is undoubtedly guilty, but her reasons, except for the general viciousness of women, are not clear. Chaucer's and Malory's characters are innocent; suspicion falls on them because of misogyny alone. In Elizabethan and Jacobean drama, poison is used frequently and ingeniously as a murder weapon by both women and men, and the motives are always clear. In addition, poison in these dramas stands as a symbol of a society's moral malaise.

THE DIVORCE DEBATE: ALICE ARDEN

Society's sick center is marriage. In these dramas, characters marry for the wrong motives, chief among them being material gain and social climbing. Their emotions are engaged elsewhere, if at all. The sickness in marriage manifests itself in sexual infidelity and murder, usually in that order. As one critic points out, Lady Macbeth is an unusual murderess in that lust is not one of her motives.[45] It has always been a truism in poison lore that the unfaithful wife poisons her husband to gain freer access to her lover. In societies in which a woman's best path to financial and social gain is marrying a rich man and waiting for him to die, the motivation for this is increased. In these dramas, women poison to achieve, to safeguard, or to avenge the loss of power.

In *Arden of Feversham* (1590) and Ben Jonson's *Sejanus* (1603), women follow the pattern much feared in misogynistic lore. By poisoning their husbands to marry their lovers, they seek gains concomitant upon the second marriage. In Thomas Middleton's *Women Beware Women* (1657), the anarchy loosed upon the world has its source in a failed marriage, its symptom in infidelity, and its result a destruction that spreads beyond the loveless couple.

Poison lore in Elizabethan England included, in addition to the archetypal image of something dangerous to eat, imaginative variations. In "The Audience and the Poisoners of Elizabethan Tragedy," Fredson Bowers mentions such techniques as envenomed letters and perfume. Bowers attributes to the Elizabethans a combination of sophisticated knowledge of poisons and terrified superstition about their efficacy. Unlike the Middle Ages, when actual cases of poisoning were rare, "the most casual reading of Elizabethan annals shows case after case of poisoning," especially of husbands by wives with adultery as the motive.[46] Such is the historical source of the play *Arden of Faversham*, the notorious murder of Thomas Arden by his wife in 1551.[47] The play based on this is the "first full-scale portrait of a murderess presented on the Elizabethan stage."[48] Alice's first attempt on Arden's life illustrates contemporary notions about poison as a woman's weapon.

The play opens with the intersection of those two prime concerns of bourgeois life, money and love. Arden has succeeded in the former—he has just received letters patent on all the lands of the abbey of Faversham—and conceded defeat in the latter—his wife has given her wedding ring to her lover, Mosby. Arden's world is "concerned not with passions in the purified form they often take in tragedy, but with matters such as class and property. . . . Arden is offended not just because Alice is dishonouring him but because she is doing so with a social climber."[49] Arden's naive confidant, Franklin, advises him to take a philosophical approach to this mishap in love: "it is not strange / That women will be false and wavering" (I, ll. 20–21). Franklin suggests that Arden, rather than express jealousy, let Alice's heart grow fonder by spending time away from her in London. Against his better judgment, Arden agrees. This is an obvious mistake, since if Alice is unfaithful with her husband nearby, she will be a weaker reed still in his absence.

Enter Alice Arden, a misogynist's dream—deceptive and deadly. Expressing surprise at her husband's early rising, she teases him: "Had I been wake, you had not rise so soon" (I, l. 59). Having roused Arden's suspicions by calling out Mosby's name in her sleep, she devises a false explanation of it. Hypocritical too is her lamentation for Arden's departure. All of this causes the too-trusting Arden to deny the evidence of his own senses, like the equally gullible cuckold, Januarie, in Chaucer's "Merchant's Tale," and to allow his wife to persuade him that the perceptible evidence—seeing the ring on Mosby's hand, hearing his sleeping wife call Mosby's name—means nothing.[50]

In soliloquy, Alice explains her motives for wanting to kill Arden. In her lust for the power and freedom of widowhood, Alice is a vicious fictional daughter of the Wife of Bath. She wants free access to her lover, and more than that, she wants to inherit Arden's money. She has married above her own social status and, in surviving Arden, would inherit not only his money but also his position, enabling her to have Mosby and power over him. With Arden's money and a widow's independence and status, she would bring a solid basis for mastery to a second marriage; in return, Mosby would achieve upward social and financial mobility. The running title's description of Alice as motivated by the "unsatiable desire of filthie lust" (2) is only partially true; lust for power in marriage is Alice's prime mover. To this end she wants Arden dead.

The plot Mosby contrives illustrates the credulity with which an Elizabethan audience would approach poison lore. The ancient belief that poison
could penetrate the body through any of the senses persisted:

> I happened on a painter yesternight,
> The only cunning man of Christendom,
> For he can temper poison with his oil
> That whoso looks upon the work he draws
> Shall, with the beams that issue from his sight,
> Suck venom to his breast and slay himself.
> Sweet Alice, he shall draw thy counterfeit,
> That Arden may, by gazing on it, perish.
>
> (I, ll. 227–34)

The cunning man, a male witch with the witch's characteristic knowledge
of poisons, can amplify Alice's own malevolence. Looking upon an image
of Alice, Arden will die. Mosby unintentionally sees Alice as basilisk, an
unflattering but accurate acknowledgment of her malevolent influence. Neither he nor she recognizes the implications of the envenomed portrait. To
Alice, the plan is impractical because of the strong possibility for misdi-
recting the poison:

> Ay, but, Mosby, that is dangerous;
> For thou or I or any other else,
> Coming into the chamber where it hangs, may die.
>
> (I, ll. 235–37)

So they consult the painter (also promising him the hand of obliging Sue,
Alice's serving woman and Mosby's sister) for "some other poison ... such
as might be put into his broth, / And yet in taste not to be found at all" (I,
ll. 279–81). The painter obliges, and Alice goes off with the deadly dram,
which is to be secreted in Arden's "drink / Or any kind of broth that he
shall eat" (I, ll. 283–84).

The next episode illustrates by contrast the concept of poison as a woman's weapon. Alice exits to make what she intends to be Arden's last breakfast. Mosby remains, to be confronted by Arden on the matter of adultery.
There is some swordplay and accusatory talk of male weapons large and
small, but a full-fledged duel is averted by Mosby's deception and Arden's
too-swift forgiveness. Yet the men confront each other openly, even if dis-
honestly on Mosby's part and foolishly on Arden's. Meanwhile, the more
deadly and unacknowledged enemy, Alice, is preparing her secret weapon.

Ever so kindly she presents it to Arden: "Husband, sit down; your breakfast will be cold" (I, l. 360). He immediately tastes the poison (obviously
the painter did not make it to specifications, which were "in taste not to
be found at all" [I, l. 281]). In Holinshed's *Chronicles*, the *Arden* play-

wright's source, an explanation lies in Alice's ineptness in following a simple recipe. The painter has told her to pour the poison into "the bottome of a porrenger" and milk on top, "which circumstance she forgetting, did cleane contrarie, putting in the milke first, and afterward the poison."[51] In both source and play, Arden stops eating: "There's something in this broth / That is not wholesome. Didst thou make it, Alice?" (I, ll. 365–66). While those who see Arden as a tragic innocent point to the "magical ability of a saintly person to detect poison in his food,"[52] the failure of the poison can also be traced to natural causes, chief among them being failures in knowledge of the current state of the art. In Avicenna's authoritative discussion of poisons in his *Canon Medicinae*, he mentions poison as being commonly administered *in vinum*. This procedure becomes a staple of poison lore. For example, in Gaspar of Sarnana's *Papal Garland Concerning Poisons*, written circa 1348 for Pope Urban V, the writer raises the question "why poison is recognized with more difficulty when mixed with things having a strong taste." Somewhat anticlimactically, he explains this by saying that the strong substances "distract the attention."[53] Bland broth will not do. The intoxicating effects of wine make the victim more likely to drink first and question later. Too, in the evening a man's defenses are lower—he is tired and hungry—so Alice's decision to administer the poison at breakfast, when Arden is alert, rather than at dinner, is a mistake. Alice's plot thus fails through ignorance of the proper administration of poison. To cover her mistake and prevent further investigation of the broth, Alice flings it to the ground in a feigned tantrum, impersonating a housewife irritated at a demanding husband: "There's nothing that I do can please your taste" (I, ll. 368).

In Holinshed, the survival of Arden is attributed to an undramatizable reaction: "Then he took horsse and road toward Canturburie, and by the waie fell into extreme purging upwards and downewards and so escaped for that time."[54] Since laxatives and vomitives are the preferred remedies in poison lore (they are tried, to no avail, on the ailing Arcite in Chaucer's Knight's Tale, who suffers from a venomous swelling or infection), nature saves Arden in Holinshed. The *Arden* playwright gives him a more dignified remedy in the universal antidote, mithridate, which Arden's friend Franklin carries on his person, testimony to the general fear of poisoning in Elizabethan England. Alice histrionically offers to eat the antidote as if it were poison: "Then should my cares and troubles have an end!" (I, l. 388). Arden, a man of trusting nature, cannot comprehend the degree of duplicity his wife possesses, and he reassures her of his trust. Again, against all evidence he lowers his guard. This loving forgiveness leads to his destruction.

Arden departs for London, and Alice and Mosby lament the failure of their plot: "This powder was too gross and populous," too obvious (I, l. 425). Mosby begins to back off from the relationship with Alice on the excuse that, to avoid a duel with Arden, he had promised "never hereafter to solicit" Alice (I, l. 430), and he intends to keep is word. The "striking of bargains," as Alexander Leggatt points out, is central to the play.[55] But it is only men who feel obliged to keep their word. Alice laughs to scorn this idea of a binding oath; she points out that "oaths are words, and words is wind, / And wind is mutable" (I, ll. 436–37), that she has broken her own marriage oath already, and that the oath can be evaded by linguistic hair splitting: if he cannot "solicit" her, she can "importune" him. While words mean nothing to Alice, yet Mosby still clings to his determination to keep his oath to Arden "unbroken whilst he lives" (I, l. 440); so Alice, taking advantage of Mosby's verbal error, the unclear pronoun reference, and incidentally contradicting herself on the issue of the importance of words, assumes that this means Arden's death must be hastened to shorten the time span covered by the oath. The passive Mosby allows her to initiate a new plan involving hired thugs ominously named Black Will and Shakebag.

If ever murder was premeditated, this one is; in fact Alice does little else in the play but premeditate murder. The whole play is devoted to further attempts to carry out the failed plot. Of the adulterous couple, Alice is the more active plotter, far more so than Mosby, who makes several attempts to back off from both the relationship and the murder plot. At one point he allows Alice to think she has "incurred his wrath" (I, l. 122); at another he breaks off entirely (I, l. 190); he even halfheartedly suggests that they "give it over" and let Arden live (XII, l. 64). But Alice can get their love and the plot back on course each time. His passivity in both love and murder is indicated by the nature of the dialogue. His conversation with Alice consists largely of questions to her on how the plot is going. Mosby's one attempt to initiate his own plot is a quixotic plan to acquire an envenomed crucifix. It would work by transmitting its poisonous influence through the air, like the envenomed portrait of Alice which she earlier rejected as impractical. Like all poisons that were believed to operate through the senses of sight and smell, both crucifix and portrait cannot be precisely targeted and so kill all in the vicinity indiscriminately, perhaps even the poisoners. The painter Clarke suggests protecting themselves by wearing tight-fitting spectacles and stuffing a rhubarb leaf in the nose. Despite this elaborate planning, Mosby's suggestion comes to nothing; indeed he seems to forget it, leaving the matter of the murder in Alice's competent hands.

Protected only by his own sweet innocence and the platitudinous advice of his friend Franklin, Arden survives multiple attempts on his life foiled by the merest coincidence. The plot outcome is, of course, Arden's death, but in a fashion clumsier and less easily concealed than a successful poisoning would have been. Mosby criticizes Alice for this: "to acquaint each stranger with our drifts" (I, l. 578) is to risk discovery. Poisoning being a secret crime, none other than the poisoner and the supplier would have to know; this would lessen the chances of discovery. It is a domestic crime requiring no outside help, no Black Wills and Shakebags with their male strength but also their conspicuousness. The Elizabethans believed with their forebears that poisons could be adjusted to work over time and simulate natural illness; the possibility of a time-release poison is constantly debated in the medical literature and shows the confusion in the medical sources between poison and infection or contagion. With a slow-acting poison, murder might never be suspected, and even if it were, the perpetrator has excellent alibi possibilities. With the failure of the poison plot, Alice and Mosby wind up with irremovable bloodstains and with a corpse obviously not dead of natural causes that most inconveniently bleeds anew in the presence of its murderer. Alice pays for not using the conventional female weapon.

Adulterer and murderer, Alice seems a latter-day Juvenalian character. Motivated by those two notorious drives of women, sexual lust and power lust, Alice betrays her husband on every possible level. Her duplicitous behavior throughout makes it hard to tell when, if ever, she speaks truth. She lies to virtually everyone in the play, including Mosby. So it is difficult to see her conversion in extremis as sincere; rather she seems to be acting the expected role of "Christian penitent"[56] much as she acted, say, the dutiful wife or the doting mistress. The key word in the running title that describes Alice's character is "discimulation"; she is all falsehood, all pretense.

As murderer of her husband, she is guilty of treason under English law, rebellion being as serious in the commonwealth of the family as disorder in the state. But Alice's evil has spread beyond her, and so must punishment: Mosby, his sister Sue, the servant Michael, Bradshaw, Black Will, and Shakebag all die too. Mosby's final words point the misogynistic moral: "Fie upon women!—this shall be my song" (XVIII, l. 34). But his blanket accusation is not the whole explanation of the events surrounding the death of Arden of Faversham. Rather it is the diseased state of marriage, the disorder in the family caused by marriage's becoming a vehicle for sexual lust and power lust, which leads to death and destruction of guilty and innocent alike.

Late in the play, when Arden's murder becomes an end in itself after so many abortive attempts, Alice still has clearly in sight the two motives for the crime, love and power:

> Why should he thrust his sickle in our corn,
> Or what hath he to do with thee, my love,
> Or govern me that am to rule myself?

(X, ll. 83–85)

The way Alice's thinking reflects the disruption of the natural order of things is apparent. The legitimate husband is the usurper, thrusting his sickle into the lovers' corn. He is irrelevant, but so is Mosby himself since Alice's intention is to rule herself in both senses of the term: to rule in her own right (over Mosby) and to be her own boss. The Chaucerian theme of women's "maistrye" and "soverayntee" links Alice Arden with the Wife of

Bath, with Alice being the dark underside of the Wife's desire for self-determination.[57] But if Alice is power driven, it is partially because the men around her are weak, inadequate to play the role of governing her. Like an early draft for a Hedda Gabler, Alice Arden is one of those heroines for whom the domestic drama is enacted on too narrow a stage to allow scope for their driving ambitions. The result is disastrous not only for her but for the whole society of which she is part.

The notoriety of the Arden case, plus the popularity of the play, has been explained by critic Catherine Belsey as a response to "Alice Arden's challenge to the institution of marriage." At the time of both crime and play, a shift from arranged economic marriages to marriages based on mutual affection was in progress. The great divorce debate in which John Milton figured so prominently showed the "polarization of conflicting definitions of marriage." To the Anglicans, marriage was indissoluble; to the Puritans, marriage depended on continuing mutual consent. A proponent of the latter viewpoint, John Rainolds, writing *A Defence of the Judgment of the Reformed Churches* in 1609, saw divorce as a solution to the problem of murder. The hated husband is in real danger:

And how can he choose but live still in fear & anguish of mind, least shee add drunckennesse to thirst, & murder to adultery: I meane least he serve him as *Clytemnestra* did *Agamemnon*, *Livia* did *Drusus* as *Mrs. Arden* did her husband? (Quoted in Belsey 95)

Thus both play and case became evidence in the case for divorce. The unloved husband needed a way out with his life. This fear of murder exaggerates but is nevertheless based on reality. "The existing historical evidence gives us no reason to believe that there was a major outbreak of women murduring their husbands in the sixteenth century. What it does suggest, however, is a widespread belief that they were likely to do so."[58] It is as if men sensed that for women, widowhood was a preferable condition, and so perceived themselves as endangered. Since Roman times, a widow was *sui juris*, her own mistress. In the Middle Ages, "childless widows often regained full rights over property in France, Italy and Spain. In such cases we may say that the death of one partner was the legal liberation of another."[59] Although the divorced woman would by no means have the legal independence (or money) of the widow, nevertheless at a time when women were beginning to see the single choice of a marriage partner as less than irrevocable, men might well begin to see divorce as an improvement. At the very least, it would give women like Alice Arden an option other than murder.

THE POWER PLAY: LIVIA

The irony of the theme of poison lady as murderer is that the same objects and qualities that a woman like Alice Arden uses to evil ends could be used to legitimate ends. Alice wants mastery and sexual satisfaction but feels she must be rid of Arden to acquire both. Her drive and determination organize this misguided project in spite of the incompetence and faltering commitment of others. Without attempting to reconstruct Alice as heroine, it is clear that for her, poison is an instrument of her own power, and she uses it with initiative, independence, and self-determination.

These characteristics of Alice are all the more noticeable when she is compared to Livia in Ben Jonson's *Sejanus*. Livia is a pawn in Sejanus's quest for power. Instead of being an initiator for good or ill, she is a tool. Therefore, although she seems to fit the image of the venomous woman, in fact she does not, because it is Sejanus, not she, who wields the power. She serves his power needs, not her own.

The character of Livia is a byword in poison lore for the treacherous wife, but in Jonson's play she appears merely pathetic. Her husband, Drusus, is son of Tiberius, emporer of Rome, and next in line for the throne. Sejanus is a favorite of Tiberius and thus in competition with Livia's husband. To eliminate him, Sejanus seduces Livia and enlists her aid in the plot to poison Drusus. In Jonson's argument that prefaces the play, he describes the basic situation thus: Drusus, jealous of Sejanus's influence with his father,

struck him publicly on the face. To revenge which disgrace, Livia, the wife of Drusus (being before corrupted by him to her dishonor, and the discovery of her husband's counsels) Sejanus practiseth with, together with her physician, called Eudemus, and one Lydgus, an eunuch, to poison Drusus. This their inhuman act having successful and unsuspected passage, it emboldeneth Sejanus to farther and more insolent projects, even the ambition of the empire.[60]

The argument articulates several basic concepts of the play. If the rivalry between Drusus and Sejanus was exacerbated by a male-to-male insult, then male-to-male open combat, not sly poisoning, should have resulted. Yet even given the use of poison rather than combat, the plot still operates in a way that renders Livia unnecessary. It is not her plot or her poison; she does not even administer it herself; her role is limited to consent. The poison is made by her physician, Eudemus, and administered by Drusus's eunuch, · Lydgus; why Sejanus thinks he needs Livia at all is unclear. He does not at any point allege that he loves her; his attitude toward women in general is callous. In *Sejanus*, the real world is the male world of political ambition, to which women are irrelevant except when employable as implements. Given Livia's minimal importance to the plot, Sejanus's romantic encomium to Livia is hypocritical:

> Royal lady,
> Though I have loved you long, and with that height
> Of zeal and duty—like the fire, which more
> It mounts, it trembles—thinking nought could add
> Unto the fervor which your eye had kindled;
> Yet now I see your wisdom, judgment, strength,
> Quickness, and will to apprehend the means
> To your own good and greatness, I protest
> Myself through-rarefied, and turned all flame
> In your affection.
>
> (II, ll. 24–33)

As stock Machiavellian villain, Sejanus cannot be given the redeeming virtue of true love for Livia; neither is she any more than a stock villainess— gullible, greedy, grasping. Sejanus knows that her desire for power motivates her love for him. Therefore, what better appeal than to her "masculine" qualities as well as her "feminine" ones?

> Such a spirit as yours
> Was not created for the idle second
> To a poor flash as Drusus, but to shine
> Bright as the moon among the lesser lights,
> And share the sov'reignty of all the world.
> Then Livia triumphs in her proper sphere,
> When she and her Sejanus shall divide
> The name of Caesar.
>
> (II, ll. 33–40)

Livia's reaction to this, her drive for power, is not analyzed; Jonson leaves her character undeveloped. Her major function seems to be to stand for feminine deceptiveness in marriage, hardly an outstanding feature in a play devoted to male duplicity in politics.

To expand on this theme, the planning scene of the play is followed by a symbolically significant scene between Livia and her physician, Eudemus. Drusus has sent for his wife, in preparation for which meeting Livia has Eudemus make up her face with a "fucus" or cosmetic, gives her "a dentifrice ...to clear [her] teeth" and a "pomatum...to smooth [her] skin" (II, ll. 79–81). Face painting is always a symbol of deception and false seeming in Jonson,[61] since it is used with the intention of improving (in Jonson's terms, falsifying) her appearance to "hold the heart" of Sejanus, the agent of her increased power:

> Some will think
> Your fortune could not yield a deeper sound
> Than mixed with Drusus, but when they shall hear
> That, and the thunder of Sejanus meet—

Sejanus, whose high name doth strike the stars,
And rings about the conclave, great Sejanus,
Whose glories, style, and titles are himself—
The often iterating of Sejanus,
Then they will lose their thoughts, and be ashamed
To take acquaintance of them.

(II, ll. 94–103)

At the same time as he is improving her appearance before she meets her husband, Eudemus is advising her to ally her fortunes with Sejanus, cosmetic and advice forming together a pattern of deception. The painting of the face in Renaissance tragedy is, as Annette Drew-Bear points out, an external indication of inner corruption, especially deception, "assuming false faces."[62] In addition, as the audience would realize, the ceruse or white lead Eudemus uses to make the "fucus" is itself a deadly poison. The use of poisonous substances in the making of cosmetics is also discussed by medical writer Antonio Brasavola. Writing in 1534, Brasavola asserts that silver sublimate, one such ingredient, affects the female body adversely indeed: "Women use it to whiten their skin but at great cost, since the teeth decay, the breath takes on a bad odor, the eyes cloud, the skin wrinkles and they are seized by apoplexy and rush to a sudden death."[63] The white lead Eudemus uses on Livia has a similar effect. It renders the lady as unattractive without as she is corrupt within. The neat confluence of symbols gives moralists like Thomas Tuke a prime opportunity to draw a physical-spiritual analogy. In his formidably titled 1616 treatise, *A Discourse against Painting and Tincturing of Women. Wherein the abominable sinnes of Murther and Poysoning, Pride and Ambition, Adultery and Witchcraft, are set foorth & discovered*, Tuke sees an inevitable continuum: making up the face, murder, pride, adultery, and witchcraft are all manifestations of the same evil force, and all feminine.[64] The point of intersection is knowledge of deceptive tactics and substances, which enables a woman either to paint her face or to commit adultery or to murder, as the spirit takes her.

Although Jonson's play was performed in 1603 and Thomas Tuke's treatise is dated 1616, the ideas Tuke expresses are far from new. It is obvious from the space Jonson devoted to a scene of face painting in the midst of a murder plot that Jonson made the same connection as did Tuke among adultery, deception, poisoning, and cosmetics. Tuke's treatise is a long diatribe against women's use of cosmetics, which he sees as manifesting assorted character defects. The first and cardinal sin is pride, since a woman who is attempting to improve upon what God gave her is obviously interested in raising herself above her allocated slot in his creation. Since, Tuke reasons, not everyone is rich or noble, not everyone need be beautiful either. There can be no other reason for the use of cosmetics than lust. With "vile drugs adultering her face," she "closely allures the adulterers embrace" (B3ᵛ). By the same token (and probably obtaining them from the same source), this same kind of woman "will not sticke to stoope to practise love-potions by charms and socerie" (43). In an age when physical appearance was thought to mirror the state of the soul, changing the face flouted God's truth and substituted artifice for nature. A woman who would deceive about the color of her cheeks would deceive about other things. She goes "disguized," in a false guise, "masked" in "antifaces"; because she "beares two faces," men "misesteeme" her. She is a "false coyner," a "show," a "mimique." Her ability thus to transform herself smacks of sorcery:

> She is a sickly woman alwaies dying,
> Her color's gone, but more she is a buying...
> She is *Medea*, who by likelihood
> Can change old *Aeson* into younger blood,
> Which can old age in youthful colours bury...

(B2ʳ)

Because of cosmetics, the sick look well, the well look sick, and the old look young. The result is that men are deceived and trapped into unwise marriages: "If she be *unmarried*, shee desires to be *mistaken*, that she may be *taken*" (60). How are men to know what constitutes the truth of such a creature? Tuke tells the story of a deceived husband who married a "glorious idoll," only to find that her beauty was due only to cosmetics, "such poisons one would lothe to kisse." He thought his wife was "a lasse, / Young, fresh, and faire." But when the poisonous cosmetics have taken their toll (or perhaps when, safely married, she stops using them), her real self emerges:

> my lovely, lively bride
> Is turn'd a hagge, a fury by my side,
> With hollow yellow teeth, or none perhaps,
> With stinking breath, swart cheeks, & hanging chaps,
> With wrinkled neck, and stooping, as she goes,
> With driveling mouth, and with a sniveling nose.

(B3ʳ)

A man cannot make a wise choice of a wife under these circumstances. If "to deceive men with counterfit wares" is unjust, so it is "to deceive them with a disguised countenance" (4). If the appearance of her merchandise for sale is not as represented, Tuke regards this as "injustice with feigned shewes to endeavour to cousin others" (4). The annoyance of a bilked consumer blocks any thought of the possible unwisdom of marrying on the basis of appearance alone. Tuke sees it as poetic justice that the substances that are used to deceive are themselves "corosive and byting" (B4ʳ), causing a remetamorphosis, which restores synchrony between the inner and the outer woman. Who would want to kiss a "woman of polluted lipts" (A3ʳ)? It goes without saying that the unlovely lady is unlovable.

Despite the formidable title, Tuke's treatise never gets to a discussion of murder. But it is obvious that for him pride, adultery, deception, and the use of poisonous substances form a moral continuum. He would see Jonson's Livia as fitting his description neatly: hoping to advance her situation in life and to satisfy her adulterous lust for Sejanus, she poisons her unsuspecting husband, Drusus. What else can you expect from a woman who paints her face?

But Livia, while she is deceiving with a false face, is also being deceived as well. Drusus dead, Sejanus shows little interest in her. In fact, he mentions her only once more in the play—in a discussion with Tiberius in which he attempts to cement his alliance with the emperor by asking for the now-widowed Livia's hand in marriage. It is clear, however, that for Sejanus, this is negotiable; there is no suggestion that he has ever loved Livia, and when the emperor fails to assent immediately, Sejanus drops the idea. He speaks of Livia no more in the play. As he left his wife for her for political ends, so he abandons all thought of Livia—it seems the playwright forgets her too—when she has served her plot purpose in abetting the murder of Drusus, the obstacle in Sejanus's rise to power. Livia fades from the scene, neither independent enough nor formidable enough to be a factor for good or evil, excluded from the male world of power politics.

THE LONGEST MURDER: LADY ESSEX

Although her name is a byword for the traitorous wife, Livia in Jonson is a cipher by comparison to Alice Arden. But these poison ladies in literature could hardly compare with Frances Howard, Lady Essex. After 1613, when she poisoned Sir Thomas Overbury, no piece of literature involving a woman poisoner would fail to remind the reader or theatergoer of the famous case. The convoluted events surrounding the Overbury murder, where illicit sex and sleazy politics combined in a fashion more worthy of melodrama than history, illustrate as effectively as a piece of literature the themes surrounding the image of the venomous woman.[65]

Overbury's fate resulted from his entanglement in the love life of his patron, Robert Carr, later Viscount Rochester, still later earl of Somerset, who was himself a protégé of James I of England. The events leading to Overbury's death began in 1606 when Frances Howard, then thirteen, married Robert Devereaux, earl of Essex, then fourteen. This arranged marriage was not, and was not intended to be, consummated. The two children returned to their premarital activities, Frances home to mother and Robert back to the Continent to complete his education. In 1609, Essex, then a comparatively mature seventeen, returned to England to claim his bride, then sixteen. But in the meantime Frances, Lady Essex, had fallen in love with Robert Carr and intended to divorce her husband to marry him. Overbury had been aiding this love affair and keeping in Carr's favor by writing love letters and sonnets for him to send to Lady Essex. Meanwhile the whole Howard family was pressuring her to admit Lord Essex to her bed, to no avail. By this time Lady Essex was Carr's mistress. What to do?

Enter two characters: Simon Forman and Ann Turner. The former, a magician and astrologer, and the latter, a Celestina come to life, a dressmaker, abortionist, and maker of love potions, team up to help Lady Essex. Just as if she were a character in a *venefica* story, Lady Essex consulted these two and received two potions to shape the behavior of two men: one to cool off Essex, another to warm up Carr. Thus Lady Essex hoped to keep her marriage unconsummated, giving her grounds for divorce so she could marry the ardent Carr.[66] The hapless Essex, according to his protégé Arthur Wilson, was subjected to Forman's " 'natural magic' " and " 'subtlety' ": " 'for no linen came near his body, that was not rinsed with their camphor compositions, and other faint and wasting ingredients, and all inward applications were foisted on him by corrupted servants, to lessan and debilitate the seminal operations.' " Another contemporary commentator attributes Essex's impotence versus Frances to sympathetic magic rather than poison: " 'At last they framed a Picture in Wax, and got a Thorn from a Tree that bore Leaves, and stuck upon the Privity of the said Picture, by which means they accomplished their desire.' " The poisons worked only when Essex was near Frances; when he was away from her, he recovered. Being then "hard put to keep him at bay," Frances, according to Arthur Wilson, resorted to " 'an artifice too immodest to be discovered, to hinder penetration.' " As if all that were not enough, Frances also discouraged Essex by simple obnoxiousness, " 'calling him "cow," "coward," and "beast." ' "[67]

Whether the potions, devices, effigies, or Lady Essex's own behavior was the cause, by 1612 the Essexes were in the Stuart monarchy's version of divorce court, the grounds being nonconsummation caused by impotence. By this time Lord Essex wanted to be rid of his troublesome wife but not at the expense of his reputation as lover and future marriage prospect. One kind theory dreamed up by the king's Divorce Commission was that Essex was bewitched; the result was impotence toward his wife, *maleficium versus hanc*, but toward no other woman in the world. The divorce seemed in the bag. Reenter Overbury, who had shifted sides in the dispute: a Howard marriage would be more demanding than a clandestine affair, plus his patron, Carr, would be too firmly allied to this powerful family and too often away from court to serve what Overbury saw as his own political interests. Overbury tried to discourage the affair by cutting off his literary output on behalf of Carr, but to no avail. When Lady Essex began to suspect that Overbury would reveal what he knew about her relationship with Carr (her alleged virginity was a piece of evidence in the divorce case), she became his implacable enemy. She decided to kill him. Meanwhile Overbury had fallen out of favor with James by gossiping that through his influence over Carr, he influenced James as well. To get rid of Overbury, James offered him an insignificant ambassadorship. When Overbury refused to be thus removed from the scene, James clapped him into the Tower, thus inadvertently providing Lady Essex with a captive victim.

After one abortive attempt involving one Mary Woods, known as Cunning Mary, a competitor of Mrs. Turner in the potions-and-poisons trade, Lady Essex returned to her original supplier, Mrs. Turner, who was "always ready in a crisis with useful acquaintances in the lower reaches of the medical profession,"[68] and put her in contact with an apothecary who could supply a time-release poison to kill Overbury slowly, as a wasting disease would. They settled on red arsenic but apparently decided to add to the venomous arsenal. The process of administering it was a drawn-out affair, involving a steady stream of tarts, venison pasties, and jellies sent to the now-imprisoned Overbury. In an episode for which the term *overkill* should have been invented, they were stuffed with "a fine range of poisons ... 'Arsenic, Lapis Costitus, Mercury Sublimate, Cantharides and Great Spiders.' "[69] Inevitably, unless Overbury had a gargantuan appetite, a lot or two of these envenomed goodies must fall into the wrong hands: a warder's wife finished off some soup and became violently ill; a deliverer licked his fingers and promptly lost his hair and several fingernails.

But Overbury did not die. The situation was complicated by the fact that Overbury (and his patron Carr as well) was in the habit of using vomitives to render himself ill and thus manipulate the emotions of King James. Overbury also seemed to be a chronic user of medications not prescribed by a doctor for treating various imaginary ills. In fact, most of the people in this odd story used drugs and potions to nonmedical ends. So often did Overbury do this that it obscured the effect of the real poison. Perhaps, too, he had built up some immunities. So despite broth, jellies, and pasties, he had to be finished off by a sublimate of mercury enema administered by a bribed apothecary's assistant.

Throughout what must certainly be one of the longest murders in history, the obtuse Carr seems not to have known of his lady's scheme. With Overbury dead and the divorce granted, Lady Essex and Carr (now Lord and Lady Somerset) could have lived happily ever after, aided by medical ignorance: "In an age when chemical analysis was impossible and medical evidence wholly unreliable, it was extremely difficult to get at any certain truth in poisoning cases."[70] Were it not for an attack of conscience on the part of the apothecary's assistant, who made what he thought was a deathbed confession, all involved would have gone free. Underlings like Mrs. Turner were hanged, but not Lady Essex, who was pardoned, presumably having suffered enough. Thomas Tuke mentions the execution of Mrs. Turner approvingly, commending the state's wisdom in convicting her, but not mentioning Lady Essex at all. As a prime example of seeing all the world from the perspective of one's hobbyhorse, Tuke connects Mrs. Turner's artifice in fashion with her propensity to poison. He depicts Mrs. Turner as repenting of the former but mentions the latter not at all. Tuke movingly describes Mrs. Turner as dying with words of fashion advice upon her lips, condemning a style she had popularized, the wearing of starched yellow ruffles; she expires "exhorting the assistants with much earnestness to leave off their yellow bands, and of garish fashions, the very inventions of the devil."[71] It is as if both Tuke and Mrs. Turner have missed the point of her execution.

The Essex case, fact that reads like fiction, is more important than any of the many other actual murder cases involving women and poison in that it had an impact on literature because of the notoriety of the people involved. While the memory of the case remained fresh, any literary poisoning (especially in that most public art form, the drama) reminded the audience of Frances Howard and her love problems. Thomas Middleton in particular was influenced by the case in his unsuccessful play *The Witch*, staged only once, probably in 1615 or 1616. The political allusions in this play might have been so controversial as to account in part for the play's failure, so when Middleton depicts women as poisoners again, in *Women Beware Women*, probably first staged in 1621, he eliminates the roman à clef aspects and draws on a more remote historical source.[72]

UPWARD MOBILITY: BIANCA

When Thomas Middleton used the name *Livia* for his pivotal character in *Women Beware Women*, a name that had long been associated with venomousness, he did so to call attention to her function as source of evil in the play, which culminates in the poisonings of the masque. While Middleton found a character named Livia in an English translation of the French source of the Isabella-Hippolito subplot,[73] he surely must also have known the old story of the poisoner Livia, as did Jonson. Unlike Jonson's play, in which Livia is depicted as a passive tool in the hands of Sejanus, Middleton's character is powerful. Although it is the other two important women characters in the play, Bianca and Isabella, who actually use poison, Livia is its ultimate source; she is the chief exemplar of the moral corruption that permeates the world of the drama. It has often been noticed that in *Women Beware Women*, poison functions as part of an imagery system that includes images of disease and decay as well, serves as an expression of sexual corruption, often in the service of material gain, and culminates in the poisonings of the masque scene. The fate of the characters who die by poison expresses the connection between unhallowed sex and death. Sexual excess is described "in terms of food and eating,"[74] especially "gluttonous feeding,"[75] or consuming something deadly. So it is appropriate that the deadly sin of lust, which kills the soul, be metaphorically expressed by poison, which kills the body. The poison within is expressed as a plot element: "Lust has utterly corrupted its victims, and its actual and metaphorical infection has become poison."[76]

In addition to these concepts, commonly noted by critics, there is another significance to the image of poison in *Women Beware Women*. Isabella's and Bianca's use of the weapon of the weak throws attention on the key concept of feminine weakness in the play. If Bianca and Isabella are "void of moral stamina,"[77] one reason is that they are portrayed against the background of the misogynistic concept of the weak reed. In this image, women are envisioned as clinging vines, unable to stand alone, requiring a strong prop around which to wind, and manifesting a propensity to fall into sin when deprived of this prop. As a fourteenth-century Florentine put it, " 'The female is an empty thing and easily swayed: she runs great risks when she is away from her husband. Therefore, keep females in the house, keep them as close to yourself as you can."[78] A commentator contemporaneous with Middleton, Richard Braithwaite, agrees: "How subject poor *Women* be to lapses, and recidivations, being left their owne Guardians, daily experience can sufficiently discover. Of which number those always proved the weakest, who were confidentest of their owne strength."[79] Implied in the image is the need for women to be protected, guided, supported, and made secure, a traditional function of male relatives. Women in Bianca's and Isabella's society need the "context of a whole network of family relationships that ought to guarantee social and moral order."[80] Their feeling of a need for protection is a realistic response to their vulnerability. While weakness is a personal trait, vulnerability is a result of the lack of social position and power. The two traits need not be combined in the same person, but in this play they are, in both the young women. Their security lies in alliances with powerful men—licit if possible, illicit if necessary.

In the traditional wedding ceremony, the bride is escorted down the aisle by her father, her arm hooked through his as if she needs physical support, then turned over to the new protector to be escorted through life in the same way. The ritual dramatizes the unspoken belief that a woman cannot walk alone and so should not forsake one protector until she has another lined up. To maximize her security, customary supports must be maintained. The idea of feminine weakness explains Bianca's rapidly shifting allegiance from Leantio to the Duke, the secrecy of Isabella's liaison with Hippolito, and the vulnerability of both to Livia's manipulations. Both young women are indeed weak; they perceive themselves as weak; they need a man to guarantee their security; then they use deception to maintain whatever degree of security they have achieved through this man, even to the use of poison, the weapon of the weak, to destroy anyone who threatens their precarious position. For Bianca especially, the concept of weakness inherent in the image of poison is an important element linking the two Biancas, the radically different characters she becomes in the course of the play; in fact, the woman she becomes between the time she takes the poison and her death is yet a third Bianca.

The woman of whom Isabella and Bianca should beware is Livia; she can be the "catalytic agent of all the evil which takes place in the play"[81] because she is not a weak woman. Unlike the malleable Livia of earlier literature and of the Jonson play, who, a victim of her adulterous passion and Sejanus's ambition, allows herself to be used as an instrument to remove her husband from Sejanus's path to power, Middleton's Livia is the initiator of action. Compared to the other three women in the play, Livia is in the strongest position socially and economically. First, she is a widow, an independent woman who "never mean[s] more to marry" (I, ii, 51),[82] a "typical survivor,"[83] retaining the social position and money of her two late husbands without their inconvenient physical presence. Second, unlike Leantio's mother, also a widow but poor, Livia is insulated from weakness by her money. Finally, unlike Bianca and Isabella, she is mature; she corrects Fabritio's compliment to her (he calls her sweet and witty) as condescending, fit for a girl of sixteen and not the "blown" and "wise" adult woman she is (I, ii, 48–49). Therefore, unlike Bianca and Isabella, she has no need to ally herself with an older man; like the Wife of Bath, she can afford, both psychologically and financially, a purely sexual liaison with a younger man. She is a worldly sophisticate who "enjoys manipulating other people"[84] for the pleasures of exercising power and chooses to use this skill to corrupt Bianca and Isabella. What she is doing is not merely illicit matchmaking. She is destabilizing their relationships with men, relationships that are the two younger women's only assurance of security. Bianca and Isabella begin the play as innocent girls and degenerate into venomous women. In the process, they are passive channels through which Livia's evil spreads, instruments rather than agents.

Evil as she is, however, Livia panders to but does not originate base tendencies already existing in the other characters and in the larger society. The characters' basic needs are the usual ones: sex and the security provided by money and material possessions. In Livia's case, she has money and so can buy sex. For her, a third motivation enters: power. Her main drive is to demonstrate her ability to manipulate people by appealing to their basic needs:

> I can bring forth
> As pleasant fruits as sensuality wishes
> In all her teeming longings. This I can do.

(II, i, 30–32)

Sexual and financial corruption reign in this society, giving Livia plenty of material with which to work.

In the subplot, the groundwork for Isabella's and Hippolito's sexual corruption is laid in the custom of the "mercenary, enforced marriage,"[85] which renders a woman powerless to determine her own future. Guardiano and Fabritio are arranging a marriage between the former's Ward and the latter's daughter. Each is casual with respect to the effect of their plan on the happiness of the young; both assume that love before marriage is unnecessary. If sexual fidelity is an important moral norm, then the loveless marriage is clearly undesirable, and the play is a "powerful criticism of the education of women and of the *mariage de convenance*."[86] In accepting this custom, Fabritio is the more guilty in his carelessness of his daughter's happiness, since, as Livia points out, the choice of a marriage partner is far more significant for a woman than it is for a man: a woman "takes one man till death," which is "a hard task" (I, ii, 34–35). It is not equally hard for a man, says Livia, because a man

> tastes of many sundry dishes
> That we poor wretches never lay our lips to:
> As obedience forsooth, subjection, duty, and such kickshaws,
> All of our making, but served in to them.
> And if we lick a finger then sometimes,
> We are not to blame; your best cooks use it.
>
> (I, ii, 40–45)

Freedom is a food served by women to men; men consume the whole dish, while the curious cook merely takes a taste. The homely domestic analogy, treated humorously by both Livia and her hearers, trivializes an important concept: the limitations on women's freedom imposed by the marriage choice and women's attempts to assert individuality by making another choice. In literature, when poison is used as a murder weapon against a husband, its intent is usually to undo a mistaken marriage choice. In this play, poison is used as an instrument of revenge against those who are impeding a woman's choice. In both cases, limitations on women's lives cause them to take drastic measures to achieve, preserve, or avenge the loss of whatever limited gains they have made through making their own decisions.

As the play opens, Isabella has little choice. Like Bianca, she is a young woman in love. She and her uncle, Hippolito, are "like a chain" (I, ii, 68), linked together in a relationship in which the as-yet-unrecognized sexual element has so far been successfully sublimated. The idiotic, lusty, and vulgar Ward is a completely inappropriate choice for Isabella's husband, his main qualification as a husband being his deceivability and his wealth. So Isabella naturally sees marriage, even when women have a choice as she does not, as a limitation on women's freedom, their dowries a way to "buy their thraldoms, and bring great portions / To men to keep 'em in subjection.... Men buy their slaves, but women buy their masters" (I, ii, 169–76). Happiness in marriage is possible if the partners sincerely love each other; but even this is in spite of the institution, not because of it:

> That Providence that has made ev'ry poison
> Good for some use, and sets four warring elements
> At peace in man, can make a harmony
> In things that are most strange to human reason.

(I, ii, 179–82)

Isabella's father's cynical advice that she use marriage to support herself and have illicit affairs does not at first appeal to her. It is obvious that her father and her husband, "those who should protect and care" for her in her feminine weakness, "have no understanding of her emotional needs."[87] But she is a good daughter and prepared to make the best of the arranged marriage, and her conventional goodness is also shown in her immediate rejection of her uncle's declaration of love.

In the main plot, the opposite kind of marriage, the "romantic, unenforced marriage"[88] of Bianca and Leantio, is also flawed. Both have made a mistake: they have married for sex when they value money much more. Leantio makes his money in trade and has the material outlook of his class, while Bianca is a "gentlewoman" (I, i, 11). Leantio has married above himself, acquired a "most unvalued'st purchase" (I, i, 13), a treasured new posession, his "masterpiece" (I, i, 41). With "his merchant's *petit bourgeois* pride in securing a possession more dazzling than all his competitors,"[89] he installs his new acquisition in his house among his other collectibles. He wants to safeguard the treasure of Bianca's virtue, which is "all her dowry.... Like jewels kept in cabinets" (I, i, 54, 56). Leantio's mother warns him that Bianca is a woman who might have inherited a large fortune were it not for her marriage and has acquired expensive tastes. Women are accustomed to being provided for at least according to the condition of their upbringing, and most hope to surpass that. How will Leantio manage? Leantio hushes his mother for putting ideas into Bianca's head; he wants the treasure house of her thoughts locked up too. So far, he is convinced that she is "in a good way to obedience" (I, i, 75) and contented to "keep close as a wife that loves her husband" with "all conditions that [his] fortunes bring her to" (I, i, 88–90). One justification for Bianca's behavior is that she does not like to be kept close, locked in a cabinet; she later criticizes Leantio for his desire to "mew [her] up / Not to be seen" (III, ii, 138–39), like money in the bank. The prudent factor even expects a prompt return on his investment. His wife's one goal, according to Leantio (but never Bianca), is to produce children. This description of Bianca seems a projection of his own wishes to see his investment in her increase. Since he has had to balance "time spent getting money" against "time spent in sexual intercourse,"[90] he is concerned about efficiency and waste avoidance. He will, he tells his mother, "follow [his] business roundly, / And make [her] a grandmother in forty weeks" (I, i, 108–9). In the meantime, for the duration of his upcoming trip, he will leave his "jewel...cased up from all men's eyes" (I, i, 170), sequestered in his house, guarded by his mother:

Old mothers know the world, and such as these,
When sons lock chests, are good to look to keys.

(I, i, 175–76)

As the play beings, Bianca's motivations seem simple: she is a very young and inexperienced woman who has given up all thoughts of material gain to marry the man she loves. But this decision has placed her in a condition of destabilized security, social weakness. She has forsaken friends, fortune, and her country to elope with Leantio. Therefore she is totally dependent on him for protection and for her position in society. If, as critic Christopher Ricks points out, "Middleton's aim is to connect the world of money with the world of love,"[91] then for women the connection to money must be made through their sexuality, since women have no other access to money than by allying themselves with a man who has it. Leantio thinks of being a husband in terms of sexual possession, so he misunderstands his role as protector and provider. He thinks of his wife as a possession; she needs possessions provided by him. Both have a possessive streak, a lust for owning objects, which in their youthful idealism they failed to realize. Leantio has a limited ability to provide the possessions on which Bianca's sense of security is based. She is in a shaky position: having just forsaken the customary props—family wealth and the arranged marriage to carry on the security of her childhood—she is especially vulnerable to an appeal to her sense of diminished security: "she realizes that...she has exposed herself to a situation which may have unforeseeable dangers beyond the simple power of her will."[92] Leantio does not understand this. He is not an aristocrat who can say "farewell all business" (I, iii, 16) and spend his time in "banquet and toy and play" (I, iii, 33) with his lady love. Rather he must be up and doing early in the morning, busy at business,[93] to make his living and support his new "purchase." But Leantio, with his mercantile mind, does not understand that in his hurry to provide for Bianca's material well-being, he is depriving this "isolated and frightened girl"[94] of whatever psychological security his presence provides.

Livia exacerbates these basic problems centering on sexual freedom in the subplot and money and security in the main plot. Both young women have weak moral principles that do not hold up under any temptation that seems to offer promise of solving these problems. Isabella's sexual needs, which will clearly not be satisfied by her planned marriage to the Ward, render her vulnerable to any excuse that will justify their satisfaction. Livia's task, then, is to convince Isabella that Fabritio is not her father, so therefore

Hippolito is not her uncle; this lie conveniently "reduces unthinkable incest to acceptable adultery."[95] Isabella is easily persuaded and seeks no further substantiation even for so important a matter. This surface gullibility manifests a moral superficiality. Livia cautions her to be careful not of what she does but of what is found out: "Nothing o'erthrows our sex but indiscretion" (II, i, 164). Not what is, but what appears to be, is important; concealment is desirable. The misogynistic commonplaces come to mind: woman's fickleness and instability, her shifting moods, her weakness when deprived of a strong protector, her proneness to deception and concealment.

Isabella's main motive is sexual, but her security needs mandate that the affair be concealed. When Isabella "learns" from Livia that Fabricio is not her father, another consequence could result: she does not need to obey him and marry the Ward; she could then marry Hippolito since he is not a true relative. But operating openly in this way never occurs to her. One reason for this is that she never really believes the paternity story in the first place. Another reason is that she does not want to lose a living father—with all the security he provides—to claim a dead one. So she "freely prefers an illicit liaison to a chaste rebellion against her father's authority.... We cannot expect a girl who is supinely obedient to a foolish father to cut herself off from family and society by proclaiming her illicit ancestry. She is a true child of her time, brazen enough to have a 'friend' but too weak to defy social conventions."[96] It never occurs to Isabella to take advantage of that "largeness in [her] will and liberty" of which Livia speaks (II, i, 160) to assert independence from the man to whom she no longer believes she owes obedience. Through deception she can hedge her bets, maintaining alliances with husband, father, and lover at once.

In the case of Bianca, security needs predominate over sexual needs. Bianca is vulnerable even before the seduction scene commences because she has lost her moral prop, her husband, and now is dependent on another weak reed like herself, his mother. Livia's first task is to remove even this protection by causing Leantio's mother to relax her watch over the treasured possession. This Livia accomplishes by flattering the mother: Livia alleges she cannot do without her company, and Leantio's mother is enough of a social climber to be flattered. As M. C. Bradbrook points out, the mother-in-law's virtue collapses just as fast as Bianca's.[97]

The famous chess scene in which Bianca is separated from her watchful mother-in-law, ostensibly to look at Livia's upstairs rooms and pictures, is an emblem of the misogynistic commonplace of the weak reed. In rapid succession, Bianca has left her family and fatherland, been left by her husband, and is now temporarily separated from her husband's delegated caretaker. Alone this way, she is a pawn in the more clever hands of Guardiano, Livia, and the Duke. Guardiano's tactic of showing her first Livia's possessions, her "fairer ornaments" (II, ii, 311), then the Duke himself, "a better piece / Yet than all these" (II, ii, 313–14), shows that both he and the Duke sense her vulnerability to the lure of beautiful possessions, the Duke being chief among these. Critical language used to describe this scene invariably connotes weakness. Bianca cannot stand alone; her "virtue simply collapses."[98] Briefly resisting seduction, Bianca calls upon religion and virtue; but the Duke's appeal to her unsatisfied desire for money and security puts an end to all resistance:

> She that is fortunate in a duke's favor
> Lights on a tree that bears all women's wishes;
> If your own mother saw you pluck fruit there
> She would commend your wit, and praise the time
> Of your nativity. Take hold of glory.
> Do not I know y' have cast away your life
> Upon necessities, means merely doubtful
> To keep you in indifferent health and fashion—
> A thing I heard too lately, and soon pitied?
> And can you be so much your beauty's enemy
> To kiss away a month or two in wedlock,
> And weep whole years in wants for ever after?
> Come play the wise wench, and provide for ever;
> Let storms come when they list, they find thee sheltered.
> Should any doubt arise, let nothing trouble thee;
> Put trust in our love for the managing
> Of all to thy heart's peace.

(II, ii, 370–86)

Comparing this scene to the temptation of Eve in *Paradise Lost*, one critic points out that, like Satan, the Duke knows that "temptation is most successful when it appeals to a woman's prudence and her aspiration."[99] The Duke indeed appeals to her need for protection and higher social status. The Duke, an older and more solidly established man than Leantio,[100] can offer Bianca "shelter . . . built of sturdier stuff."[101] A "wise wench" will allow herself to be provided for by allying herself to his wealth and power.[102] Women have always been advised against casting away their lives on unsound romantic alliances, have always been encouraged to make the financially prudent marriage; indeed her own mother would approve her substitution of a rich man for a poor one. The money and possessions of the Duke "provide concrete assurance of security" and symbolize his "dependability as provider and protector."[103] Bianca needs this; besides, if she does not yield to him voluntarily and if he forces her, as he suggests he will, she risks losing both his approval and that of her husband, a situation that would leave her abandoned in a strange land without father or kinsmen to avenge her honor. Alone in this place, she needs "some sort of accommodation with a society to which she is a stranger."[104] The Duke, as leader of that society, can surely provide her with a secure—even if illicit—position within it and the hope of a still better position in the future.

Bianca's first reaction to her loss of virtue is extreme: she sees herself as corrupt, decayed, blasted, infected. Her beauty is the "fair that caused the leprosy" of her moral downfall (II, ii, 425). Life is no longer worthwhile: "Come poison all at once" (II, ii, 426). This first reaction of Bianca foreshadows the scene in which she meets her death by kissing the Duke's lips, envenomed by the poison she herself meant for the Cardinal, and forms part of the interrelated imagery pattern of food, infection, sexual corruption, and poison. When first corrupted, she knows it; her revulsion at her own behavior is the correct moral stance. The disease causes her to loathe her life and reject her beauty, which contributed to her downfall. But she adjusts herself very rapidly in a process familiar to moralists. The first sin causes a moral reaction, but subsequent sins become habitual, and the sinner's eventual callousness precludes repentance. Livia knows this:

> Her tender modesty is sea-sick a little.
> Being not accustomed to the breaking billow
> Of woman's wavering faith, blown with temptations.
> 'Tis but a qualm of honour, 'twill away.
> A little bitter for the time, but lasts not.
> Sin tastes at the first draught like wormwood water;
> But drunk again, 'tis nectar ever after.

(II, ii, 471–77)

Temptation causes women's fidelity to waver. Livia does not suggest that their faith should stabilize but rather that they grow accustomed to the motion of yielding to temptation.

Bianca's adjustment to the "breaking billow" of her wavering faith, "the hardening of the spirit" of which moralists speak,[105] is facilitated by the increased security achieved through her relationship with the Duke. Yet even in the process of betraying Leantio, she shows her similarity to him. Her petulant demands for the trappings of the good life—cushion cloth, cutwork, and a green silk quilt, "some pleasant lodging i' th' high street . . . near the court," where she could have the "sweet recreation for a gentlewoman / To stand in a bay-window, and see gallants" (III, ii, 47–50)—is matched by Leantio's own. In the scene in which Livia courts Leantio, he shows himself to be as materialistic as Bianca but without the excuse of feminine weakness. Livia, the initiator of the relationship, motivates him exactly as the Duke did Bianca, with the lure of money and possessions:

> I pray let's walk, sir.
> You never saw the beauty of my house yet,
> Nor how abundantly fortune has blessed me
> In worldly treasure; trust me I have enough, sir,
> To make my friend a rich man in my life,
> A great man at my death . . .

Come, you shall see my wealth; take what you list;
The gallanter you go, the more you please me.
I will allow you, too, your page and footman,
Your race-horses, or any various pleasure
Exercised youth delights in; but to me
Only, sir, wear your heart of constant stuff—
Do but you love enough, I'll give enough.

(III, iii, 357–62, 368–74)

House, treasure, wealth, race horses, pages, footmen—the male equivalents of cushion cloth, cutwork, green silk quilts, and a house in the high street—cause Leantio to fall as quickly as did Bianca. That Leantio understands the nature of this quid pro quo is apparent in the structure of his response: "Troth then, I'll love enough, and take enough" (III, iii, 375). For all his protestations, his love is as shaky as was Bianca's; his "life's wealth" (III, iii, 307) can be replaced by other worldly possessions. Thus, in the important scene when he and Bianca encounter each other, both in their ill-gotten finery, when he calls her a "whore" and a "strumpet" (IV, i, 61, 62), he is guilty of the grossest application of the double standard. Both have traded virtue for the fulfillment of needs unrealized when they made their romantic marriage.

Isabella's and Bianca's unhappy fate can be attributed to an unhappy conjunction of their own weaknesses, the machinations of stronger people, and their dependent position as women in a patriarchal society. Isabella surely allows herself to be deceived. Yet she also "longs for freedom"[106] and so is predisposed to believe any story that will encourage her to express her individuality through choosing Hippolito. When Bianca blames her limited upbringing rather than her own choices for her ill fortune, it is, as many critics have pointed out, a rationalization; yet it is also an accurate statement of the limitations placed on the lives of women, an "inevitable consequence of the way she was brought up."[107] Maids are indeed kept "so strict" that "restraint breeds wand'ring thoughts" (IV, i, 31–32). Restraint breeds desire for rebellion, and she would grant a daughter of hers a freer upbringing. Not that this would prevent a fall such as Bianca's, but rather that it is pointless to restrain freedom, since girls "fetch their falls a thousand mile about" (IV, i, 39), no matter how strictly they are kept. Both young women sense the narrow scope of human freedom in women's lives in their society. Instead of a life shaped by many choices, a woman has only one choice that really matters: the choice of a man.

Bianca is more rebellious than Isabella since she makes two unacceptable alliances: one by eloping with Leantio, another by betraying him with the Duke. In both cases she is trying to shape her own life, however misguidedly. When the first choice proves unsatisfactory, she feels she is not determined by it but has the right to make another choice. The only way to make a change in her station in life (it is the easiest way, even today, for a woman to improve her financial lot) is to ally herself with a wealthier and more powerful man. Sexual rebellion is a form of self-determination for both Bianca and Isabella, one of the few available to them as women in their society. Yet a strong irony exists in the fact that even these choices are less than truly free because of Livia's engineering. Instead of helping the young girls toward a greater degree of freedom from society's traps, Livia sets them "deadly snares" (V, ii, 211), as Bianca realizes too late.

Bianca undergoes a greater transformation in the course of the play than does Isabella, indicated in their differing motives for the use of the poison. When to avenge Leantio's death, Livia reveals the trick that has led to their incest, Isabella tells Hippolito that they must leave each other's sight:

> for our very eyes
> Are far more poisonous to religion
> Than basilisks to them.
>
> (IV, ii, 138–40)

While here Isabella uses the traditional basilisk image as a metaphor for sinful sexuality, the possibility of a poison literally being transmitted through the atmosphere is a recurrent question debated in poison lore, appearing in literature in the suggestion of the poisoned portrait and crucifix in *Arden of Faversham*. Before the clear differentiation of poisoning and contagion, the concept of an envenomed atmosphere was postulated as a cause of disease. As in the Petrarchan tradition, love enters through the eyes, so the venom of incestuous love poisons the spirit through this vulnerable sense. Isabella's and Hippolito's relationship ends in the acknowledgment of moral corruption. But the end of incest does not bring about a restoration of truth and virtue. Unlike Hippolito, who challenges Leantio to a duel, Isabella desires to "practise...cruel cunning" (IV, ii, 148), to "dissemble" forgiveness (IV, ii, 184) of the apologetic Livia, herself dissembling. It is fitting that Isabella chooses for her weapon of revenge a poison that envenoms the atmosphere and kills her too, a fitting symbol of the moral miasma surrounding Livia and encompassing Isabella herself.

Bianca's different use of poison as murder weapon is equally fitting. When Bianca first perceives herself as a sinner, after succumbing to the Duke's embraces, she cries, "Come poison all at once" (II, ii, 426); she sees herself as totally corrupted and decayed and momentarily considers suicide by poison, which would envenom the body as sin has the soul. This original reaction becomes muted as she grows accustomed to a state of sin, to living on poison. The Cardinal, continuing the analogy between moral and physical disease, describes the marriage of the Duke and Bianca as a garment covering "leprosy and foulness" (IV, iii, 17). Bianca's genuine belief is that they are the "converted sinner[s]" (IV, iii, 56) in which heaven rejoices, and their marriage is a vehicle for their repentance, not their continued lustful-ness. The Cardinal's opposition to this viewpoint makes him her implacable enemy against whom revenge must be taken.

The peculiar moral blindness of Bianca and the Duke in their attempts to legitimize their love has always been a problem in interpreting the play. Apparently basing his action on the idea that one sin is preferable to a habit of sin, the Duke murders Leantio (thus freeing Bianca for marriage), and Bianca plans to kill the Cardinal (thus removing another barrier). Both seem to believe that murder is a less serious crime than adultery. In Middleton's *The Witch*, the outcome of one of the four plots hinges on this concept. The Duchess is being tried for adultery and for the murder of her husband. When she pleads guilty to murder but professes herself innocent of adultery, her intended victim, the Duke, rises from a feigned death and forgives her on the spot. If in this play "a woman's honor is damaged more by the act of adultery than the act of murder,"[108] so in *Women Beware Women*, at least according to the shared values of Bianca and the Duke. The Duke "vowed no more to keep a sensual woman"; if, in order to "make a lawful wife of her" (IV, iii, 31–32), he must murder her husband, so be it. The end justifies the means.

Their behavior can also be clarified by reference to the pattern created by the poison imagery. If, according to homeopathic theory, a dose of venom drives out venom, then by analogy one sin, however grievous, is preferable to a habit of sin. This leads to the surprising moral conclusion that one murder (each—neither knows about the other's plans) is preferable to the continuing moral poison of an adulterous union. This odd analogical rea-soning shows not only the pair's moral obtuseness but also their similarity: the Duke's "willingness to take the steps necessary to marry Bianca"[109] is paralleled by her own efforts to marry him. Of the two, however, the Duke is the less self-interested. Although he has nothing further to gain, Bianca has the opportunity to move from concubine to Duchess, surely a way to "take hold of glory," as the Duke urged her to do in the seduction scene.

Much of the critical debate on Middleton's play as tragedy has focused on the character of Bianca, specifically the question whether she has suffi-cient nobility to experience a truly tragic downfall. Whether Bianca's fate is seen as "the promise of a fine flowering that is destroyed"[110] or, on the other hand, the dreary tale of a "profoundly, incurably commonplace" young girl,[111] a "thoroughly mediocre person,"[112] even a "contemptible weakling,"[113] the problem is complicated by the drastic dissimilarity be-tween the Bianca of the beginning of the play and the woman she becomes. The split between the sweet, unformed girl who married Leantio and the worldly courtesan has been described as so discontinuous as to constitute two Biancas. But this is hardly startling. Theologically, sin's consequence is to distort the human personality, male or female, so it is natural that the sinful Bianca is "a changed being."[114] In addition, two expectations concerning women are relevant to Bianca's change, both related to the central concept of woman's weakness. First, women's overall character is considered totally on the basis of their sexual morality. Second, women are expected to adapt themselves to whatever role their sexual alliances prescribe.

At the beginning of the play, Bianca is a virtuous young wife. Once she becomes a fallen woman, she would, of course, be expected to be totally changed, reflecting her sexual corruption. Acquainted with sin, she becomes bold (II, ii, 439–40); her whole personality, even her manner of speaking, changes. Before the seduction, she spoke briefly and demurely in response to questions but not calling undue attention to herself. After, she speaks forcefully, bluntly, even vulgarly, and at greater length. The theatergoer would see a complete metamorphosis in her demeanor and tone of voice. One critic points out that the seduction of Bianca is like the death of Hamlet's father, an event "of such a magnitude as to challenge the character's beliefs concerning the nature of life and of the universe."[115] It is a turning point, a death of the old virtuous self; she must now arrange an "accommodation to corruption."[116] It is clear from the tenor of these critical comments that a sexual lapse is of such magnitude that it compares to death and decay. A woman cannot make immoral sexual choices and be a fine person otherwise. Bianca must be a virtuous wife or a whore; no middle ground exists.

Aside from the moral dimension, there is a social dimension as well. As Leantio's wife, she occupies a lower station in life than she does as the Duke's mistress; she is expected (as women are expected today) to change completely to fit the life of the man she loves. "For Bianca, the new position of mistress to the Duke means removal from the status of a hidden possession to that of treasure on display: from merchant-class values to those of the aristocracy."[117] It is expected that she will be able to make this upwardly mobile adjustment with as little resistance from a fully developed strong personality as possible. She is supposed to be malleable and flexible, with little underlying identity. In Chaucer's "Merchant's Tale," old Januarie hopes to shape his young wife, May, like warm wax; he sees this as one of the several advantages of marrying a young, unformed girl. Similarly, Livia has encouraged Bianca to be morally adaptable, to grow accustomed to the waves of faith and winds of temptation. It is appropriate that the fallen Bianca change from a "self-effacing, virtuous girl" to a "strong-minded even aggressive woman wholly adapted to the hypocrisy and compromise of Florentine society"[118] as her new position demands. This is simply a change from being Leantio's "sweet wife"[119] to being the Duke's mistress, an acting out of role expectations. Adaptability is a function of weakness; her sense of self is supposed to be thinly developed so that, chameleon-like, she can blend into the life of the man whose life she shares.

So of course there are at least two Biancas. As act V begins, she is the "fair duchess" (V, ii, 1), ready to begin a new and better life after the elimination of the Cardinal. Instead, she becomes a third Bianca, without husband or lover, a woman alone, nobody's wife and nobody's mistress. Here at last, we should be able to see her true character, in the brief interval between the death of the Duke and her own. What we see is a combination of the traits exhibited earlier: Bianca kills herself partially out of repentance, partially out of love for the Duke, but also because she cannot bear to live alone. Her suicide by poison is a logical culmination of the idea of feminine weakness. As in the case of Isabella, the misdirected poison turns upon herself. Both women attempt to avenge their wrongs on external enemies but, through ignorance and incompetence, end by punishing themselves.

Bianca's voluntarily joining the Duke in death expresses two of her main character traits: acting impetuously, even idealistically, when motivated by love; and an inability to live without a man's protection. In her death for love, on one level she can be seen as redeemed and ennobled. Sharing a kiss and a cup of wine are symbolic expressions of unity, even if it is a unity in sin, the poisoned "cup of innocence" symbolizing the "staining of white Bianca."[120] Although the lovers began their relationship in the poison of "unholy lust," which grew into a desire for "the sanctity of marriage,"[121] so, when Bianca kisses the envenomed lips of the Duke and drinks the poison that killed him, her physical destruction becomes a moral antidote. Joining their spirits in death is a fitting repentance for the illicit mingling of their bodies in life. The "cursed poison" has fulfilled her earlier wish, at her seduction, to destroy her beauty and make her inner and outer reality synchronous: "A blemished face best fits a leprous soul" (V, ii, 205). Having passed through her earlier naive innocence into worldly experience and thence into a new state of higher spiritual development, she rejoices in an unselfish act:

> Yet this my gladness is, that I remove,
> Tasting the same death in a cup of love.
>
> (V, ii, 220–21)

More than the loss of the world's goods, she regrets the loss of the Duke. For at least her dying moment (and in Christian theology, all can be won or lost at this point), she is restored to her original "whiteness," the idealistic purity that led her to forsake all to marry Leantio. It would be a moral paradox if her relationship to the Duke were to be redemptive for her after all, but so it seems to be. She dies thinking of her beloved, not herself—the only one in the play who does so (Isabella dies without a parting speech). It is as if the physical poison she ingested becomes antidotal to the moral evil that has suffused her system. Operating within the tradition of the medieval morality play, Middleton is also making use of the medieval sin/poison, repentance/antidote, physical/moral analogy system. As would be believed in the medicine of Middleton's day, one poison drives out another. Bianca's death, a death for love, is redemptive; her self-poisoning is an act of repentance that drives out the venom of sin. It is not orthodox theology (Bianca dies a murderer and a suicide), but it is good drama.

And yet there is a drastic ambiguity about her death. Bianca, kissing the dead Duke, describes her own action in language that strongly implies an inability to envision herself as an independent being, living and breathing on her own:

> Give me thy last breath, thou infected bosom,
> And wrap two spirits in one poisoned vapour.
>
> (V, ii, 193–94)

Taking the poison to die with her lover is an acknowledgment that Bianca cannot conceive of the possibility of outliving her role as mistress to the Duke. She can live alone for only a few minutes. This is a weak reed indeed; deprived of her prop, she dies. If she lived, she would have to face the consequences of her murder attempt on the Cardinal, who, as the Duke's heir, is now the head of state. And she would have to do this without benefit of any man's protection. "However infected their love may be, it is all she has to cling to"; without the Duke, "she realizes her complete isolation."[122] Looking around her, she sees herself out of place at a court without the Duke, among "strangers / Not known but by their malice" (V, ii, 206–7); it is at this point that she drinks the poison. Bereft of father, brother, husband, or lover, having no son, away from her country, Bianca is truly alone in the world, fallen from duchess to stranger, and cannot survive. Her inability to stand on her own undercuts any nobility she gains from her act of repentance and love.

Perhaps the problematic nature of the play as tragedy is rooted in this ambiguity. The waste of a potentially noble character is a main component of tragedy. With woman's lesser potential for greatness in a patriarchal society, the potential for tragic waste is correspondingly less. All the more so is this true in the bourgeois society Middleton depicts, where crass monetary values replace the fate of kingdoms. In this society, women's only opportunities lie in their alliances with rich and powerful men, so their failures can be only "domestic tragedy."[123] On one level, Bianca dies loving and repentant, but on another she also succumbs to weakness because she is unable to envision a life without men in which she faces the consequences of her actions without the shelter of their protection. Worse, the agent of her fall is another woman; as David Holmes points out, the title also means, " 'Women beware yourselves.' "[124] Livia's machinations can work only because they draw on a preexisting tendency in Bianca: her vulnerability to seduction by a man who promises her a greater strength than her own. When in the last moments of her life she has repented of her sexual corruption, when the physical poison has driven out spiritual poison, what remains is an essential weakness, an emptiness, which makes it impossible for her to live alone.

POISON AND DOMESTICITY

As if in tacit acknowledgment of the criminal justice truism that women who commit domestic murders are seldom dangerous to the larger society, the murdering woman in literature is often treated with sympathy, as Middleton treats Bianca. Even the worst offenders can be portrayed with redeeming traits. In *The Book of the City of Ladies*, Christine de Pisan is a Renaissance revisionist in her reinterpretation of old stories concerning famous women.[125] The book is an antimisogynistic tract, antidote to the kind of compendium of stories about evil women such as the Wife of Bath's husband, Jankyn, was so fond of reading in the evenings. In it, she summarizes the relevant biographical data and accomplishments of a variety of ladies who are envisioned as inhabitants of her idealized city; it is a kind of *Who's Who* of important women, all of whom are in some way construed by Christine as good, whatever violence this does to the authorities so beloved in her day. Whether the ladies are fictional or historical, Christine ignores their flaws, so obvious in earlier versions of their stories.

Medea, for example, is depicted as having made a coolly rational decision (influenced only slightly by an excess of pity) to help Jason find the Golden Fleece. She aids him with "charms ... enchantment ... expertise." When Jason betrays her and marries another, she "turned despondent, nor did her heart ever again feel goodness or joy." The image of the depressed displaced homemaker replaces that of the raging, passionate sorceress of Euripedes' drama. No mention is made of Medea's killing Jason's bride or her own small sons. Rather, Christine concludes on a note of pity for the loyal Medea, "who would rather have destroyed herself than do anything of this kind" to her disloyal husband Jason (189–90).

Christine's treatment of Arachne is similarly divergent from the usual interpretation of this character. In Ovid's *Metamorphoses* (Book VI, 163–67), Arachne is a poor young woman living by weaving; so skillful is she at the loom that she arouses the jealousy of Pallas. Arachne refuses to acknowledge the goddess's inspiration; "she'd rather hang herself than bow her head," and in fact attempts to hang herself. Pallas saves her, but for this act of domestic hubris she punishes Arachne by transforming her into a spider, "the tenuous weaver of an ancient craft." So Arachne weaves—and hangs—for all eternity. As Edith Hamilton notes, "The fate of this maiden was another example of the danger of claiming equality with the gods in anything whatsoever."[126] Thanks to Arachne, the spider becomes a symbol of the propensity of women to weave nets to ensnare men (although in Ovid, Arachne herself does no such thing), again stressing the male fear of entrapment in the domain of the female; a related idea is the conspiratorial plotting of women.

But for Christine, Arachne is noteworthy as an early pioneer of the textile industry. Thanks to her "marvelously subtle mind," she was

the first to invent the art of dyeing woolens in various colors and of weaving art works into cloth, like a painter, according to the "fine thread" technique of weaving tapestry. She was marvelously skilled in all kinds of weaving. Moreover, she is mentioned in the fable which says she was the one who competed with Pallas who changed her into a spider. (81)

The metamorphosis becomes a mere aside; Arachne's real importance lies in her contribution to technology:

She was the first to invent a way of cultivating flax and hemp, along with harvesting and breaking them, as well as steeping and hackling the flax, spinning it with a distaff, and weaving linen. It seems to me this technique was quite necessary for the world, although many men have reproached women for practicing it. This Arachne also invented the art of making nets, snares, and traps for catching birds and fishes, and she invented the art of fishing and of trapping strong and cruel wild beasts with snares and nets, as well as rabbits and hares, and birds too; no one knew anything about these techniques before her. This woman, as far as I can tell, performed no small service for the world, which has still derived and derives much ease and profit from it. (82)

Christine herself is a bit of a weaver here as she embroiders the story of Arachne with these many accomplishments. Christine never reverts to the idea of metamorphosis or to the common misogynistic notions surrounding the ideas of weaving and ensnaring. Rather, she diverges into a disquisition on whether new inventions truly benefit the world (according to Boccaccio, they do not; according to Christine, they do). So for Christine de Pisan, in the pantheon of good women, Medea deserves a place for her unrequited loyalty and Arachne for her technical creativity. Every woman who lives in Christine's City of Ladies, however unpromising her previous reputation, can be creatively rehabilitated.

In considering women who kill by poison, one must take care not to emulate Christine in reconstruction beyond recognition. Whatever the provocation, poisoners are always cold-blooded domestic murderers, betrayers at board and usually in bed too, serpents in a man's bosom. Yet their actions are extreme responses to difficult situations encountered by many women. Studies of actual murders, like Mary S. Hartman's *Victorian Murderesses*[127] and Patrick Wilson's *Murderess: A Study of the Women Executed in Britain since 1843*,[128] provide insights into literary murderesses as well. Both see women who murder as basically ordinary women facing ordinary problems. Hartman says that in killing, they are "responding to situations which to some degree were built into the lives of their more ordinary middle-class peers."[129] As befits their usual confinement to the domestic sphere, the situations that provoke murder are domestic. Wilson says that "the vast majority of murders by women spring from circumstances within their family lives which they find intolerable."[130] Like Jones, Wilson stresses that women never kill strangers: they "kill the men who are at the center of their lives."[131] Even today, women seldom kill outside the domestic circle. And in the cases Hartman and Wilson studied, poison is clearly a woman's weapon. It is used stealthily and, even at that fairly recent date, with relative impunity, given medical ignorance. So serious is the crime considered that poisoners usually were executed, while women murderers who used other weapons generally were not. For motive, Hartman describes it as the poisoners' "attempt to enhance their own authority in relation to fathers, husbands, and other domestic authorities."[132]

Intolerable domestic circumstances drive the female poisoners to kill the men at the center of their lives, so, of course, Pertelote and Guenevere must be innocent. Pertelote's hen-coop conditions seem quite cordial. Despite occasional bickering with her husband, she seems far from powerless; she has authority in being chief wife and worthy opponent of Chaunticleer. Guenevere has no motive to poison Gawain; he is not the man at the center of her life. Both are victims of stereotyped thinking on the part of their accusers. Lord Randal's lady is guilty, but since ballad conventions demand mystery, her motive is suppressed.

Among the guilty, Deianira is the most pathetic, clinging in total dependence to Hercules, like a living version of the poisoned shirt she unwittingly offers him. Her fate and his illustrate the absolute damage to both because of her lack of autonomy. Life is not worth living without him; his love is so important that she will take extreme measures to ensure it. This is destructive to both of them. Livia in *Sejanus* is somewhat sympathetic in that she is a victim of Sejanus's deception, as well as her own lust and ambition. The premise of her crime is that it will guarantee her Sejanus's love, but he loves only himself and power. Livia, Machiavellian though she is, has no scope to rise to power on her own. She can improve her life by facilitating Sejanus's rise, but when she does, she is cast off, losing husband, lover, and path to glory all at once. Bianca too is restricted by the norms of her society in advancing in any way except by allying herself with the Duke. Any barrier to this must be eliminated. Yet she too is the victim of the manipulation and deception of others, thus not entirely a free agent for good or evil.

These several murderers have redeeming qualities nevertheless. Love is their motivation. Livia's and Bianca's goal, however mistakenly pursued, is to establish a love relationship more favorable to them than their former one. They seek a better life. Had circumstances or their own characters been different, they might have become better people in the process.

The truly insidious murderer is Alice Arden. Lustful and power driven, deceitful and hypocritical, she has no redeeming virtue. But as a social statement, the play contributed to the divorce debate. Society had become increasingly aware of the inability of people who made a wrong marital decision patiently to suffer the consequences until the death of one of the partners. The contemporary response to the Alice Arden story and play showed increasing awareness that the opportunity to make a second, third or fourth choice must be offered—by means short of murder.

3

Venefica: Healer and Witch

Her old nurse's name was Thessala, who was skilled in necromancy, having been born in Thessaly, where devilish charms are taught and wrought; for the women of that country perform many a charm and mystic rite.

CHRÉTIEN DE TROYES, *Cligés*[1]

'Tis a common practice of some men to go first to a witch and then to a physician, if one cannot the other shall.

RICHARD BURTON, *Anatomy of Melancholy*[2]

In *The Heptameron*, Marguerite de Navarre tells the tale of a woman whose husband, an apothecary, is insufficiently amorous.[3] In fact, he takes no notice of his wife at all, "except in Holy Week, by way of penance." One day this neglected wife overhears her husband tending to a customer, another woman in similar plight, who asks the apothecary for " 'some medicine that might change' " her husband. The apothecary prescribes a love potion for her to "put...in her husband's soup or on his roast."

Several days later, the customer reports success, and the apothecary's wife, eavesdropping again, decides to administer the same to her own husband. Her opportunity arises several days later "when her husband began to feel a chill in the stomach, and asked her if she would make him a broth." Into the broth goes the aphrodisiac, but she gives "no thought whatsoever to weight, measure, or dosage." The result is that he becomes ill and is saved only with the aid of the apothecary of the queen of Navarre. The deluded man learns his lesson: he has prescribed for someone else a drug he would not willingly take himself. He also admits that "his wife had only acted properly, seeing that she had merely wished to make him love her." The *Heptameron* storytellers, discussing the outcome, avoid the obvious issue: the wife's secret administration of "some medicine that might change" her husband as a devious and illegitimate arrogation of power.

In poison lore, the apothecary's wife would be called a *venefica*, or potion-maker: a character, usually female (as the noun's gender indicates), who concocts a potion to be administered to a victim, usually male. In the Middle Ages and the Renaissance, the purpose of the potion is to govern male behavior, so it is a powerful symbol of female dominance and, conversely, loss of male control. The *venefica* is a stock character who represents the dark and devious underside of legitimate feminine roles: nurturer and healer. She recurs in literature throughout the Middle Ages and Renaissance but with variations appropriate to her function in the work in which she appears. In most instances of her appearance in the Middle Ages and Renaissance, the *venefica* is associated with witchcraft but also with healing. Also, her function is split off from that of the seductive woman, who is a separate character. Responsibility for the potion is thus diffused between them and the image of power dissipated. Since sexual power is separated from intellectual power, neither woman is very threatening, and a lighter tone is maintained. But with Spenser's Acrasia, a change occurs. As befits the serious moral allegory of *The Faerie Queene*, the *venefica* and the seductress become one person, and the element of healer drops out. The consequence is the depiction in that Renaissance epic of a character whose skill and seductiveness make her a powerful agent of evil.

This development really represents a return to the archetypal *venefica* Medea, witch-woman, potion-maker, murderer by poison and sword. Her homeland, Thessaly, becomes a byword for witchery. In fact, Medea's ability to use both characteristically male and characteristically female murder weapons make her, in Boccaccio's words, "by far the best trained woman in evil-doing," an arch-villainess indeed.[4] She can dismember her brother and knife her two sons, if not with equanimity, at least without shrinking from the deed. Worshipper of Hecate, she is a creature of a passion served by knowledge of the magic arts. Ovid attributes Jason's success to Medea's "deeper magic," "dark arts," and "gathered herbs." She even rejuvenates his dying old father by making, from plants and roots and with the aid of Hecate, "a magic potent drink that dissipates / Old age and fills old veins with manly blood." Throughout Ovid's description of her, she is a combination of witch-woman and herbal healer. And her healing works: Aeson is restored to his forty-years-younger self through Medea's potions. Yet she is equally capable of tricking the daughters of Pelias into stabbing their father by pretending that she intends to pour "new life, the blood of youth" into his severed veins. She does nothing of the sort, of course; motivated mainly by a desire to "keep her evil wits as sharp as ever," she finishes off Pelias and "tossed his torn remains into boiling water."[5]

As Sophocles does in *Trachinian Women*, Euripedes takes the Ovidian story and renders it more complex by developing the stock character of the jealous wife into a woman sinned against as well as sinning. Yes, Medea is evil, but she has also employed her evil arts in the service of Jason, a customary role even if, in her case, carried to extremes. With every other aging wife abandoned for a younger woman, Medea cries betrayal. Her grief becomes as excessive as her love had been, and the carrying out of revenge is facilitated by her knowledge of magic arts. If Jason has been unmanly in breaking his word, she will be unwomanly in killing their children.

Her murder of Creon's daughter by the agency of the poisoned dress and tiara is an appropriate revenge. Hating the beauty of the younger woman, which lured her husband, Medea destroys not only the bride but also the bride's beauty, so that she dies ugly:

> Save to her father, she was unrecognizable.
> Her eyes, her face, were one grotesque disfigurement;
> Down from her head dripped blood mingled with flame; her flesh,
> Attacked by the invisible fangs of poison, melted
> From the bare bone, like gum-drops from a pine-tree's bark—
> A ghastly sight.[6]

Medea knows that no woman can resist a gift of splendid clothing, so the vain young girl will thoughtlessly try on the gift immediately, even if the giver is a well-known witch with a grudge against her. Creon's daughter is a victim almost as much of her own stereotypical feminine vanity as of Medea's deception. It is rare in literature that one woman uses poison on another; the fairy tale in which Snow White's stepmother poisons her with comb and apple is reminiscent of Medea's story in the motivation of jealousy of the younger woman's beauty. But in the Euripedes play, it is clear that Medea intends Jason as the true victim; the bride's death is only the best means to the end, which is Jason's suffering.

Unlike Deianira, who cannot make the poison and uses it accidentally, Medea is the true literary ancestor of the *venefica* tradition. In addition to being a maker of deadly potions, she is a healer, a knower of remedies. In Ovid, she rejuvenates Jason's father, and in Euripedes she presents herself as an infertility specialist. She promises Aegeus, in return for refuge after her planned crime, an end to his childlessness: "I know certain drugs / Whose power will put an end to your sterility. / I promise you shall beget children" (39). Here Medea foreshadows the *venefica* character who aids the sexual intentions of others as well as her own. The components of the character split off in the literature of the Middle Ages and do not fuse again until Spenser presents his seductive witch, Acrasia. Medea, sexual woman and witch, is too powerful.

WISE WOMEN

The potion-maker in the Middle Ages is not readily distinguishable from female medical irregulars of all sorts, from housewives to midwives, who treated most of the injuries and illnesses of the time. Most medieval women could concoct "potions, powders, confections, ointments, and plasters."[7] Preparing these herbal remedies must have seemed very like an extension of a woman's culinary duties. In medicine, a skilled amateur might well be as effective as an apothecary or physician. In the Paston letters—correspondence dating from about 1422 to 1529 documenting the personal relationships and business transactions of a large, busy Norfolk family—we see the men consulting their wives from afar as to the remedies for particular illnesses, and we also see the women's distrust of physicians and preference for their own remedies.[8] "For God's sake," writes Margaret Paston to John Paston, "beware what medicines you take from the London doctors. I shall never trust them because of your father and my uncle, God rest their souls."[9] Upper-class ladies were responsible for health care too; in fact they had additional responsibilities given their men's propensity for getting wounded in wars and tourneys. As one commentator points out, it is common in the romances to see "*des demoiselles soignant de leurs mains blanches les chevaliers blessés*."[10] White hands or no, the dressing of wounds was a required feminine skill.

On a slightly more professional level, women such as the apothecary's wife in Marguerite de Navarre's tale could have a place in the health care system. In the fourteenth century, a woman could be trained in a medical specialty, even to the rank of physician, by a father or husband, and thenceforth practice on her own.[11] In 1374, the French parliament decided in favor of a woman charged with illicit practice of medicine. She was a barber-surgeon (as distinct from a university-educated physician) who had been apprenticed to her father. The parliament dismissed the suit against her, allowed her to practice again, and ordered that the confiscated tools of her trade be returned to her.[12] A woman could then practice medicine much as the Wife of Bath conducted her business, as a *femme sole*.

By far the most approved form of medical practice for women was obstetrics and gynecology. The *sage-femme*, or midwife, was considered preferable to the male physician, however well trained, on the grounds of modesty. One Francesca, the wife of a physician of Naples, was herself admitted to the practice of surgery in 1321 on the grounds that "it is better, out of consideration for morals and decency, for women rather than men to attend female patients."[13] But most women healers were not professionally trained or licensed. The fourteenth-century translator (from Latin into English) of the eleventh-century gynecological tract *De passionibus mulierum* justified his endeavor on the grounds that the female healer, unlettered in Latin, still needed up-to-date (only three centuries old) information so that women could treat each other "wt. owtyn shewyng here dysese to man."[14] Their herbal remedies included contraceptive and abortifacient potions.

Although women were seldom permitted to attend a university, there are records of licensed women physicians in the fourteenth and fifteenth centuries, thanks to the vagaries of local ordinances.[15] Most women learned their medicine empirically, by hearsay or trial and error; some were apprentices to trained males; the literate in Latin could have access to the same material used to train physicians; the literate in the vernaculars had to wait for translations. In general, then, women practiced medicine on various unofficial levels during the Middle Ages, and this phenomenon is reflected in the literature of the time. Fictional healers in medieval literature include Pertelote, the hen-coop housewife, prescribing a home remedy for indigestion; on a more professional level, Queen Isolde treating wounds and infections with balms, plasters, and medicinal baths; and even a psychologist, Dame Brisen in Malory's *Morte Darthur*, treating Lancelot's insanity.

In the romance particularly, fictional exigencies require quick cures. Treatment can be described in realistic detail, but the hero must recuperate rapidly and return to the fray, lest the plot languish.[16] Such rapid cures lend an aura of magic to the proceedings and render the perpetrator suspect; anyone that powerful can be dangerous too. Again in the *Morte Darthur*, Morgan le Fay (Book II, Chapter 9) can cure Sir Alexander's wounds, but she can also keep him with her for a twelvemonth and a day by means of a magic potion. Queen Arnive in Wolfram von Eschenbach's *Parzifal* is a skilled practitioner, but she attributes her success to the power of Kundry, the sorceress: " 'What can be done by medicine she has enabled me to do.' "[17] The medicine of the old wives could indeed be a combination of home remedy and incantation, rightly rejected by the trained physician; yet on the other hand, there is also simple misogyny in this aura of suspicion surrounding women in medicine.[18]

The reason is the connection in the popular mind between women healers and witchcraft. By the fourteenth century, female healers were increasingly regarded as "in league with devils and demons."[19] In 1511, an act of the English Parliament accused various medical irregulars of using " 'sorcerye and witchcrafte.' "[20] This belief in the possibility of supernatural aid reinforced the general belief in women as deceptive and therefore possibly poisoners. Since she who knows the drugs that heal must also know the drugs that kill, accepting a potion from a woman was a risky business. As late as 1669, in a case referred to the courts by the medical faculty of the University of Leipzig, the decision was definite: "Women are by no means to prepare medicines."[21]

The association of witches and poison was a very old idea even in the Middle Ages. Ovid speaks of witches who use magical formulas, sympathetic magic, and aphrodisiacs, but he speaks of them only to discourage his readers from consulting them. His stock figure, the old bawd who dispenses all of these and practical advice too, takes up residence in literature as one kind of *venefica* character. Typical of Ovid's commonsense approach is his skepticism with regard to the potion's powers; Ovid thinks that carefully cultivated erotic skills are far superior. As he points out, Circe and Medea should not have needed artificial assistance, and in fact both failed to keep their lovers even with such aid:

> Don't mess with Thessalian witchcraft—
>   That love-charm torn from the brow
> Of a foal is no good. Not all Medea's herbs, not every
>   Spell and magical cantrip will suffice
> To keep love alive—else Circe had held Ulysses,
>   And Medea her Jason, by their arts alone.[22]

He calls aphrodisiacs "poison" even while he suggests a recipe for them (pepper, nettleseed, camomile, wine, white Megarian onions, colewort, eggs, Hymettus honey, pine nuts [*The Art of Love*, II, ll. 415–25]). He will teach his reader the modern methods: "Witchcraft's ways are outdated" (*Cures for Love*, l. 251). His arts—sexual techniques—are more reliable. On the other hand, Ovid seems to believe, or perhaps pretends to believe, that witches can concoct anaphrodisiacs; he blames impotence on witches' brews. This belief will recur in witchcraft lore since it provides a handy external agent to blame for a sexual failure:

> Perhaps some Thessalian hell-brew has ruined
>   My physical urges...
>   Maybe *that* was the trouble, made worse
> By embarrassment when I couldn't, the final humiliating
>   Blow to my masculine pride.
>
> (*Amores*, III, ll. 27–28, 36–37)

Like Pliny in his *Natural History*, Ovid connects love charms (which Pliny calls "*Thessalam herbam*") with witches.[23] Even as Ovid argues against belief in these, he testifies to the prevalence of the belief in his audience, a belief that was to last for hundreds of years in medical literature and popular thought.

Witches were long connected with poisons in general and with love potions in particular. The Latin term *veneficus*, or its more common feminine form, *venefica*, was synonymous with *poisoner* or *sorcerer*, at least through the sixteenth century. The power of love potions could take two forms: to promote love or to obstruct it. In the medical field, the question of whether love could be engendered by a potion was discussed by Peter of Abano (who flourished in the late thirteenth and early fourteenth centuries); Peter said it could without reservation. Later, Daniel Sennert (1572–1637) and Elias Heinrich Henkel (1689) said it could arouse lust in general but not directed to a specific person.[24]

The converse question—whether witches could cause male impotence—

was an even hotter one. Fear of this alleged power resurfaces constantly in witchcraft lore. Aquinas discussed it twice and said that witches can indeed do it.[25] Lord Essex got his famous divorce in 1613 on the grounds that he was bewitched into impotence toward his wife only, *maleficium versus hanc*. In between Aquinas and Essex, there were complaints that the claim of *impotentia ex maleficio* was "abused . . . to secure annulments." In cases of *frigiditas*, a man could have sex with no woman; but in the case of what we now call secondary impotence, the phenomenon was so puzzling that no explanation could be found except *maleficium*. So (in the absence of grounds like *incompatibilitias*) it became a recognized cause for annulment in Gratian's *Corpus Juris Canonici* (c. 1140). Even as late as the middle of the seventeenth century, a prayer against impotence refers to the problem as caused by *maleficium*.[26] In a painting by Hans Baldung-Grün (c. 1484–1545), *The Bewitched Groom and the Witch's Curse*, a witch gloats over a comatose young man with a wilted flower protruding from his codpiece.[27] The image sums up the fear of impotence projected onto a presumed cause, the witch-women. It is but a small psychological step to project the blame for sexual failure onto all women.

As the *venefica* is associated less with healing and more with witchcraft in the intensely misogynistic witchcraft lore, all women came to be seen as potential potion-makers. All women, not just witches, learn in their traditional roles as "cooks, nurses, midwives, and keepers of the home" how to "gather the herbs that can cure or poison"; all women "know the charms or the potions that can cause hatred or love, fertility or impotence."[28] Poisons, potions, drugs, medicines: these are synonymous, as the French term used by Chrétien, *la poison* ("potion") suggests, and all are regarded as the province of the powerful female. Fear of mysterious female power to shape events through a substance deviously administered permeates works on witchcraft.

The fear of the witch's supposed power to deprive man of rational control or even of life itself is nowhere so obvious as in James Sprenger's and Heinrich Kramer's *Malleus Maleficarum* (1486),[29] described as "the most important and most sinister work on demonology ever written" (47)[30] and also a classic of misogyny. In it, women are seen as "wheedling and secret" enemies (45), whose natural weapon is poison. Even an ordinary housewife will resort to *veneficium*, the art of poisoning, at the least provocation:

So Theophrastus says: If you hand over the whole management of the house to her, but reserve some minute detail to your own judgement, she will think that you are displaying a great want of faith in her, and will stir up strife; and unless you quickly take counsel, she will prepare poison for you, and consult seers and soothsayers; and will become a witch. (45)

If a man escapes with his life, he must still fear women's use of witchcraft to control his sexual nature. Ovid joked about "a magician giving [his] member a local anesthetic" (*Amores*, III, l. 35), but he may have believed it too. Kramer and Sprenger surely do; they devote a great deal of attention to the problem. The witch controls what Kramer and Sprenger call the "virile member"; she can cause impotence or satyriasis or deprive a man of potency entirely. Since Sprenger and Kramer draw a fine line between witches and other women in general, it is clear that their obsessively recurrent image—the lost virile member—expresses strong fear of dominant women.

Even more interesting on the topic of the potion than Kramer and Sprenger's fulminations is Reginald Scot's *Discoverie of Witchcraft*, published in 1584 as a refutation of *Malleus Maleficarum*.[31] By this time, witchcraft was no longer viewed as it had been in earlier times, as concerned with such matters as "curing ailments"; now it was seen as a "fearful evil rapidly overspreading the land."[32] Scot systematically refutes Kramer and Sprenger, denying the existence of phenomena such as shape shifting, incubi, succubi, and making off with the male member. Scot does not believe in the power of witchcraft to inhibit sexuality, but he does concede a point: the relationship between witches and poisoning. In fact, for Scot, "poisoner" is the definition of *witch*: "Sometimes a murtherer with poison is called a witch. . . . And at this daie it is indifferent to saie in the English toong; She is a witch; or, She is a wise woman" (88).

The equation Scot establishes joining poisoning, witchcraft, and special knowledge is crucial: the witch is "wise woman," and a major thing she is wise about is *veneficium*. He translates Exodus 22 as "You shall not suffer anie poisoners, or (as it is translated) witches to live" (89). As in the days of the children of Israel, *veneficae* exist in Scot's day, and they are more likely to be women than men. The murders they commit are a total reversal of the proper order of things:

Trulie this poisoning art called *Veneficium*, of all others is most abhominable; as whereby murthers maie be committed, where no suspicion maie be gathered, nor anie resistance can be made; the strong cannot avoid the weake, the wise cannot prevent the foolish, the godlie cannot be preserved from the hands of the wicked; children maie hereby kill their parents, the servant the maister, the wife hir husband, so privilie, so inevitablie, and so incurablie, that of all other it hath beene thought the most odious kind of murther. (94)

Of this magic art, the concoction of "love cups" is the "principall part . . . which indeed are meere poisons, bereaving some of the benefit of the braine, and so of the sense and understanding of the mind. And from some it taketh awaie life, & that is more common than the other" (96). He cites Livia and Lucia (98) just as the Wife of Bath's husband Jankyn did so long before (III.D. 747–53). Skeptic though he is, he has no doubt that one feature of witchcraft that cannot be debunked is poisoning and that "women were the first inventers and practisers of the art of poisoning" (93). Later, James I in his *Daemonologie* rehashes the same issue: witches exert control over the sex act, learn "uncouthe poysons" from the devil, and are likely to be women.[33] Still later, in *The Displaying of Supposed Witchcraft* (1677), John Webster uses the terms *witching* and *secret poysoning* as synonyms and adds to the witches' repertory "philters and receipts whereby they do much hurt and mischief."[34]

This belief in the power of the witch finds its way into both literature and life. In Fernando de Rojas's *Celestina* (c. 1499), the title character has the multifaceted career attributed to the *venefica*.[35] She is "wise woman" (176), witch, whoremonger, and general facilitator of all women's ends. On the one hand, she is a "kinde of Phisicien" (241) who knows "convenient medicines...remedie of infirmities" (175), including charms for the toothache. Like other healing women, she is "skilful in hearbs" (81). On the other hand, she is also "an old bearded woman...a witch, subtill as the divell, and well practis'd in all the rogueries and villanies that the world can afoord" (33), including repairing "crackt maidenheads" (40). Since she is a "Perfumeresse" and cosmetician as well, she keeps a "chamber full of Limbecks" (41) for yet another sideline, making love potions.

In *Celestina*, the relationship of the *venefica* and the sexual woman is reversed in that it is the young man, Calisto, who comes to Celestina for a philter to make his lady, Melibea, fall in love with him. With much ado and long incantations to the devil, Celestina makes the concoction from such ingredients as bat's blood, cat's skin, dragon's wings, and "oyle of serpents" (75). She uses the resultant mixture to anoint a "clew of yarn" (76) and transmit it to the intended victim in her additional role as yarn seller. The lady duly falls in love and is seduced, leading to the disastrous conclusion resulting from ingesting this "poysoned morsell" (Melibea refers to love itself, not the "clew"), from taking this "serpent within [her] body" (again love, or maybe Calisto himself [175]).

In his *Anatomy of Melancholy* (1621), Robert Burton repeats the same beliefs that have permeated literature and life for so long, even mentioning the bawd Celestina as a "wise woman" who can "give a dram, promise to restore maidenheads, make an abortion if need be, keep down their paps, hinder conception, procure lust, make them able with Satyrions"—in short, perform some functions that we would associate with health care and other functions connected with magic. Along with many other examples, including referring the reader to *Malleus Maleficarum*, he quotes Erastus's *De Lamiis* to stress that witches make "philtres 'to force men and women to love and hate whom they will, to cause tempests, diseases,' &c., by charms, spells, characters, knots—*hic Thessala vendit Philtra*."[36]

Therefore throughout this period, beliefs perpetuated in witchcraft lore are reflected in literature. The custom of entrusting medical matters to women, coupled with the belief that the witch could control love and hate, even life and death, through the concoction of potions, forms the basis for the image in literature. In Marie de France's *lai* "Les Deus Amanz," a typical *venefica* comes to the aid of two young lovers.[37] A widowed king is trying to prevent the marriage of his daughter by requiring her suitor to perform an impossible task:

> it was decreed and destined that he
> would have to carry her in his arms
> to the summit of the mountain outside the city
> without stopping to rest.
>
> (ll. 35–38)

Since this king has placed an artificial obstacle between his daughter and a legitimate and proper marriage, artificial means are needed to overcome it. The daughter's true love, the son of a count, wants her to elope with him. But she insists that he meet her father's requirements and sends him to her aunt, who lives in Salerno, site of the famous medical school, and has "practiced the medical arts for so long / that she's an expert on medicines" (ll. 98–99). The aunt gives the young man a potion that will make him strong enough to meet the father's requirements. The aunt is a typical medieval *venefica*. She is trained in orthodox medicine; at that time, a woman could study medicine at a school such as Salerno even if she were not considered a degree candidate. Like many another woman practitioner, she operates on the fringe of an increasingly professionalized medical establishment, such operations being characterized by traffic in magic and sorcery. So when the young man goes to her for help, she uses two lines of treatment: medicines (to make him naturally stronger) and potions (to make him supernaturally stronger and instantaneously, "the moment he drank it" [l. 140]).

Back in his native land, he presents himself for the challenge. His lady love, however, seems not to have much faith in the efficacy of the potion since she goes on "literature's first crash diet":[38]

> she fasted and dieted,
> cut down on her eating,
> because she desired to help her lover.
>
> (ll. 164–66)

The young man has his potion at the ready as he carries the lady up the mountain, but he inexplicably procrastinates about taking it. The sweetheart urges him—indeed nags him—to take it, but he does not, saying he does not want to stop when he is doing so well. Of course, he dies, and she with him of the mandatory broken heart. Both are buried on the side of the fatal mountain.

In this story, both potion and potion-maker work toward a legitimate end but are oddly peripheral. The potion is powerful but only if taken. The tragic denouement results from the self-deception of each of the three principal characters, who act from motives that they will not or cannot admit, and so do not use the obvious means for solving the problem. The father sets impossible standards for the daughter's suitor; he does not want to give up his daughter at all but will not admit it. The daughter refuses to elope and insists that her lover meet her father's irrational norm; she cannot break free of her need to please her dominant father, whom she still sees as the standard of male prowess. The lover has a magic potion but refuses to use it; he wants to prove to his beloved, to himself, and above all to her father that, unaided, he is superior not only to all the previous suitors but to the father as well. The contest is between the two men; the lady is the prize. Although the power of the *venefica* could have influenced events, it does not because of the peculiar psychological problems of the characters.

MEDIEVAL POTION-MAKERS: ISOLDE AND THESSALA

The relationship between the king's daughter and the aunt in Salerno (with regard to the potion, the young man is a mere errand boy) represents the typical division between the *venefica* and the younger woman whose love life is affected by the administration of the potion. The best-known example of this pairing of women is Queen Isolde and her daughter, Isolde, in the Tristan story. The elder Isolde has the combination of magic and healing skills characteristic of the medieval wise woman. Thus, she is the only one in the world able to cure Tristan of his poisoned wound; yet at the same time, she makes a potion that does not merely encourage but compels the affections of those who drink it, giving Tristan a wound more serious than the one of which she cures him.[39]

Tristan received his physical wound in hand-to-hand combat with Morold, enemy of his liege lord, King Mark of Cornwall. Morold chooses single combat with Tristan as a way of settling his differences with Mark, and much is made of the tradition of the worthy opponent, but Morold is guilty of deception in envenoming his sword. Although Tristan wins the battle, he appears doomed to die since " 'no physician or medical skill can save' " him except that of Morold's sister, Queen Isolde of Ireland, who is " 'versed in herbs of many kinds, in the virtues of all plants, and in the art of medicine' " (134).[40] Morold attempts to bargain with Tristan, exchanging his sister's cure for his own life, but Tristan refuses to spare his lord's enemy even at the possible cost of his own life, and chops off Morold's head. Morold's body is returned to Ireland in pieces. Queen Isolde and her daughter lament vociferously, but Queen Isolde has the presence of mind and the medical skill to perform a post-mortem surgical procedure. She closely examines Morold's head wound and with a forceps removes from it a fragment of Tristan's sword embedded in it. This piece of evidence will later identify the disguised Tristan.

Tristan's wound becomes infected and gives off an unromantic stench. After Cornwall's best doctors fail to cure him, Tristan realizes he has no recourse but to Queen Isolde. He goes to Ireland disguised as the harpist Tantris and lands a job as the younger Isolde's music instructor. This proximity calls Queen Isolde's attention to his medical condition. Characters like the Queen, "female healers who tend the hero's wounds," are common in the romance,[41] and Queen Isolde is a particularly professional representative of the type. She is apparently accustomed to dealing with such situations and is in no way put off by Tristan's unpleasant symptoms. She seems not so much to sympathize with Tristan as to welcome the opportunity to demonstrate her skill when she declares herself his doctor: " 'I will restore your life and body to you in perfect health and looks. I can give or refuse: both are in my power!' " (145).

The Queen is in general depicted as a woman of strength and presence. She is often described as "well-versed," "wise," "skilled," "discerning." She is a respected political adviser to her husband, included in the meetings of his counselors. In all her appearances in the story, she seems a managerial type, used to decision making and accustomed to being in a position of authority. It never occurs to her, or to anyone else, that she might consult her husband before making a decision. In the case of the marriage proposal made to Isolde by Tristan on behalf of Mark, she presents the decision she has made to the King, who defers to her judgment (181). In addition to her knowledge of medicine, she is also depicted as able to foretell the future by means of "secret arts." However, in the matter of Tristan's true identity, she is inexplicably ignorant, and her firm decision to give him medical aid places her in the ironic position of rescuing her mortal enemy, the killer of her brother.

Meanwhile, as Tantris, he is tutor to Isolde, an "enchanting girl . . . blessed by fortune" (147–48). Even in that alluring relationship, male teacher and female student like Abélard and Heloïse, there is still no indication that Tristan and Isolde have fallen in love. Tristan and Isolde are described as ideal representatives of their type, and so there is no reason why they should not fall in love. But Tristan's emotions are firmly in the service of his reason; he has come to Ireland to be cured of his wound, not to get another one. When Tristan is strong enough to return to Cornwall, he sings Isolde's praises to King Mark but shows no reluctance to act as Mark's go-between. Although Mark has promised not to marry, that Tristan might be his heir, his court counselors, jealous of Tristan, convince him that a politic marriage between him and the sole heiress of Ireland would put an end to the hostilities between those two chronically warring nations. Tristan consents, not wanting to be responsible for leaving the land without an heir, and sets off once more to Ireland to woo Isolde for Mark.

A barrier to this union is overcome when Tristan slays a dragon, a "cursed fiendish monster" that "had burdened the land and the people with such an excess of harm that the King swore by his royal oath that he would give his daughter to whoever would make an end of it, provided he were a knight and of noble birth" (159). Tristan does this, ridding Isolde of an unwelcome (because ignobly born) suitor; but in the process he is (again) envenomed by the dragon's tongue. Tristan's vulnerability to poisons of all sorts is a recurrent motif in his legend. Queen Isolde resumes her role as healer. She doses him with theriac, the universal antidote for poison in literature which could not be found in life, the quest for which in medieval poison lore is equivalent to the search for the philosopher's stone in alchemy. Cured again, Tristan has also sufficiently ingratiated himself with Queen Isolde to cause her to swear a solemn oath that " 'no ill shall befall' " him in Ireland (167). Unlike some other literary ladies, she does consider herself bound by her oath, even when Tristan's real identity is revealed. Ironically, however, she is accidentally forsworn when Tristan drinks the potion that will eventually destroy him. But technically she is guiltless even of this, as neither this misfortune nor its consequences befall him in Ireland.

Meanwhile, Isolde is becoming attracted to Tantris—"she scanned his body and his whole appearance with uncommon interest" (173)—but worries that he is beneath her in station. Isolde's curiosity about the minstrel Tantris is a response to a recurrent motif in the story, Tristan's shifting identity. From earliest childhood, Tristan's true identity is unclear to both Tristan and others. The lie of Ruai li Fontenant, while it protects Tristan, also obscures his parenthood; Morgan accuses Tristan of bastardy. Tristan changes fathers, names, and appearances often, variously disguised as a merchant, a pilgrim, a minstrel, a leper. At one point Mark and the barons ask the same question that Isolde does: " '*Who is Tristan?*' " (98). Her curiosity about how so noble a knight could have so low a social rank impels her to examine his armor for clues, whereupon she discovers his broken sword, which matched the fragment taken from Morold's skull. All her attraction turns to hatred because now she thinks she knows who Tristan is: her kinsman's killer. But Tristan's real identity will emerge only after he drinks the potion. The only consistent element in his character, the only real answer to the question, "*Who is Tristan?*" will be "Isolde's lover."

The question of the potion's power is inseparable from the state of mind of Tristan and Isolde before taking it. In Malory's version of the legend, Tristan and Isolde are well on their way to being in love before taking the potion. Gottfried's version, however, strengthens the impression of the potion's efficacy by exaggerating Isolde's revulsion against Tristan upon her discovery of his true identity as Morold's killer. She wants revenge and is deterred only by Queen Isolde's reminding her of the oath of protection. This leads the elder Isolde to a brief meditation on the ironies of power: she can heal or destroy and has healed the one she would destroy.

She, her daughter, and Brangane take counsel among themselves and accept Tristan's proposal that Isolde marry Mark. This has several advantages. First, there is no question that Mark, unlike Tristan in disguise or the overweening Steward, has appropriate rank to marry Isolde. Second, though Tristan has won the right to marry Isolde by killing the dragon, he does not want to do so; he is acting only as Mark's representative. Third, such a marriage uniting warring kingdoms might well end the kind of violence that led to Morold's death and Tristan's wounding. Finally, a marriage to Mark would get Isolde out of the uncomfortable position of being won in marriage by an enemy of her family. Isolde's anger is somewhat assuaged, Tristan has carried out his mission, and the marriage is arranged. Any passing attraction between Tristan and Isolde is gone.

Then the potion is prepared. In an age of prearranged political marriages such as the one now planned between Isolde and Mark, love is unnecessary. Queen Isolde is unusual in hoping for a loving marriage for her daughter, a life in which her yet-unseen husband will love her above all others and she him: "They would share one death and one life, one sorrow and one joy" (192). This intensity is usually reserved in literature for the extramarital relationship. Apparently Queen Isolde does not agree with Andreas Capellanus's famous dictum that "love cannot exert its powers between two people who are married to each other."[42] Centuries before the idea of marrying for love became current, Queen Isolde wants for her daughter a marriage more like a love affair. She is a woman ahead of her time in this. Yet at the same time she is an astute politician, cementing an alliance between two previously warring nations.

Because she knows "secret arts," she need not leave the matter to chance or even to her daughter's own abilities to secure the love of Mark. In attempting to determine her daughter's life, she is using her power in an interfering and manipulative way, always a temptation to mothers. She does not ask Isolde's consent but gives the potion to Brangane to be administered secretly, but only to Isolde and Mark: " 'Beware lest anyone share with them.... This brew is a love-philtre!" (192). Her maneuver turns upon her as the object of her daughter's passionate love turns out to be their family's mortal enemy.

The philter's drastic effects are again stressed by the scene immediately preceding Tristan and Isolde's drinking it. Isolde is desolate: "she was leaving her homeland...and all her friends...and was sailing away with strangers," one of whom had killed her uncle, to marry a man she has never met. Tristan tries to console her, but to no avail: " 'I hate you!.... You killed my uncle!' " Still trying to cheer her, Tristan "called for something to drink" (193–94).

Both are trapped for life in the potion's fateful power. All loyalty and honor are cast aside as Tristan and Isolde continually deceive his lord and her husband. Their lives thenceforth are determined by the constant quest to satisfy their passions, "wild and raging" as the sea into which the horrified Brangane throws the remainder of the love drink (195). Brangane's words are fulfilled at last: " 'that flask and the draught it contained will be the death of you both!' " (205). Their whole lives are shaped in the image of the poison. Tristan's "life was poisoned" (284); Isolde's "death and life had poisoned her" (285). There is no escape; neither can ever love another.

In poison lore, a homeopathic remedy—like cures like—is often prescribed; Tristan's marriage to Isolde of the White Hands can be seen as an attempt at such a cure. Tristan seems to hope that the nominal similarity of the two women drive out the venom of the illicit love that is destroying his life; but this attempt is futile. He and the first Isolde are " 'too bound up with one another' "(302), and he is impotent with his wife. Only the first Isolde can arouse or satisfy his passions. The second Isolde serves only as a pathetic excuse for his love effusions to her namesake. This discourteous behavior to his wife shows the extent of the corruption caused by the potion. The lie he tells to excuse his sexual failure expresses a paradoxical truth: he is indeed ill, of a " 'bodily infirmity' " (310), an envenoming, which permeates his being and renders his marriage an empty shell.

It is fitting that death comes to Tristan as a result of being "wounded through the loins by a lance bated with venom" (341). His death is, as his life had been, a manifestation of his point of vulnerability, his Achilles' heal: the compulsive sexual attraction caused by the potion. No physician has the power over his sexuality that his lady Isolde has. No physician has the curative powers of her mother the Queen, so "the poison cruelly torments him" (341). He is separated from his physician and his consolation by the illegitimacy of their love. At this point in the tale, the name confusion worsens. Queen Isolde and her daughter begin to fuse into one person, which is suitable to the nature of Tristan's wound. On the one hand, Queen Isolde has power to cure all envenomed wounds, even this one. On the other hand, Tristan's sexuality is totally bound up with the younger Isolde because of the power of her mother's potion. Without her, he is impotent, without power. The wound in his loins is a graphic image of the inevitability of his destruction as a result of the passionate love that renders him helpless in her absence: " 'Our death was hidden in that potion, and never shall we recover from it!' " (344).

As his condition worsens, he loses the hope of Queen Isolde's restoring his physical health and longs only for his love, who can be brought to him in the fitting disguise of " 'a physician-woman who has come to heal [his] wound' " (345). Here his life recapitulates that of Rivalin, his father, who, while lying mortally ill, receives his lover, Blancheflor, in disguise as a "physician-woman," a meeting that results in the conception of Tristan. Tristan sees women as potential healers, but, as his mother failed to cure his father and indeed died herself, so Isolde cannot cure Tristan, being as sick as he is. Her ship is delayed by unfavorable winds; Tristan dies in the arms of the wrong Isolde; and the lovers are united only in death. Isolde's death is a " 'drinking of the same cup' " (353), an inevitable sharing of the fate foredoomed by their drinking the love philter.

In the Tristan legend, the mother is strong and the daughter weak. The formidable Queen thinks she can use her magic arts to bring her daughter happiness. In a way she is right in not wanting her daughter to languish, passions unengaged, in a practical marriage. She wants her daughter to have a passionate love. But she wants to control the situation totally, so that this love will be contained within the socially acceptable arrangements she has made, the marriage to Mark. She wants her daughter to experience an all-consuming love but within a marriage that suits the family's and the nation's needs, as well as Isolde's own. Queen Isolde knows that the extremes of passion are antisocial and wants to manage her daughter's life in such a way as to channel these drives. The paradox is that through the misdirection of the potion, her attempt to enhance a socially acceptable love results in the exact opposite: a love in conflict with society.[43]

Sensing her own power and her daughter's relative powerlessness, the Queen plans her daughter's life, and the plan backfires. Once separated from the dominant mother, Isolde cannot receive any assistance from her. Queen Isolde never again plays a role in the story; she becomes a shadowy figure, whose reaction to the mishap is never discussed, who is distinguished by her absence from the scene of the disaster she has caused. The mother determines the direction of the daughter's life and then leaves her alone, "at sea" as Isolde is when she drinks the potion, away from the safe harbor her mother afforded. She offers no solution to the problems her interference has caused. After this, Isolde is on her own. This is most apparent at the end, when Tristan lies dying of a wound Queen Isolde could have cured if she were there. The Queen's power sets the plot in motion; the young couple are at the mercy of events. The older, wiser woman makes the choice; the young, vulnerable couple bear its results. If "Tristan did just as Adam did ... took the fruit which his Eve offered him and with her ate his death" (280), then there is no role for Queen Isolde in this scenario but that of serpent.

The confusion among the three Isoldes and the word play resulting from Tristan's marriage to the third Isolde stress the point of the domination of Queen Isolde. She makes/names her daughter in her own image and tries to predetermine her life. This has consequences also for the third Isolde, pitiful substitute, kept on hand as a possible *remedia amoris* and excuse for poetic exhortations to her name, not herself. She is a poor copy of Isolde, who is in turn a pale reflection of her mother. As Joan Ferrante points out, the fact that the two younger Isoldes have the same name "suggests that the hero's love is his own creation ... the image he created of his love as he wanted her to be";[44] but this is also true of the elder Isolde, whose influence shapes the lives of the younger women and of Tristan as well. With the best of intentions, the Queen as *venefica* has undone her work as healer and unwittingly taken revenge on Tristan at last. But the potion-maker typically tries to control the male only; Queen Isolde has controlled, and finally destroyed, her daughter too. She is a forceful figure of the too-powerful mother who scripts the story of her daughter's life and then withdraws from the scene, leaving the daughter to play out her tragedy, alone on an empty stage.

The tragic tale of Tristan and Isolde turns into comedy in Chrétien de Troyes's twelfth-century romance *Cligés*.[45] In this anti-Tristan tale, "the elements of tragedy found in the Tristan legend are undercut and eliminated," especially the crucial potion, which here becomes "an illusion-making concoction."[46] In the *Cligés*, Thessala is the *venefica* and Fenice the heroine of the love story. Fenice is in love with Cligés but betrothed to his uncle, Alis. Her morals require that she be unlike Isolde, who was shared by lover and husband. In pursuit of this goal, she consults her nurse, Thessala, who prepares a potion that, imbibed by Alis in the wedding wine, induces each night a dreamful sleep in which Alis thinks he has made love to his wife but has not. Thus Fenice preserves herself for her lover alone.

Thessala is depicted as both healer and necromancer. On the one hand, she can " 'cure the dropsy, gout, quinsy, and asthma' "; she is " 'so expert in examining the urine and the pulse that you need consult no other physician.' " On the other hand, she says she " 'know[s] more than ever Medea knew of enchantments and of charms.' " She is a combination of the Ovidian nurse, of Medea, also native of the land "where devilish charms are taught and wrought" (130), and of the medieval healer; in the fused wisdom of these roles, she can easily remedy Fenice's lovesickness by treating her husband, Alis.

"As she diligently prepares and tempers her potions," Thessala is deceptive as the devil himself. To her potion she adds "spices in abundance to sweeten and temper it ... [and] give it a sweet and pleasant fragrance" (133). Poison concealed in a sweet substance is St. Jerome's metaphor for the deceptive nature of evil: "Poison is not good unless smeared in honey, and vice does not deceive, except under the appearance and semblance of virtue."[47] Again operating by subterfuge, Thessala causes Cligés to administer the potion to his uncle, both men being unaware of its nature. So Alis is deceived, and Fenice reserves herself for Cligés; a side effect of the treatment is that the marriage of Fenice and Alis is rendered invalid by virtue of nonconsummation.[48]

Thessala's skills are again useful when Cligés and Fenice decide to elope. Fenice, wanting to conceal the elopement, decides to feign death. Thessala prepares another potion, which leaves Fenice "cold, colourless, pale, and stiff ... yet she would be alive and well, and would have no sensations of any kind" (162). When Fenice feigns illness in preparation for her feigned death, Thessala's actions show her medical skills. In an oddly realistic note for a romance, Thessala is shown as knowing enough about urinalysis to substitute a dying woman's urine for Fenice's to deceive the physicians, who solemnly agree that "the urine was very bad" (165).

These "aged physicians from Salerno" (166) do not believe that Fenice is dead, and to prove their point, they resort to more and more extreme measures, including pouring hot lead onto her palms and roasting her on a grate. The heroic treatment they render may be a clue as to why the unlicensed alternative healers were so popular in the Middle Ages. Drastic though they are, these measures do not cause Fenice pain, since she is protected by the anesthetic effect of the potion. Nevertheless, hot lead and grilling injuries require treatment before she can be restored *in corpore sano* to her lover. Thessala is again at the ready, with "a very precious ointment" (170) and also "plaster, and remedies" (172). Thessala's skills thus are such as to enable her to outwit, and to undo the damage caused by, the trained and licensed practitioners from the famous medical school. Yet at the same time, other, more suspect powers are implied in the French term *mestre*, which is often applied to Thessala. Its connotations include both medical skills and magic.[49] She is an artificer who uses her powers to control affairs through manipulating men. Ever after in the kingdom of Alis, women are distrusted:

For never since has there been an emperor who did not stand in fear of his wife, lest he should be deceived by her. . . . Therefore, every empress, however rich and noble she may be, is guarded in Constantinople as in a prison, for the emperor has no confidence in her when he remembers the story of Fenice. (179)

The elements of the Tristan story are diluted by being turned into comedy. The characters in *Cligés* often seem downright silly; in fact, it is as a parody that the romance can best be understood, as Paul R. Lonigan points out. Fenice, the heroine, is a trivial girl who bases her life's decisions on hair-splitting rationalizations. For example, when she is "dead," her marriage vows presumably expire too, so her affair with Cligés can commence without fear of adultery. Cligés, the hero, is "passive throughout the affair, knowing or contributing little or nothing"; he is as much subject to the power of the women as is Alis. The latter, a diminished version of King Mark bereft of any claim to love or loyalty, had "no business being rewarded with the sweet thing" in the first place and then arrives at last in the ludicrous position in which the potion has placed him. The feigned death of his wife worsens matters rather than solves them because there is no indication that the dream-inducing effect of the potion is temporally limited: "Alis could have gone on indefinitely imagining that he had possessed Fenice. (Did he continue to have his sweet dreams even after he believed his wife to be dead?)" If he did, the effect is black comedy. In fact, Thessala is the most serious character in the romance even if the potions she makes have a comic rather than a tragic effect.[50]

After Gottfried's *Tristan*, the potion and therefore the power of the *venefica* are watered down. In Malory's *Morte Darthur*, not only is Queen Isolde much less powerful, but also her potion is diluted by the preexisting attraction between Tristan and Isolde, and as a result, the consequences of their love are far less fateful. Malory drew on a thirteenth-century prose version of the Tristan legend,[51] not on the Gottfried or Thomas version, and in general deemphasized the potion and diminished the intensity of Tristan and Isolde's love. In Malory, Tristan's association with poison has its origin in the hatred of his stepmother, who tries to poison him but instead poisons her own child and almost slays her husband, Tristan's father. For these offenses, she is deemed guilty of treason and would have been burned at the stake were it not for Tristan's intervention. As in Gottfried's version, Tristan is wounded with a poisoned sword and goes to Ireland, disguised as a harpist, for cure. Here the reason for the trip is the prophecy of a "wytty lady" that Tristan could only be cured by going "into the same countrey that the venym cam fro" (VII, 8, 238), not specifically because of any merit attached to Queen Isolde. Indeed it is the younger Isolde, a "noble surgeon" (VIII, 9, 238), who heals him, and they fall in love. When Tristan's true identity is discovered, it is the Queen, not Isolde, who is the more enraged; Isolde is "passynge sore abaysshed, for passynge well she loved Tramtryste and full well she knew the crewelnesse of hir modir the quene" (VIII, 11, 242). Each swears fidelity; rings are exchanged. The rivalry in love between Tristan and King Mark is explained by a story about a rivalry between them over the affections of the wife of Earl Sigwarides, whom both Tristan and Mark loved. Tristan seems to get the best of Mark in this situation, since this serves as motivation for Mark's desire to marry Isolde and to rub Tristan's nose in it by making him serve as go-between. This makes Isolde another in a series of ladies shared by Mark and Tristan, not the unique event she is in Gottfried. Yet Tristan is bound by his loyalty to Mark to pursue the proxy courtship as bidden.

The potion episode is then quite different in its effect on both Tristan and Isolde. Before the potion, "of all men erthely" Isolde loves Tristan most (VIII, 23, 257). Tristan has earned a boon by overcoming an adversary of the king, Isolde's father, and asks for Isolde's hand in marriage—to Mark. Isolde's father, recognizing the love between Tristan and Isolde, thinks it preferable that Tristan marry her. The political motive for the marriage—reconciling Cornwall and Ireland—drops out; Tristan is acting as an instrument of Mark's revenge on him for the rivalry over the wife of the earl. Queen Isolde makes the potion to cement the love between Mark and Isolde and gives it to be guarded by Bragwaine and also by Gouvernail, Tristan's retainer, as well. Two potion guarders prove as inept as one, and the lovers drink the potion in a cheery scene devoid of the sudden onslaught of emotion depicted in Gottfried:

So sir Trystrames toke the see, and La Beale Isode. [And when they] were in their caban, hit happed so that they were thyrsty. And than they saw a lytyll flakette of golde stonde by them, and hit seemed by the coloure and the taste that hit was noble wyne.

So sir Trystrames toke the flaket in his honde and seyde, "Madame Isode, here is a draught of good wyne that Dame Brangwayne, your mayden, and Governayle, my servaunte, hath kepte for hemselff."

Than they lowghe and made good chere, and eyther dranke to other frely, and they thought never drynke that ever they dranke so swete nother so good to them. But by that drynk was in their bodyes they loved aythir other so well that never hir love departed, for weal nother for woo. And thus hit happed fyrst, the love betwyxte sir Trystrames and La Beale Isode, the whyche love never departed days of their lyff. (VIII, 24, 258)

Brangwein and Gouvernail do not even seem to notice that the potion is lost; no flinging it into the raging sea, with all the attendant symbolism, for them. It is merely one more event in the already established love of Tristan and Isolde.[52]

In Malory, every element of the story is muted. Tristan is less ill because of his wound; Isolde less enraged at learning his true identity; the Queen less powerful; the political situation less volatile; the potion less powerful; and Tristan and Isolde less in love. This is in keeping with the psychological realism and general downplaying of the supernatural in Malory,[53] but it has the effect of turning the famous lovers into a mellow pair. "The love story is not placed firmly at the centre of interest.... Malory is more interested in Tristan as a martial hero than in his love for Isolde."[54] War, not love, is Tristan's long suit. He returns to Isolde from time to time, but she is not at the center of his life as she is in Gottfried. Like the first intensity of any other love affair, the potion's already muted effects seem to diminish over time. "Although Tristan does not reject love, he is nevertheless explicit about preferring the adventures of the battlefield to those of the boudoir."[55] He also issues the "utterly unromantic announcement"[56] of being tired of love: " 'A, madame!' seyde sir Trystrames, 'go frome me, for much angur and daunger have I as[say]ed for your love' " (IX, 1, 309). Their relationship has its adventurous moments, but overall it is far more prosaic and, most significant, fails to culminate in the deaths of the lovers. There are "no dire consequences" to the drinking of the potion; the volume of the whole romance is turned down.[57]

Malory has other powerful potion-makers who influence the lives of the heroes at various points, but Queen Isolde is not one of them. Dame Brisen, however, is. King Pelles wants his daughter, Elaine, to have a child by Sir Lancelot. But Sir Lancelot is in love with Queen Guenevere and will not lie with Elaine. King Pelles seeks the service of "one of the grettyst enchaunters that was that tyme in the worlde," Dame Brisen, who tells the king not to worry: " 'I shall make hym to lye wyth youre doughter, and he shall not wyte but that he lyeth by quene Gwenyver.' " So she concocts the potion, secretes it in wine, and the desired results are achieved. Lancelot is "so asoted and madde that he myght make no delay but wythoute ony let he wente to bedde. And so he wente that mayden Elayne had bene quene Gwenyver. And wyte you well that sir Launcelot was glad, and so was that lady Eleyne that she had gotyn sir Launcelot in her armys." She efficiently conceives Galahad, so the trickily managed encounter has significant results. When Lancelot finds out that he has been deceived, he is angry; he brandishes his sword at the recently impregnated Elaine. Perhaps influenced by the fact that Elaine "skypped out of her bedde all naked" and knelt before him, praising his knightly prowess, he forgives her. Though he swears that Dame Brisen shall " 'lose her hede for wycchecrauftys,' " he appears to forget all about this threat, and the goal of King Pelles and Elaine is achieved without much damage to anyone (XI, 2–3, 479–81).

In Malory, the *veneficae* characters are relatively benign. Queen Isolde's potion is a mere cordial to hearts already inflamed. Dame Brisen's use of the potion is deceptive but has good results: Elaine is happily "delyverde of a fayre chylde." Malory's interest is in war, the realm of the male, not in love, the realm of the female. Malory's women are not his men's primary interest and so cannot be portrayed as powerful. Add to this Malory's psychological realism, and the result is that there is no place in Malory for the *venefica*. Nothing results from a woman's potion that could not easily have happened without it.

EPIC SEDUCTRESSES

After the Gottfried *Tristan*, then, the role of the *venefica* and her potion is muted. This situation abruptly changes in the Renaissance epic, where the treatment of the love potion is deadly serious. The fears of women's power embodied in these epics are contemporaneous with the witch-hunting craze that swept Northern Europe. Attributing magic powers to the seductive female is certainly, as Joan Ferrante points out, "a way ... of rationalizing the vulnerability men felt. That is, rather than admit the weakness of lust in himself, he focused on the power that attracted him; if the power were magic, he was not responsible for giving in to it."[58] In the epic, this "fear of women's corporeality, this intense misogyny and the witch-hunting contemporaneous with it," influence the characterization of the seductress.[59] The venomous woman becomes totally witch; the element of healer drops out. The medieval *venefica* wants to control the hero's body; her Renaissance counterpart wants to do this too but also to damn his soul.

In the Renaissance epic, the "sirens and Circe figures ... are diabolical forces whose human lovers are their prey."[60] Their potions, covertly administered and insidiously spreading, are effective metaphors for their power over the hero's body and soul. The seductresses of the Renaissance epic fuse the two elements of skill and seductiveness. In the epic, the hero visits an enclosed place representing the woman's sphere of influence, a place for him "to escape *to*" but perhaps also to "be lost *in*."[61] Her desire is to keep him there, under her power; to do this, she will seduce and enchant him. So in Ariosto's *Orlando Furioso* (1516), Rogero goes to Alcina's Castle to avenge the metamorphosis of Astolfo, whom the enchantress has turned into a myrtle tree.[62] In Tasso's *Jerusalem Delivered* [*Gerusalemme Liberata*] (1575), Charles and Ubaldo come to Armida's Bower to liberate Rinaldo, who languishes there under her spell.[63] In Spenser's *Faerie Queen* (1590), Guyon goes to Acrasia's Bower of Bliss to avenge the death of Mortdant.[64] In each, a weak man has fallen into the power of the enchantress, and a stronger man must restore right order.

In Tasso and Ariosto, the tactics of the enchantresses include all the usual witchlike activities. Armida recites spells and charms, and knows as much as the witches of Thessaly (Book XVI, stanzas xxvi, xxxvii), still famous as they were in Chrétien's day. She can call spirits, raise tempests, and fly through the air; she is "demonic and magical."[65] Alcina too is a "potent witch," daily found "reading in a little book / Or mumbling words" of incantation (Canto 6, 138); she is "a malignant manipulator of illusion."[66] These two ladies use all the wiles of women and witches but no potions. Thus their evil is not absorbed into the very being of their victims, who survive. But Spenser's Acrasia is a killer; the poison she uses on Mortdant is a suitable expression of the greater corruption found in her bower.[67] As Giamatti points out, Spenser develops Acrasia as a "descendant of the Italian witches" through stressing the "traditional link between depraved sex and magic."[68] She is the only one of Spenser's women described in terms of a spider,[69] and this connection with the venomous is reinforced by Spenser's decision to characterize her as a *venefica*. Spenser strengthens the seductress with the *potu in vinum* served in her bower. Perhaps he wanted to take advantage of the association of witches and poisoning well known for a hundred years through *Malleus Maleficarum* and only six years earlier reiterated by Reginald Scot.

In the Renaissance epic, fears of entrapment and emasculation are associated with poisoning. The witch's potion keeps a man in her place under her power. The lady's bower is an exaggeration of all the comforts of home over which an idealized housewife/mistress presides. In Ariosto, it is a place of comfort and leisure, moderate temperatures, "feasts and dainty fare" (161); in short, "nice apparel, belly-cheer, and ease" (147). When he arrives at the bower, the knight puts off his arms, his "badge of identification" and symbol of his warrior calling.[70] Once inside, he is disarmed, weakened; his prowess in war does him no good here. As in the medieval romance, the structure of the Renaissance epic involves alternation between love and war, between the inner sphere of influence of the female and the larger world of masculine activity. In between killing monsters and infidels, the hero may take respite in the peaceful place to "assuage . . . sorrows past" (Tasso 316), but it is a disgrace to stay too long. The bower is an "image of the appeal and of the dangers of repose."[71] A visitor here, the hero must not become too dependent on the creature who makes him so comfortable. He must leave the garden and return to the outer world of male action as soon as possible. In fact, if the garden is a metaphor for the woman's body,[72] a womb to which the hero may retreat,[73] then, as in the case of the first womb he encountered, the point is to leave. Entrapment, domination, and loss of masculinity will result if he remains in a place that "threatens ultimately to poison, ruin men."[74] Just as the authors of *Malleus Maleficarum* express fear of the loss of the "virile member," so the "woman in the garden emasculates the hero."[75]

The ladies in the bower are conventionally beautiful themselves and also surrounded by lovely handmaidens whose function is to soften up the hero for the ultimate seduction. Tasso's description of Armida's bower is suitably steamy, with lots of naked breasts, windblown hair, and "humid eyes." In addition, both Armida and Alcina are witches. Armida recites "spells and charms" (324); she knows as much as the witches of Thessaly (326). Her desire is to have men in bondage (322); it "pleas'd her will / To conquer men," to have Rinaldo as her "thrall and bondslave vile" (328). When Rinaldo sees the light and leaves, her revenge includes typical witchiness: calling spirits, raising tempests, and flying through the air in hot pursuit. Similar events occur at Alcina's castle. Like the fish she catches in her magic net, men fear ensnarement; her bed tapestries seem to be woven by Arachne (157). Her "force of incantation" (156) can be fought only with another supernatural aid, Bradamante's ring, which restores Rogero through white magic. Tasso's and Ariosto's ladies, then, use all the wiles known to women and witches, but no potions. Thus their evil is not absorbed into the very being of the heroes, and so, unlike Mortdant in the *Faerie Queene*, they survive.

Mortdant, whose death by poison can be interpreted by those concerned with physiological realism as death by sexual exhaustion, is an object lesson in the danger of feminine power. Mortdant's problems begin when he abandons his virtuous wife for the seductress. His entrapment and destruction is a continuing problem; there are other prisoners who languish in the Bower of Bliss. The fate of Mortdant is far from unique. It falls to Guyon, the stronger man, to free them from their bondage to the dominant woman.

On his journey, Guyon hears the "ruefull voice" (II, i, 35) of the dying Amavia. She holds a newborn babe, and beside both is the "dead corse of an armed knight" (I, i, 41). She manages to retain life long enough to tell her sad story. The dead knight is Sir Mortdant, her "deare lord" who went forth to seek adventure, leaving her "enwombed of this childe" (II, i, 50). On his way, he met Acrasia, "a false enchaunteresse, / That many errant knightes hath fowle fordonne" (II, i, 51). She warns Guyon not to meet a similar fate, for her lord was undone by Acrasia, who "makes her lovers dronken mad / ... On them she workes her will to uses bad" (II, i, 52). Apparently Mortdant lingered too long in Acrasia's Bower of Bliss, for this lady, Amavia, was delivered of the child in his absence. She goes to seek him, hoping to redeem him from his current debauched state:

> "Him so I sought, and so at last I fownd,
> Where him that witch had thralled to her will,
> In chaines of lust and lewde desyres ybownd,
> And so transformed from his former skill,
> That me he knew not, nether his owne ill;
> Till through wise handling and faire governaunce,
> I him recured to a better will,
> Purged from drugs of fowle intemperaunce;
> Then means I gan devise for his deliverance."
>
> (II, i, 54)

But Acrasia's response is immediate and decisive:

> "Which when the vile enchaunteresse perceiv'd,
> How that my lord from her I would reprieve,
> With cup thus charmd, him parting she deceivd:
> *Sad verse, give death to him that death does give,*
> *And losse of love to her that loves to live,*
> *So soone as Bacchus with the Nymphe does lincke.*
> So parted we, and on our journey drive,
> Till, comming to this well, he stoupt to drincke:
> The charme fulfild, dead suddeinly he downe did sincke."
>
> (II, i, 55)

Notice the characteristic motifs connected with poison. Poisoning is associated with bewitchment, and thus a poison can act over a distance or over time or in general according to the specifications of the bewitcher. The charm, like a time-release capsule of medicine, works to kill Mortdant but at a distance from the perpetrator. When Mortdant attempts to leave the place where Acrasia is dominant, he cannot; combining poison and magic, she kills him. She would rather see him dead than free of her.

Having warned Guyon by this cautionary tale, Amavia dies. Guyon cries a bit but collects himself in time to deliver a speech outlining the moral of the story, which is moderation in all things:

> "In raging passion with fierce tyranny
> Robs reason of her dew regalitie,

And makes it servaunt to her basest part,
The strong it weakens with infirmitie."

(II, i, 57)

Having buried the luckless husband and wife, Guyon swears vengeance on Acrasia for their fate. At the same time, Guyon has to be very careful, since he has just had an object lesson in Acrasia's power.

Moving along on his journey, Guyon finally arrives at the Bower of Bliss. The usual pattern is present: the wandering man comes to an enclosed place, which is the area of woman's dominance. Much description centers on the gate that "enclosed rownd about" the garden (II, xii, 43); it seems as much designed to lure in as to keep out. On it, in the iconographic description of the visual arts so characteristic of Spenser, there is a depiction of Jason and Medea. The gate is guarded by Agdistes, god of generation, bearing a phallic staff and offering Guyon a "bowle of wine" (II, xii, 49). But Guyon knows that this is not a place of holy generation, because otherwise the additional encouragement of the wine bowl would not be needed.

Everything about the garden appeals to the senses: flowers, warmth, soft surfaces. But Guyon, who can occasionally strike the reader as something of a prig, "suffred no delight / To sincke into his sence, nor mind affect" (II, xii, 53). The centerpiece of the garden, as is only appropriate since it is a garden of temptation, is a vine-centered porch. The vines are described in terms reminiscent of Eden: they climb on a gate "in wanton wreathings intricate" (II, xii, 53). These sinuous vines form a kind of natural porch, "archt over head with an embracing vine. / Whose branches, hanging downe, seemd to entice / All passers by to taste their lushous wine" (II, xii, 54). Under this porch sits a "comely dame" (II, xii, 55) in negligé, one of Acrasia's henchwomen, and she concocts her potion from these same sensuous and weblike overhanging vines:

> In her left hand a cup of gold she held,
> And with her right the riper fruit did reach,
> Whose sappy liquor, that with fulnesse sweld,
> Into her cup she scruzd, with daintie breach
> Of her fine fingers, without fowle empeach,
> That so faire winepresse made the wine more sweet:
> Thereof she usd to give to drinke to each,
> Whom passing by she happened to meet:
> It was her guise, all straungers goodly so to greet.

(II, xii, 56)

Like the serpent of Eden, she waits under her tree to lure men into sin.

But Guyon does not fall. He throws the cup to the ground and smashes it, enraging an allegorical Excesse. Acrasia, however, has a second line of attack. Everywhere Guyon looks in the Bower of Bliss are sensual scenes:

"two naked damzelles" tossing each other up and down in a fountain, alternately concealing and revealing their "dainty partes," loosing their long hair, laughing and blushing (II, xii, 63–66). This is a bit much for our hero, who is beginning to fall into a sin of intention, feeling "secret pleasaunce" (II, xii, 65). Meanwhile Acrasia is "her selfe now solacing / With a new lover, whom, through sorceree / And witchcraft, she from farre did thether bring" (II, xii, 72). Even her garments are described in terms of the venomous: she

> was arayd, or rather disarayd,
> All in a vele of silke and silver thin,
> That hid no whit her alabaster skin,
> But rather shewd more white, if more might bee:
> More subtile web Arachne cannot spin.
>
> (II, xii, 77)

The new swain is "goodly" and "of honorable place," but he is under a "horrible enchantment" (II, xii, 79–80). As she hangs spider-like above her postcoitally dozing lover, she is described as "seeking medicine" from him; "through his humid eyes [she] did suck his spright"—drawing forth from him those vital spirits in the characteristic female fashion, to the increase of her own strength and the diminution of his (II, xii, 73). Mortdant's fate hangs over him too. The debilitating effect of sex on men might well be expressed in the liquid images Spenser uses. The belief that sexual excess is dangerous is an old one, based on the idea that the loss of vital fluids draws warmth and moisture out of the body. As Shakespeare's sonnet on lust as "expense of spirit" shows, the belief was still current in Elizabethan England. Acrasia's lover is in peril of his life, and by extension so are all other men who succumb to this or any other temptress.[76]

Guyon's battle with Acrasia must therefore be as violent and decisive as battle against mortal enemy can be. He fights her with her own weapons; he and the Palmer rush on Acrasia and the young knight and capture them in a "subtile net" against which "all her arts and all her sleights" are powerless (II, xii, 81). Like an Elizabethan Carrie Nation, Guyon breaks down "all those pleasaunt bowres and pallace brave" (II, xii, 83). Acrasia is defeated, and Guyon, like Odysseus, frees the men she has charmed into submission. However, one prisoner, Gryll, preferred being a beast and laments bitterly. Apparently it is not possible totally to overcome this strong tendency in human nature. One must "Let Gryll be Gryll, and have his hoggish mind" (II, xii, 87). Unscathed, Guyon leaves; the temptress having failed to stop him, he can continue on his journey, body and soul safe once more.

When Guyon first hears about Acrasia, she is described as making her lovers drunk to work her will, as thralling Mortdant to her will in chains of lust and lewd desire. As the "witch of incontinence,"[77] Acrasia uses potions secreted in wine as instruments of her will, to gain power over a man who has lost control of himself. Amavia temporarily helps Mortdant to regain power over himself "through wise handling and faire governaunce" (II, xii, 54). But Acrasia, "a woman whose kiss brings death," gives him a bewitched cup, which kills him.[78]

Ever since Eve, the image of woman feeding a man something dangerous has stood as symbol for her dangerous power. Guyon's behavior with regard to Acrasia's henchwoman, Excesse, demonstrates the correct male response to a woman offering a dangerous substance. Excesse concocts her "opiate" by squeezing the juice from overhanging vines into a golden cup.[79] When Guyon throws the cup to the ground and smashes it, this is "in miniature the whole of Guyon's experience of the Bower of Bliss"[80] and also the right way to handle the venomous woman. The spilled wine stains all the land, as poison suffuses the body.[81] The hero must decisively reject this malefic influence. To do otherwise is to wind up like Mortdant, dead, or Verdant, drugged and enthralled. Guyon's triumph over Acrasia and the liberation of her shape-shifted victims is possibly only because he can resist her sensual allure and her potion too.

POISON AND INTELLIGENCE

Underlying the image of the *venefica* in medieval and Renaissance literature is the fear of learned women. As Joan Ferrante points out, in the medieval romances the women are "highly intelligent and highly trained. It is their education which enables them to do unusual things."[82] Although this is true, in the *venefica* tradition at least, these intelligent and trained women are not the same women who are perceived as sexual beings. When one woman makes the potion and another uses or benefits from it, the powers are parceled out: intellect to an older, less attractive woman and sexual allure to a younger, less intelligent woman. This separation of powers is explained in another way by Margaret King in her essay on learned women of the Italian Renaissance. Such women were "urged to be chaste"; men "insisted on [their] asexuality because by means of intellect [they] had penetrated a male preserve."[83] Conversely, the Renaissance seductress is so powerful because she is also the witch, the wise woman, the knowing woman.

At first it seems odd that Shakespeare, who must have been aware of the motif, chose not to use it. His most famous poisoner is Claudius, and his potion-makers—Friar Lawrence, the master doctor in *Cymbeline*—are men too. Lady Macbeth adds a dram to the wine drunk by Duncan's guards, but her main weapon is the knife wielded by Macbeth with her encouragement. Even the witches in *Macbeth* operate by the power of suggestion and make no potion. Shakespeare's closest approximation to the *venefica* character is the Queen in *Cymbeline*. She plans to murder Pisanio and Imogen but is rendered ineffectual by the superior knowledge of the master doctor from whom she has learned various chemical procedures, but apparently not enough to be a powerful force for evil. This doctor regards her as malicious, distrusts her with possession of "a drug of such damn'd nature" (I, v, 34–36), and substitutes a harmless soporific. In this play, so powerful a character as a true *venefica* might weaken the possibility for reconciliation upon which tragicomedy depends. Thus, Shakespeare seems to have been indifferent to whatever dramatic potential his predecessors and contemporaries saw in the *venefica* character and avoided this well-known symbol of women's dangerous knowledge. Instead, Shakespeare seems to like his learned women; he does not see the intersection of intelligence and sexuality as threatening.

The more ordinary male's dislike of intelligent women is an old story. That misogynist Hippolytus hated intelligent women (like his stepmother) in particular:

It is easiest for him who has settled in his house as wife a mere cipher, incapable from simplicity. I hate a clever woman; never may she set foot in my house who aims at knowing more than women need; for in these clever women Cypris implants a larger store of villainy, while the artless woman is by her shallow wit from levity debarred.[84]

The increased potential for evil when the sexual passion of a Phaedra is united with a strong intelligence makes for a real threat to male domestic power; better to marry a "cipher." In Erasmus's *Colloquies* (1516), Antonius, who represents traditional views, says he "would not have a learned wife."[85] To render his daughters more marriageable, Agrippa d'Aubigne (1552–1630) sets a pattern for generations of advisers to women when he counsels his daughters to conceal their learning.[86] It is clear that intellectual power in a sexual being is an overwhelming combination.

One way of neutralizing the intellectual woman's power is to desexualize her by age. Another is to diminish her threat by attributing appropriately feminine selfless motives to her. In witchcraft lore, old women were considered fearful, but in literature, old women are treated more gently. The old bawd or woman healer, for example, is seldom seen as radically evil, especially because she uses her potion and the skills that allow her to produce it in the service of another. The sanctifying idea of service joins with her diminished sexual power to render her unthreatening. When, on the other hand, the potion-maker is a younger, therefore seductive, woman, and in addition selfishly motivated, she is Medea or Acrasia, truly vile.

The important determinants of a threatening woman are these three: intelligence, seductiveness, and selfishness. Selfishness is possible in a person of any age; intelligence and seductiveness are more specifically associated with maturity and youth, respectively. Intelligence, especially as manifested in learned knowledge, develops over time and so is a function of experience and maturity—of age. Seductiveness in the female is associated with youth. If such an unnatural creature arises as a young and beautiful woman who is also experienced and intelligent, who, moreover, has the capacity to use these powers in her own self-interest, she is formidable. Whether she uses poison or not, she is *venefica* or *malefica*.

This level of fearsomeness is not possible for a very young woman. However seductive she may be, she has not gained the experience time brings. She needs an older—much older—woman to advise her, but, as we have seen, separating powers weakens both characters. The characters who are the worst villainesses, Medea and Acrasia, are young enough to be attractive but not very young, not ingenues. While we cannot look for the kind of accuracy appropriate to realistic fiction, it is nevertheless clear that Medea is old enough to have been married to Jason for a long time and to have borne him two sons but not old enough to have lost her attractiveness. Nobody, not even Jason, suggests that she is past her prime as sexual woman. As for Acrasia, one of the reasons Spenser surrounds her with her henchwomen is to stress Acrasia's hierarchical superiority over them. Acrasia is leader of a cohort of women in the Bower of Bliss, is more experienced and worldly wise than Mortdant's true love, Amavia—is, in short, a woman at the height of her sexual and intellectual powers. Acrasia and Medea possess all the qualities parceled out to separate women in the medieval romance: intelligence, experience, relative youth, and sexual attractiveness. The clear implication seems to be that in this tradition, women in early middle age are most powerful, combining both sexuality and knowledge.

Returning to Marguerite de Navarre's tale of the apothecary and his wife, it is now possible to see wherein the comedy lies in this treatment of the theme. The apothecary's wife has apparently been married for some time and so must be of an age ordinarily associated with increased power, at least intellectually and probably sexually as well. But she has neither of these qualities. She is not seductive, so she is in a weak position to begin with. She is somewhat dangerous in wanting more control, in learning how to gain this control through devious means, and in perverting her role as nurturer and healer. But the action is rendered comic by her stupidity and incompetence. She is neither healer, witch, nor seductress. Even her motives are considered appropriately wifely by the fictional audience. She is not smart enough or sexy enough to be a real threat, so patriarchal order is easily restored. Even the peculiar outcome—her husband accepts all the responsibility—shows that she is too silly to be a real moral agent. Comedy, then, rests not only on absence of malice but also on absence of knowledge and skill. If she is smart, like Thessala, or attractive, like Fenice, she is a problem; if she is both, like Acrasia, she is a big problem; but if she is neither, like the apothecary's wife, she is no problem at all.

4

Woman and the Serpent

In this book I propose, with God's help, to consider diseases peculiar to women, and, since women are for the most part poisonous creatures, I shall then proceed to treat of the bites of venomous beasts.
                    ARNALDUS OF VILLANOVA (1235–1312)[1]

We and our whole community of canons, recognizing that the wickedness of women is greater than all the other wickedness of the world, and that there is no anger like that of women, and that the poison of asps and dragons is more curable and less dangerous to men than the familiarity of women, have unanimously decreed for the safety of our souls, no less than for that of our bodies and goods, that we will on no account receive any more sisters to the increase of our perdition, but will avoid them like venomous animals.
                    ABBOT CONRAD OF THE PREMONSTRATENSIAN
                    COMMUNITY AT MARCHTHAL (1273)[2]

Arnaldus of Villanova's unflattering introduction to the gynecology and venenology section of his medical handbook, *Breviarum Practicae*, and the Premonstratensians' proclamation of an end to their dual-sex monastery system epitomize an attitude with an impressive pedigree in Scripture, folklore, and literature. The serpent of Eden was often depicted as having a woman's head, to emphasize Eve's and her daughters' unfortunate propensity to sin. The lamia or *striga*, the snake turned woman, is another manifestation of this motif from the visual arts often seen in the iconography of the Fall. The serpent with a woman's face becomes the serpentine woman, the woman whose special relationship with a venomous animal makes her more fearful than either serpent or woman would be alone. The logical culmination of this identification between women and poison is the woman whose flesh is envenomed, the legendary poisoned maiden, in which the two symbols of evil fuse: the woman is the poison.

The story of the serpent-woman Lamia derives from a variety of ancient sources: Scripture, mythology, and folklore. The biblical account of the Fall is the major influence. Throughout the Old Testament, the venomous animal is a surrogate demon. Through the power of God, the good man is immune to the venom of animals (Psalms 91:13), and the ultimate hope for a righteous order on earth is symbolized by immunity to serpents: "The sucking child shall play over the hole of the asp, and the weaned child shall put his hand over the adder's den" (Isaiah 11:8). In the New Testament, the significance of the venomous animal is the same. The followers of Christ are seen as invulnerable to poison and venomous animals (Mark 16:17–18; Luke 10:19), and Christ himself uses the metaphor in castigating the Pharisees: "You serpents, you brood of vipers, how are you to escape being sentenced to hell?" (Matthew 23:33).

For early exegetes such as Ambrose, Augustine, and Jerome, the problem of the existence of poison and the venomous animal was part of the larger mystery of the existence of evil. Ambrose explains that poisons exist because they are possible, thus filling out the plethora of creation.[3] He also stresses the idea of the venomous thing as symbol of evil and the consequent power of the followers of Christ against them.[4] For Augustine, venomous things are part of the general punishment for Adam's sin.[5] Jerome uses the practice of mixing poison and honey as a metaphor for the deceptive nature of evil, which lures humans to evil by taking on the appearance of good.[6] To medieval misogynists, this metaphor seemed particularly appropriate when applied to the specific evil of sexual sin. For them, the seductiveness of women is the honey in which is mixed the poison of soul-destroying lust.

The image of the venomous animal and of poison is thus clearly a symbol of moral evil. Devious and deadly, its action mirrored the lethal effect of sin on the soul. The insidious behavior of the venomous animal reflected the malice and snares of the devil. When the idea of the venomous animal is linked to women, the significance is usually sexual, and the metaphor becomes a misogynistic commonplace.

Like Medea and Circe, other manifestations of the venomous woman, the lamia has her ancestry in Greek myth and literature. The mythological character Lamia has her own sad story. Like many another mythical lady, she is the other woman in the stormy marriage of Hera and Zeus. When Hera's jealousy is aroused, she takes revenge. She deforms Lamia so that Lamia has the face and breasts of a woman and the body of a snake. As if this were not sufficient, Hera also kills Lamia's children. In retaliation, Lamia preys on other women's children and also on young men, whom she lures to her lair and eats. This unpleasant behavior is not, however, inexplicable, when Lamia's own suffering is considered, so even in the mythological story there is some sympathy for the lamia, cannibal though she is. And—a point that is crucial in the depiction of the lamia ever after—the connection between the serpent and sex is firmly established: Lamia's shape shifting is a punishment for a sexual transgression.

In folklore, the lamia retains her status as a supernatural being. The varied elements of the lamia tradition are all connected with sex and sin. The lamia story echoes folk motifs such as the animal paramour, as in the tale of Beauty and the Beast; she is kin to mermaids, witches,[7] and vampires.[8] Hecate is her mythological, and Eve her theological, mother. When she metamorphoses, she embodies male fears of women's changeability. "Lovely maidens" were often portrayed as being "transformed into serpents, worms, and dragons" (all three being considered venomous animals).[9] If the lamia is appearing as an old hag, she wanders the night sucking blood and devouring flesh. If she is appearing as a beautiful woman, she lures men so as to dismember and devour them. Among the lamia's other baleful characteristics, along with her preference for meals consisting of children and handsome young men, is her insatiable sexual appetite.[10] She can "bring fearful dreams, eat human flesh, suck blood, or lie with devils in her role as nightmare, cannibal, vampire, and wanton (*lamiae* made 'a pact with the Devil to gratify their exorbitant sexual desires')."[11] She is an all-purpose evil being. To Andrew Tooke, author of the impressively titled *Pantheon: Representing the Fabulous Histories of the Heathen Gods and Most Illustrious Heroes*, which was popular enough to go into its thirty-third edition in 1806, she " 'plainly expresses the evil arts of wicked women.' "[12]

The lamia's unpleasant traits make her an interesting character in folk tales but a poor marriage risk. A man has to be careful that the woman he is marrying is not a lamia in disguise. Such a marriage usually involves a deceptively negotiated pact in which the husband promises not to take certain steps that would uncover her true identity. When the lamia is truly known, she vanishes, taking with her whatever goods she has brought to her marriage.[13]

In a Welsh folk tale still current in 1923, the lamia's secret is revealed when the wife exercises the right she exacted from her husband to "disappear twice a year for a fortnight." On one such occasion, he follows her and sees her cast off her girdle, whereupon she turns into a snake. When she returns home, he questions her about the absent girdle; she "blushed painfully, but would not answer." The next time she tries to go, he throws her girdle into the fire: "Immediately the woman writhed in agony, and when the girdle perished, she died." Here the husband outwits the snake-wife and triumphs.

In another version of the tale, the husband fares much worse. A man marries a woman for her money, but this wife has the capacity to change into a snake " 'from the shoulders upwards' " when angry at her husband, which happens often. The abuse he suffers on these occasions is extensive: she " 'deliberately and maliciously sucked her partner's blood and pierced him with her venomous fangs.' " This reversal of the serpent-woman shape (usually the creature has a woman's face and a serpent's body) is unattractive and deadly. She need not be seductive (her money was apparently enticement enough). Instead, the vampire element is stressed. The husband sickens and dies, and the attending physician names the cause as "a poisonous bite from a serpent, although no marks were discovered on his body." So vengeful is this serpent lady that she even sprang upon the mourners at the funeral "in serpent shape." Fortunately for all, she vanished, but a serpent prowled the neighborhood and could not be killed, so it was referred to as the " 'old snake-woman' " in commemoration of the famous citizen.[14]

These folk tales contain the basic elements of the lamia story, which influenced literary versions of it. The tale belongs to a large group with the motif of the discovery of the origins of a supernatural bride.[15] A young man visiting the country meets a beautiful girl. She appears to be virtuous and to come from a respectable background. He falls in love with her. But alas! she is a snake-woman. An older man with special powers discovers this. The lamia tries to deny her true identity but finally confesses. The plot outcome is that "the youth becomes or remains a disciple of his deliverer, and presumably stays away thenceforth from sexual pleasures." The lamia, even if she harms no one, is always punished, as if to suppress thoroughly the evil that she represents.[16]

A separate tradition, based on the pseudoscientific concept of fascination, further links the two ideas of female seductiveness and the venomous animal. In addition to its common meaning, the term *fascination* in pseudoscience means the ability to charm or cast a spell, a power thought to be possessed by the serpent and the basilisk, as well as the mythic Medusa. The victim, animal or human, that falls under the reptile's spell cannot escape, does not even try, but is "unable to control its movements once the serpent's eye has fastened upon it." Eyewitness accounts and experiments conducted as late as 1771 testify to the fascination that the concept itself has held. Eve, serpent, sin, deception, the image of the serpent stamped on the mind of the woman: all are related to the powerfully beguiling Lamia.

In Scripture, the serpent is clearly a symbol of evil. In folklore, the lamia is unambiguously evil too. In myth, however, the lamia's longing for her lost children explains her vengeful behavior. In literature, lamia characters are almost always presented sympathetically. The young man's encounter with her is more than an *exemplum* of the dangers associated with women; it becomes a test of his ability to risk. The risk he experiences operates on two levels. First, since the relationship is always sexual, the physical and moral risk of any sexual encounter is exacerbated by the combination of seductive woman and phallic serpent. Identification of serpent and phallus as male principle of generation is an ancient motif in art and folklore.[17] When woman and serpent are combined, the result is a complex combination of the problems inherent in both male and female sexuality. As woman, the lamia dominates a man by virtue of the power of her sexuality. As serpent, she embodies a man's fears of his own sexuality as well. Second, the young man is called upon to make a daring choice in risking a relationship with an unusual woman. The lamia story often includes mentor figures and normative characters who discourage the young man from loving the lamia. They feel he would be better off with an ordinary woman.

The literary uses of the lamia myth are not, however, formulaic. Each variation emphasizes a different aspect of the paradoxes and ambiguities surrounding the love of the hero for the lamia. But the hero must realize that the simple equation between woman and sin is insufficient to comprehend the real meaning of the lamia. In literature, "this story became almost completely changed in nature when the lamia began to be regarded as a symbol not of lust, but of love."[18] The hero must examine himself as well, especially his capacity to risk social disapproval. Because of the inherent caution of his own nature, he is likely to listen to the voices of the mentor figures. But to save the lamia and to become his own best self, he must go against all warnings and make the daring choice. Most often, he fails by retreating from the challenge the lamia represents.

In literature, the lamia appears to be portrayed in such a way as to diverge from the folk motif. This seems a conscious effort on the part of the authors, and the effect is a more positive portrayal of the lamia. In one of the earliest literary versions of the lamia story, Plutarch's life of Demetrius, Plutarch appears to be aware of the basic elements of the tradition concerning the serpent woman, standard even then.[19] At the same time, he appears deliberately to defy the expectations these elements engender.

Demetrius is a brave young warrior. In public life, he is "always very carefull and diligent in dispatching matters of importance" (374). He rises to great heights as a commander, triumphing in battle after battle against exalted opponents. But in private life, he has, as did his father before him, a weakness for that deadly combination, "women and wine" (373), and is "wantonly geven to follow any lust and pleasure" (374). Although he has several wives, efficiently married and replaced at death for political and dynastic reasons, he has several mistresses as well, one of whom is the "famous Curtisan Lamia" (387).

It certainly seems as if Demetrius is headed for a fall. The hero is at the height of his achievements, but he is weakened by a hereditary failing, which links him to a suspiciously named mistress. Advisers warn him away from Lamia, alleging that she is "a witche, or sorceresse" and claiming that Demetrius has "certeine markes and bytings on his necke, of a vile beast called Lamia" (399). But Demetrius disregards these warnings to attend a lavish supper given for him by Lamia to celebrate his triumph in battle. Plutarch has in place all the elements necessary for a neat *de casibus* outcome.

What actually happens is oddly anticlimactic. The banquet is a great

success. Lamia is a fascinating hostess. She performs one of the main functions of a courtesan in the ancient world by being a social asset to her man.
Like an early draft for Eleanor of Aquitaine, she presides with great "sut-
tletye" over a courts-of-love-type debate, a "prety sute commenced upon a
lovers dreame." Demetrius leaves the banquet alive and well, and Plutarch
drops the subject abruptly: "Thus enough spoken of Lamia" (400).

What has happened here? The stock plot involving the fall of the hero
has collapsed around the character of Lamia. She does not fit the stereotyped
role of fate's instrument. Oddly, however, her reality is not really complex
either. One of the reasons Lamia has aroused hostility in Demetrius's companions is the degree of Demetrius's devotion to her. He really prefers her;
he "ever kept Lamia his Curtisan with him" (397), and she had "great credit
and authority" with him (399). Presumably this is not true of his wives,
sequestered at home in their place breeding heirs and not, like Lamia, com-
peting with Demetrius's companions for attention and favor. His affection
for Lamia appears excessive to his companions, considering that to them
her only purpose would be sexual. What makes his devotion to Lamia appear
even odder to them is that Lamia is an older woman. Demetrius usually
does not like older women; he married one of his wives, Phila, "so much
against his will, bicause she was too olde for him" (399). Nevertheless he
is "so ravished with Lamia, and did so constantly love her so long together,
considering that she was also very old, and past the best" (399). How can
he be so besotted unless by bewitchment or sorcery? The advisers' attitudes
are like those found in the old folk tradition, but Plutarch suggests an equally
simple motivation more in keeping with the sympathetic literary tradition.
Plutarch says that her "sweete conversation and good grace" (387) won
Demetrius's love. It is as simple as that: the human, not supernatural, fascination
exerted by an intelligent and interesting woman, to which Demetrius has the
courage to respond. In addition, Demetrius is not the typical young man of the
lamia story. He is a seasoned warrior and lover, no ingenue, and therefore the
initiation motif is absent. As a strong man, he is able to disregard the warnings
of his advisers and follow his own inclinations without fear. He trusts his own
judgment, so the mentor figures are rendered ineffectual. Within the lamia tradition, he is as much of a hero as Odysseus.

VENOMOUS ANIMALS IN MEDIEVAL LITERATURE

In the Middle Ages, the strong influence of Christian asceticism and the
misogyny consequent upon it is expressed in the association of women with
a variety of venomous animals in addition to the serpent—basilisk, spider,
scorpion. Whatever animal is pressed into service, the purpose of the metaphor is to represent a man's fear of the physical and moral dangers of
association with females, which is really fear of the beast within himself
that is attracted to them. As the two epigraphs to this chapter suggest,

sobersided medical writers and pious clerics alike saw women as envenoming body and soul. Combine the reasonable fear of the diseases of Venus with the culturally induced fear of mortal sin; add a basic castration anxiety and fear of domination; and the result is the perception of females as the source of all evils afflicting body and soul. A few examples of how poison is seen as moral metaphor will set the scene for the specific discussion of the serpent-woman as a character in literature.

In *De Nugis Curialium* (*Courtier's Trifles*), Sir Walter Map explores the connection between women and the venomous in "A Dissuasion of Valerius to Rufinus the Philosopher, that he should not take a Wife."[20] All Women, he says, are like Circe, who "pours for you full draughts of joy . . . to delude you" (289). The charms of these "cupbearers of Babel" are "honeyed poison . . . [which will] bite as an adder, and inflict a wound that no antidote can cure" (289). Here Map alludes to Proverbs 23:31, which warns against wine, not women, but no matter: Map transfers the opprobrium from the cup to the cupbearer. All women are like Eve, whose disobedience caused the Fall; and Map compiles other examples (Samson and Delilah, Solomon and Baalim) of men brought low by women. Indeed bad women comprise the vast majority. Map, damning with the very faintest praise, says a good woman is "rarer than a phoenix" (293), which, the phoenix being unique, makes her so rare as to be nonexistent. Since bad women "swarm in such numbers" and "sting bitterly," the best course of action is to "mistrust all" (293–95). Of course, there were some good women in the past (examples included), but no more. He concludes in his advice to the philosopher, "May God Almighty grant you not to be deluded by the deceits of almighty woman" (311).

In Chaucer's "Parson's Tale," modeled on a typical medieval homily, a standard biblical and proverbial comparison is made between the basilisk and lechery. Lechery, according to the Parson, begins with the "fool look-ynge of the fool womman and of the fool man; that sleeth, right as the basilicok sleeth folk by the venym of his sighte" (X.I. 850–55). Here is the standard physical/moral analogy; just as the venomous animal kills the body, so the venomous evil of sexual sin kills the soul. For Chaucer's Parson, citing Solomon, lecherous contact with women is like handling " 'the scor-pioun that styngeth and sodeynly sleeth thurgh his envenymynge' " (X.I. 850–55). The only medicine is divine grace (X.I. 465–70). This homiletic commonplace is echoed by the preacher Thomas of Gascoigne, who regards the seductive attire worn by women as "a great allurement to sin and offers poison to those beholding it, although no one by the grace of God would drink of such poison."[21] The *Ancrene Riwle*, too, depicts Lechery as a scorpion, and Bartholomaeus Anglicus compares the spider, the "venym spynner," to the female as seductress, weaving man's destruction.[22]

Given the wide dispersion of these warnings against women's treachery, old Januarie's blindness in his trust for his young wife, May, in Chaucer's

"Merchant's Tale" is all the more an exercise in self-delusion. If it is a risky proposition for a young man to associate himself with a venomous woman, for an old man it is madness. In this tale, the imagery of the venomous animal embodies the theme of sexual deception. Both betrayers, May and Damyan, are associated with poison and the venomous animal. The squire, Damyan, is a "naddre in bosom sly untrewe" (IV.E. 1786). Strongest of Januarie's enemies is the venomous scorpion, Fortune, also a woman, whose turning wheel brings Januarie down. Having expected paradise on earth in marriage, Januarie's fall from grace is inevitable. Having constructed an Eden, Januarie should expect a serpent in it. The initial blow to Januarie's fortunes is his blindness; this fluctuation of Fate is described in terms of the venomous animal:

> O sodeyn hap! o thou Fortune unstable!
> Lyk to the scorpion so deceyvable
> That flaterest with thyn heed whan thou wolt stynge;
> Thy tayl is deeth, thurgh thy envenymynge.
> O brotil joye! o sweete venym queynte!
> O monstre, that so subtilly kanst peynte
> Thy yiftes under hewe of stidefastnesse,
> That thou deceyvest bothe moore and lesse!
>
> (IV. E. 2057–64)

This description of the behavior of the harlot goddess parallels that of her human agent May. Like the scorpion, a standard symbol of treachery that was believed to flatter before stinging, May deceptively accepts Januarie's unwelcome sexual advances to serve as a cover-up for her real love, Damyan. Moreover, the scorpion and the astrological sign Scorpio were associated with the female organs of sexuality, and consequently with lechery. This is explained in the *Ancrene Riwle* by analogy between the scorpion's body and woman's:

Salomon seið. Qui apprehendit mulierum. quasi qui apprehendit scorpionem. þe scorpiun is ones cunnes wurm þet haveð neb ase me scið sumdel iliche ase wumman. & is neddre bi-hinden makeð feir semblaunt. & fikeð mid te heaued. & stingeð mid te teile. þet is lecherie. þet it þes deofles.[23]

In view of this tradition, the death-dealing "tayl" and the "venym queynte" are unmistakable sexual metaphors in the *vagina dentata* mode, in which the specifically sexual fear of women's power is graphically represented. The harlot goddess Fortuna and her surrogate, May, are both scorpions, and Damyan in the tree is the phallic serpent in the garden.[24]

A logical extension of the woman who is compared to a venomous animal and who behaves like that animal is the woman who becomes that animal. The ancient belief in the possibility of shape shifting was still current in the

Middle Ages. Church councils and theologians debated it; Gervase of Tilbury was "typical of the popular learned opinion of the twelfth and thirteenth centuries" in his belief in it.[25] The mermaid, that fabulous beast related to sirens and lamiae, is a well-known example of the connection of the shape-shifted being with a woman, but medieval characters were equally adept at turning into dragons and snakes. The dragon, considered in the Middle Ages as a venomous beast related to the serpent, was thought to be found in faraway lands and in marvelous sizes, so it is not surprising that Sir John Mandeville considered that his adventure would be incomplete without a dragon story (53–54).[26]

On the faraway isle of Lango dwelt the daughter of Hippocrates, turned into a dragon by a goddess. Her fate is to remain this way "until the time when a knight comes who is so bold as to dare to go to her and kiss her on the mouth." The conventional motif of the knight braving danger to rescue a lady is altered here: the lady herself is the danger, and it is not clear what his reward will be, if any, should he dare to kiss the dragon. The dragon lies in a vault. One young man ventures to enter this domain but runs away in fear and for his troubles is tossed over a sea cliff by the dragon. Another young man, entering a castle and then a vault within it, finds "a damsel combing her hair and looking in a mirror, and she had much treasure round her" (54). Here the potential rewards, damsel and treasure, are clearer, but she says if he wants to be her lover, he must meet certain conditions. First, he must become a knight. Second, he must "have no fear of her, whatever shape he saw her in, for she would do him no harm, however ugly or hideous she was to his sight. For, she said, it was done by enchantment, for she was just as he saw her at that moment," (54). The young man becomes a knight easily enough, but he must decide whether to believe her promise that her fearful appearance does not correspond to an equally fearful reality. Given women's reputation for deception, this is a problem, but if he can do it, "he should have all that treasure and be lord of her and of these islands." The dragon brings material rewards, but only to the brave man, which this knight proves not to be:

And when he saw her come out of the vault in the likeness of a dragon, he had such great fear that he fled to the ship, and she followed him. And when she saw that he did not turn back, she began to wail like a thing in great sorrow. To the ship she followed him and when he had gone aboard, she turned back with a terrible cry; and soon after the knight died. And from that time on no knight has been able to see her without dying soon afterwards. But when a knight comes who is bold enough to dare to kiss her, he shall not die, but he shall turn that damsel into her proper shape, and he shall be lord of her and of the islands. (54)

The wailing woman seeks in vain for a man who can meet her needs, a strong man who dares to kiss the dragon. Such a man will have his reward, but as of Mandeville's writing, he had not yet arrived at the isle of Lango.

The fear of the female is repeated in even stronger form in Mandeville's story of an odd marriage custom:

There is another fair and good isle, full of people, where the custom is that when a woman is newly married, she shall not sleep the first night with her husband, but with another young man, who shall have ado with her that night and take her maidenhead, taking in the morning a certain sum of money for his trouble. In each town there are certain young man set apart to do that service, which are called *gadlibiriens*, which is to say "fools of despair." They say, and affirm as a truth, that it is a very dangerous thing to take the maidenhead of a virgin; for, so they say, whoever does puts himself in peril of death. And if the husband of the woman find her still virgin on the next night following (perchance because the man who should have had her maidenhead was drunk, or for any other reason did not perform properly to her), then shall he have an action at law against the young man before the justices of the land—as serious as if the young man had intended to kill him. But after the first night, when those women are so defiled, they are kept so strictly that they shall not speak to or even come into the company of those men. I asked them what the cause and reason was of such a custom there. They told me that in ancient times some men had died in that land in deflowering maidens, for the latter had snakes within them, which stung the husbands on their penises inside the women's bodies; and thus many men were slain, and so they follow that custom there to make other men test out the route before they themselves set out on that adventure. (175)

The damsels with serpents within them are a logical culmination of the risky journey into the lady's domain, which is also found in the dragon story. The services of Freud are hardly necessary to see the significance of these stories. The basic concept, serpents within, is allied to the *vagina dentata* superstition and to the belief in the witch's ability to steal the male member. Both stories express strong fear of castration or death in intercourse. A related image is that of women's hair, used as a symbol of entrapment. Mandeville's dragon lady is also depicted as combing her hair because a woman's flowing hair is often seen as a snare, web, net, or noose.[27] Medusa's hair serpents, as well as the spider's web, are related images, linking the long-haired woman to the venomous animal. The image of a man caught in or choking on a woman's hair is yet another way of expressing the physical and moral threat of women's bodies. Yet again like Mandeville's dragon lady, the serpentine woman is often depicted as bringing with her rewards of various kinds, rewards available only to the man brave enough to win and keep her.

The death/sex correlation in interpretation of animal behavior is apparently based on fact. In a popular college textbook, *Animal Behavior*, the author has chosen for a cover design, out of all possible animals and all possible behaviors, a photo of a "female grass mantis consuming her mate ... during copulation."[28] The author explains that this does not jeopardize the future of the grass mantis population: "If a mature male's head is removed . . . the male's abdomen probes about professionally and copulation occurs normally."[29] This contemporary account is remarkably reminiscent of the bestiary tradition in that it invites interpretation. Referring to the identical behavior in the praying mantis, Carl Sagan seeks meaning in this phenomenon, in a manner similar to that of a medieval bestiarist, by interpreting the behavior thus:

The heads and bodies of anthropods can briefly function without each other very nicely. A female praying mantis will often respond to earnest courting by decapitating her suitor. While this would be regarded as unsociable among humans, it is not so among insects: extirpation of the brain removes sexual inhibitions and encourages what is left of the animal to mate. Afterwards, the female completes her celebratory repast, dining, of course, alone. Perhaps this represents a cautionary lesson against excessive sexual repression.[30]

With the twentieth-century interpretation of the behavior of the grass mantis couple, the behavior of Mandeville's men can be seen as motivated by fear of loss. Once having entered the dangerous realm of the female, will the hero emerge intact? Only the brave man dares. Most men are more like those in Mandeville who let others "test out the route" first. Only the first who penetrate into the dangerous terrain are in danger; the latecomers are safe enough. Those "other men," the sexual pioneers, are the fearless ones, the ones who might indeed kiss the dragon or deflower the maidens, but they are "set apart to do that service"; they are "fools of despair," a special group not typical of the average male. The man who does not fear this journey is unusual. Too often, the male protagonist of a venomous-woman story is more like the failed knight or the cautious husbands and draws back in fear from the encounter with the venomous woman. It takes a special man to win her and to keep the rewards she brings with her.

MÉLUSINE

The story of Raymond and Mélusine in *The Tale of Mélusine*, a four-teenth-century romance about a married couple, is based on the multiple problems surrounding a man's relationship with a serpent-woman. In romance literature, couples often love but seldom marry; this work is an exception, an unusual combination of a fantastic romance plot and a realistic exploration of marriage's multiple challenges. It is little read today, which is unfortunate, because this story of one medieval marriage has contemporary resonances in that it analyzes the special requirements of marriage with an unusual woman. Mélusine is very unusual: one day a week she is a serpent from the waist down. Therefore her marriage to Raymond requires adaptation of a rule-bound institution to her particular needs. The marriage fails, but the attempt highlights the weaknesses of both the institution and the individuals. The weight of the institution supports Raymond as the more powerful partner; but in this marriage, Mélusine, as a supernatural being, dominates. As long as Raymond accepts this unorthodox arrangement, he shares in her power; when he reverts to a typical marital relationship, all is lost.

Mélusine is a supernatural being, which raises the question of whether she is good or evil. The case can be effectively made that Mélusine is a demon because she is associated with the serpent, biblical symbol of evil, and therefore can do no good.[31] This argument, however, is undercut by the evidence in the tale that she does indeed do good acts, and morally neutral acts, along with some questionable acts. She is both Eve and Mary. Like her husband, she has faults, and this is what makes the tale a psychologically realistic commentary on marriage.

Whether as femme fatale or supernatural helpmate, the serpent woman exists in literature in relation to a man and often children but because of her unusual nature has problems working out her fate in the context of family life. The visual image of her mythic ancestor, Lamia, influences iconography of the Fall in that the devil tempting Eve is often depicted as having a woman's face, often Eve's own face, and a serpent's body, stressing Eve's sinful pride. For her transgression, Eve suffers through her children, whom she will bear in pain and doom to death. Both Eve and Lamia violate rules and are punished; these well-known rebels would be in the mind of any medieval reader of *The Tale of Mélusine.*

The tale exists in two fourteenth-century versions, one in prose by Jean d'Arras (completed about 1394)[32] and the other in verse by Couldrette (completed about 1396).[33] Both were probably based on a common unknown source,[34] both were translated into Middle English by unknown translators,[35] and both were written at the request of noble patrons[36] to commemorate Mélusine, from whom the lords of Lusignan claimed descent.

Mélusine's story begins with the meeting of her parents, Elynas and Pressine. They meet at a fountain and fall in love at first sight in appropriate romance fashion. As a condition of the marriage, Pressine requires that her husband never see her in childbed. (In one of the many variants, the condition is that he shall never see her naked;[37] the matter of the condition usually involves some area of privacy that the husband must not violate.) Elynas agrees, the marriage is solemnized and consummated, and the result is triplet daughters. Prodded by his jealous son by an earlier marriage, Elynas violates the ritual childbirth period and his vow. Although she loves Elynas, he has broken faith, and so Pressyne takes the three little girls and leaves the kingdom, leaving Elynas so sorrowful that he is considered mad and deposed. Thus the pattern is set: break the promise and lose all.

Pressine raises her three daughters on Avalon. Every morning she takes them to a high mountain from which they can see the lost paradise, their father's kingdom. When she is fifteen, Mélusine, the eldest, punishes their erring father by imprisoning him on a mountain. In retaliation, Pressine, who still loves her husband, condemns Mélusine to be a serpent " 'fro the navyll downward' " (15) every Saturday. Her only possibility for a normal life on the other six days (and, despite her unfeminine behavior in taking revenge against her father, she does want a normal woman's life) is to find a man who will agree not to see her on Saturday. If she can find him, she will live a " 'cours naturell,' " beget a " 'fayre lynee,' " and die " 'a naturel & humayn woman' "(15). But if he breaks his promise she will be a serpent-woman until the Judgment Day and have the morose duty of heralding the death of the lords of Lusignan, her descendants, by appearing as a serpent on the castle tower. Although the other two sisters are also punished, it is only Mélusine who must repeat her mother's own failed quest, for a man who will accept her with unusual conditions and, most important, keep his promise. Mélusine's happiness in life and salvation in the afterlife depend on his keeping faith.

Again like her mother, Mélusine meets her future husband at a fountain, the Fountain of Soif or thirst, located in a forest wherein Raymond is wandering disconsolately because he has accidentally killed his lord. Mélusine immediately demonstrates the unusual powers characteristic of the snake-woman by knowing who he is and what his problem is.[38] Like the thirst that the fountain's water slakes, each has a need that the other can fulfill. She knows that he has killed his lord " 'as moche by myshap as wylfully' " (30), and she can help him: " 'Forsouthe, Raymondyn, I am she after god that may best enhaunse the in this mortal lyf, and all thyn adversdytees & mysdedes most be tourned in to wele nought avaylleth to the for to hyde them from me' " (30). He is at the bottom of Fortune's wheel now; with her help, his adversity can be overcome. She assures him that her supernatural knowledge does not come by " 'fauntesye or dyvels werk' "—she is " 'of god, and my byleve is as a catholique byleve oughte for to be' " (31). She and God are going to help him if he marries her, which she expeditiously proposes. Since he knows he is in need and she has the power to help him but does not know about her need and his power to help her, she has the upper hand in the relationship from the start. She exacts the commitment she needs from him and makes it part of their marital pact:

"Ye muste promytte to me, Raymondyn, upon all the sacrements & othes that a man very catholoque & of good feith may doo and swere, that never while I shalbe in your company, ye shal not peyne ne force your self for to see me on the Satirday nor by no manere ye shal not enquyre that day of me, ne the place wher I shalbe." (32)

Raymond agrees and binds himself to her on her terms. How binding the betrothal, or *sponsalia*, a secular and private agreement between the couple, was considered to be is still being explored by medievalists. Whether this agreement constitutes the marriage, which is later ratified by repetition before a priest and witnesses, is a question that churchmen debated throughout the Middle Ages as the church attempted to assert greater control over unruly unsanctified unions.[39] The *sponsalia* between Raymond and Mélusine is still more problematic in incorporating a contingency into the contract, a questionable practice. Nevertheless, whatever the orthodoxy of the situation, Raymond as a knight is bound by his word.[40]

In addition to his obligations under the finer points of canon law and *courtoisie*, Raymond can also be seen as a hero in the *de casibus* mode, the working out of whose fate involves rising to a high position and falling therefrom.[41] While Mélusine's nature is the central issue in the legend, Raymond's fidelity is the key character trait. As long as he keeps faith, he rises on Fortune's wheel, and this happy ascension begins when he meets Mélusine.

Their efficient courtship is remarkably unromantic. Although the snake-woman is often seen as the very embodiment of seductiveness,[42] Mélusine is business-like. She proposes Christian marriage, not soul-destroying lust. In the visual arts, Mélusine is sometimes depicted in mermaid pose, comb in one hand and mirror in the other,[43] yet she is never described in the tale as concerned about her beauty. She is not even particularly seductive; during their brief courtship, she does not attempt so much to seduce Raymond as to negotiate a prenuptial agreement with him. Thus the conventional association of hair with the web, snare, or net does not apply to her. In fact, what is most characteristic of Mélusine is her refusal to fit into predetermined categories.

Mélusine is as good as her word; she not only helps Raymond out of his predicament but also forms the base for his power. When the king's body is discovered, she advises Raymond to lament more loudly than anyone else. This certainly is deceptive but hardly demonic, since Raymond did not murder the king. Mélusine further advises that when the new earl of Poitiers shall ask for his vassal's homage, Raymond " 'shal demande a yefte for the salary & remuncione of alle the servyse that ever ye dede unto his fader' " (38–39). This assertive act involves asking for as much ground as will be covered by a hart's skin. The lord, thinking that this will be a little patch of ground, assents. But Mélusine causes Raymond to buy a magical skin, cut the skin into thongs, and with these thongs surround a large piece of land that the lord, bound by his rash promise, will have to give Raymond. Thus Mélusine brings land, the basis of feudal power, to Raymond; her dowry is her supernatural wisdom.[44] This coup establishes a pattern: Raymond goes home to Mélusine for advice, goes out to execute her plans, triumphs, returns for more advice, and triumphs again, finally achieving great success dependent on her powers. She has her sphere of activity, he has his; she remains stationary in customary wifely fashion, he roams and returns; but she is clearly the dominant partner.

At Mélusine and Raymond's wedding, Raymond's lord is surprised at its suddenness and at the fact that Raymond does not seem to know his bride's " 'lynee.' " Who is she? The serpent-woman always conceals her identity, else she would not be able to win, and test, the love of a mortal. But social order demands proper procedure to ensure the marriage's validity and legitimacy, including the proclamation of the banns of marriage, which has been evaded. Such inquiry is intended to prevent just such a marriage as Raymond and Mélusine are contracting, one based on concealment of an *impedimentum ad matrimoniam* (albeit one that is hardly likely to be mentioned in canon law). Although both the earl and Raymond are reassured by Mélusine's large retinue, suggesting noble lineage, the mystery remains. The lord is concerned that his vassal is making an unsuitable marriage, reflecting the medieval concern with lineage and inheritance, but the marriage choice of the individuals overrides this seigneurial disapproval.

The couple has a big wedding with the usual trappings: lots of food, lavish service, jousting, a dance, and bedding of the bride, with blessings supplied by the local bishop. At this last event something peculiar happens (in d'Arras but not in Couldrette). The countess of Poitiers and her ladies serve their office as eleventh-hour sex educators: they "did endoctryne her in suche thinges that she ought for to doo." But Mélusine "was ynough purveyed thereof," or, as the marginalia comments, "knows everything" (55–56). This sexual knowledge could imply that she is not a virgin, but this would surely be elaborated upon. It seems more important as an indication that Mélusine is a fully mature and knowledgeable woman, reinforcing the idea of power. In bed, before the marriage is consummated, rendering it indissoluble,[45] Mélusine unromantically reminds Raymond of the promise that is part of his wedding vow and the consequences to him if he breaks it. She will be a dutiful—and ordinary—wife in every way but one: he must respect her privacy. Raymond renews his vow; she cautions him several times more; finally the marriage is consummated, and they beget Uryan, the first of their ten sons.

Immediately Mélusine embarks on her primary career as builder and cultivator. Whenever Raymond is out on an adventure (previously directed by her, of course), he comes back to find that "with her own hands as the head of a work crew," she has built something marvelous: towns, fortresses, towers, castles, abbeys, noble Lusignan itself.[46] These achievements are seen as supernatural because they are done so quickly. In these projects, she acts not as Raymond's representative but on her own. She does not ask for his authorization or approval; in fact, he always seems surprised at her building projects when he returns, like a husband whose wife has rearranged the furniture. At one point, he can hardly recognize Lusignan because she has built a whole town around it in his absence. In addition, she clears fields and devotes them to agricultural production.[47] For his part, Raymond is becoming so powerful in the region "thrugh the polycye & good governaunce of Melusyne" (104) that all the princes of Gascony and Brittany fear his displeasure. Raymond conquers, Mélusine consolidates; they are successful business partners. Through Mélusine Raymond has acquired land, lineage, and wealth; as Le Goff observes, "Mélusine is the fairy of medieval economic growth."[48]

Although her duties as political and military adviser and city planner do not prevent Mélusine from becoming a prolific mother, there is a problem. Each of her ten sons has an unusual birth defect: Uryan has ears big as a fan handle; Geffrey has a long tooth; Anthony has a lion's claw growing out of his cheek; Reynold has only one eye, with which he can see sixty-three miles. The most deformed son, appropriately named Horrible, has three eyes, one in the middle of his forehead; he is so evil that at age four, he kills two of his nurses. In an age when physical deformity was thought to mirror moral depravity, clearly there is something wrong with Mélusine's lineage, but Raymond never objects.

When the eldest son, Uryan, is eighteen, he and his brother Guyon go off to seek their fortune as knights errant. Apparently primogeniture is not the custom, and the land, commodious though it is, will have to be subdivided among these many sons. Without asking Raymond, Mélusine gives permission for this, outfits them with ships and provisions for 80,000 men, gives them a long lecture on the proper behavior for young knights (comfort maidens, counsel widows and orphans, do not covet your neighbor's wife, watch out for false flatterers, distribute largesse, and keep your promises), and off they go. They too, like Raymond, are very successful; they slaughter enemies by the thousands and marry the daughters of kings; their brothers do similarly, all at great length.

Mélusine and Raymond have now reached what would be middle age in realistic fiction. He has kept his promise, and she has aided him. They have achieved worldly success and raised a large family. Raymond has respected his wife's privacy on Saturdays, but so strange is this custom that an interfering relative, Raymond's brother, the earl of Forests, reports to him that people gossip that she is seeing a lover on those days. Mélusine's lineage had been questioned before, and Raymond was able to restrain his curiosity; but infidelity casts greater doubt than low birth on the integrity of the line. In any case, argues the brother, Raymond has a right not to have any aspect of his wife's life concealed from him. Raymond's jealousy and possessiveness are thus aroused. As is typical of family life, problems do not come one at a time. Children, while a major end of marriage, can also be a mixed blessing. One of the sons, Geffrey, he of the long tooth, proves to be more trouble even than Horrible. These two elements—sexual jealousy and problems with children—interact to trigger the double crisis of the romance.

The first phase is described by both authors but with more evocative symbolism by Couldrette. The chamber in which Mélusine spends her Saturdays is a room of her own with a vengeance; it has a door of iron. Enraged and jealous, Raymond girds on his sword and asserts his ownership rights. With this inappropriate—and characteristically male—weapon, he intrudes upon her privacy, in a way that suggests psychological rape, especially when he has agreed, in Mélusine's careful phrasing worthy of a lawyer, not to force himself on her (32). In d'Arras he breaks down the door; in Couldrette he pierces a hole in it, through which he spies on Mélusine. "A wicked curiosity," editorializes the page heading. There she is: "within the bathe unto her navell, in fourme of a woman lymbyng her heere, and from the navel dounward in lyknes of a grete serpent, the tayll as grete & thykk as a barell, and so long it was that she made it to touch oftymes" (297). Raymond is immediately repentant; in Couldrette he stops up the hole with "a litell cloute" and melted wax (11.2818–19). The deed is done; the breach of promise cannot be repaired. Raymond does not reveal her secret. Mélusine knows what he has done but does not let him know that she does. Although deception is increasing on both sides, in Couldrette the discovery is followed by a touching scene of marital reconciliation. That night in bed, Mélusine, "swetly all naked," sees that Raymond is troubled and offers to " 'hele' " him and make him " 'all hole' " if he confesses his problem to her. He misses the opportunity to increase the level of honesty between them, but nevertheless he wins her sympathy through feigning illness; he whines about " 'brennyng' " and " 'coldnesse' " (11.2906–47). This is the only time in either Couldrette or d'Arras that Mélusine acts seductively, and it is within her marriage for healing and consolation. For a while, sex solves everything; but it is clear that Raymond and Mélusine are lapsing into conventional role behavior. Their unusual marriage is crumbling.

The consequences of the deed do not occur immediately, as seemed to be implied by the prophecy. It is as if the terms of the curse have been changed enough for an element of decision on the part of Mélusine to be introduced, lending greater realism to the couple's eventual breakup. The outcome awaits the further complication of the problem with the son Geffrey; it is his evil, not that of his serpent mother, that triggers the outcome. Geffrey, who has a terrible temper, is enraged because another brother, Froimond, has become a monk. In d'Arras, his rage is circularly explained; he is angry because he is by nature wrathful. In Couldrette, Geffrey is angry because he does not want his brother to " 'leve chivalry' " (l. 3262). Mélusine and Raymond, on the other hand, rejoice at having their very own intercessor at God's throne. But Geffrey, "in wode rage" (l. 3291), burns down the abbey and all the monks, including his brother. Like Eve, Mélusine has birthed a fratricide. Although Raymond blames Mélusine's poor nurturing and worse lineage for Geffrey's action, it is clear that anger and irrationality are part of Raymond's emotional lineage, not Mélusine's. Raymond is de-

scribed in d'Arras as "perced with yre" so that "al rayson naturel was fled
& goon from hym" (314). Mélusine, on the other hand, is almost too
philosophical. She explains to him that what has befallen them is caused
by factors outside themselves: God's foreknowledge of events, the evil lives
of the monks that allowed God to punish them through the agency of
Geffrey, and the character of Geffrey himself. Mélusine says they can undo
some of the evil by endowing the abbey to rebuild it (313–14). But this
appeal to reason cannot persuade Raymond. Apparently Mélusine has
shown herself to be so powerful that it is to Raymond as if she is responsible
for everything that happens.

    If the spoken word sealed their covenant, so it is broken. Publicly, before
her retinue, Raymond turns against Mélusine, blaming her for this family
fall from fortune, revealing her secret, and by his words fulfilling Pressine's
curse:

"By the feyth that I owe to god, I byleve it is but fantosme or spyryt werke of this
woman and as I trowe she never bare no child that shal at thende have perfection,
For yet hath she brought none but that it hath some strange token...sawe I not
also theyre moder o that satirday, whan my brother of Forestz to me brought evyl
tydynges of her in fourme of a serpent fro the navel dounward?...Goo thou hens,
fals serpente by god!" (311, 314)

    Mélusine's life—and afterlife—are ruined:

"Halas, my frend! yf thou haddest not falsed thy feythe & thyn othe, I was putte
& exempted from all peyne & tourment, & shuld have had al my ryghtes, & hadd
lyved the cours natural as another woman...but now I am, thrugh thyn owne dede,
overthrowen & ayen reversed in the grevouse and obscure penytence, where long
tyme I have be in, by my aventure: & thus I must suffre & bere it, unto the day of
domme & al through thy falsed but I beseche god to pardonne the." (316)

    Managerial to the last, she proclaims her last wishes for her children. No
sentimental mother but mindful of her duty to the kingdom, she calls for
the killing of her son Horrible to prevent the " 'grete dommage' " he could
do (318). Despite this preventive measure, she prophecies that the land shall
ever after be troubled by political instability. Then she "in fourme of a
Serpent flough out at a wyndowe" (319), leaving a print of a curious anatomical feature, her "foote serpentous," at the "basse stone of the wyndowe," which still "apereth at this day" (320). She returns for two reasons:
to foreshadow the death of one of her many ancestors and to visit her two
youngest children, which she does every day, "& held them tofore the fyre
and eased them as she coude" (322). In some visual images, she is breast-
feeding them, echoing the motif of the nursing Madonna.[49] Except for this,
never after is she seen as a woman, but for all eternity she watches over

the fate of her descendants, functioning in the context of the family, which was her downfall.

The fate of the rest of the characters is mixed. Geffrey kills his uncle, the earl of Forests, for his part in the family tragedy. Raymond resigns his lordship, becomes a hermit, and dies penitent. The other sons have further adventures and are successful; their progeny includes the lords of Lusignan for whom d'Arras and Couldrette wrote.

The interpretation of the chracter of Mélusine is the central issue in Mélusine criticism, and much of it focuses on the many sources and analogues to this legend. Sir Walter Map has his own version, yet another of the many stories he offers in evidence to Rufinus the Philosopher as to why he should not take a wife. The variations between Map's version and the d'Arras-Couldrette version highlight certain positive attributes of Mélusine in the latter two versions.

In Map, one Henno-with-the-teeth falls in love with a beautiful girl whom he came upon accidentally.[50] She is dressed in gorgeous attire but weeping. She has been accidentally abandoned by her father (a wind blew his ship away when she was ashore, he afloat) on their way to get her married to the king of France. Although she expects them to return for her when her absence is discovered, at the moment when Henno meets her, she is in distress, alone with only a maid, and needs his protection. On the one hand, Henno should be wary of the impact on his potential lineage of this lady of mysterious origins; but on the other hand, his protective instincts are aroused by her plight. He "brought her into his home and took to himself in marriage that brilliant pestilence, he committed her to the care of his mother, and she bore him beautiful children" (347).

This mother-in-law and Henno's wife were both ardent churchgoers, but the wife had an odd habit:

She fulfilled every comely duty in the sight of men, except that she shunned the sprinkling of holy water, and by a wary retirement (making the crowd or some business the excuse) anticipated the moment of the consecration of the Lord's body and blood. Henno's mother noticed this; her proper suspicion made her anxious and, fearing the worst, she set herself to spy out with the closest watchfulness what it meant. (349)

The wife's avoidance of the consecration, the most sacred part of the liturgy, bodes ill. Some hidden truth about the mysterious lady must emerge; it does, with the help of the spying mother-in-law:

In order to learn the reason she made a little hidden hole looking into the chamber and kept secret watch there. She then saw her at early morning on a Sunday, when Henno had gone out to church, enter a bath and become, instead of a most beautiful woman, a dragon. (349)

She tells her son about this; they bring a priest to exorcise the demon by means of an *Asperges*, a sprinkling of holy water, and with that the dragon-lady flees through the roof, shrieking horribly. The misogynistic moral of the story is not explicit (Map digresses a bit, comparing the dragon-lady's rising through the roof to the equally marvelous ascension of Christ), but in the context of his epistle to Rufinus, it is clear: a beautiful woman probably is not good. Her innocent demeanor and apparently virtuous behavior are snare and delusion. A man cannot believe in her words or deeds. There is always something unpleasant that she is concealing, which, when revealed, will destroy all. She is one way when you are with her, another way when she is alone. And since what she changes into is a venomous animal, she and all other women are like the hybrid creature Map mentions in the epistle, "a chimaera...armed with the tail of a rank viper" (291).

Yet Map's story and the story of Mélusine are very different. There is no promise for the hero to break, so he remains a blameless victim of mistaken identity. The active role belongs to the mother-in-law, who is protecting her son from a demon; any woman who cannot tolerate the consecration or an *Asperges* is surely no fit daughter-in-law. Unlike Mélusine, Henno's wife is a serpent on Sunday; Mélusine's serpentine day being Saturday, she can profess herself, as she repeatedly does, a good Catholic, and perform all religious duties as a normal human woman. Finally, more sympathy is generated for Mélusine as herself a victim: of her father's betrayal of her mother, of her mother's curse, of her own husband's betrayal, and finally of her pathetic loss of children. Mélusine is a far more complex character than her briefly sketched analogue in Map.

In the most recent book published on the Mélusine legend, the author sees Mélusine as an ambiguous creature—attractive as a woman, repulsive as a serpent, yet not diabolical, rather a "victim of a malediction." The motif of the marriage of the mortal with the supernatural being is an expression of the human desire to unite with the supernatural, thus "elevating oneself above the human condition" to achieve "happiness, wealth and power." The prohibition is a "method of proof which permits the superior being to find out whether his partner is worthy of his love.... Respect for the pact is the condition which the man must satisfy to gain access to the higher world. The pact is never respected, which proves that the man cannot elevate himself to the level of the gods, incapable as he is of keeping his word."[51]

In *The Tale of Mélusine*, this cosmic failure is expressed as domestic failure. It is the "story of a conditional marriage"[52] in which Raymond is given the opportunity to prove that he can be a fit partner for a superior woman. Mélusine's modification of the marriage vow indicates an inability to be bound by the conventional institution. The marriage vows in the form acceptable to the church do not allow for reservations or continuing contingencies. Nevertheless, Raymond keeps his word for many years, proving himself worthy of her love and sharing in her power.

Finally the inertia of the institution drags him down. Nonconformity to usual marriage practices causes suspicion and jealousy. According to custom, if not law, the husband owns his wife's time. She should have no secrets from him, since marriage gives him the right to know her in every sense. Female privacy carries with it the threat of infidelity, which is intolerable as the ultimate violation of property rights. When Raymond reasserts the power he has given his word to renounce, he becomes unworthy of her love and loses her power.

The promise and the marriage based on it are broken. Neither Raymond nor Mélusine seeks any church sanction for this separation, even when Raymond confesses to the pope. Marriage is seen by both as a private affair, contracted between the two parties but requiring the consent of no one else. The lord's objection does not stop it, nor does the bishop's blessing render it indissoluble. The contract lasts as long as the couple can live in mutual fulfillment of needs, each being a fountain of thirst to the other as they were when they first met.

For all the connection with the demonic, the serpent-woman is no guiltier than her fully human spouse. Her initial act of arrogation of power—and this as a natural being—is to usurp the male prerogative of revenge, and she remains dominating ever after. She is rendered extraordinary by her mother's curse; nevertheless, her main goal is to live a normal woman's life as wife and mother. Finally, however, Raymond proves himself too normal, too ordinary to remain united to a supernatural being, and Mélusine's nature cannot be shaped to the common mold of matrimony. Her fate is painful but symbolically fitting. For all eternity, her private self, her Saturday self, becomes her only real self.

NINETEENTH-CENTURY VARIATIONS: GERALDINE AND LAMIA

As in Plutarch, the literary lamia is often portrayed sympathetically, and Keats, Holmes, and Hawthorne modify the sources further to make her more sympathetic still, until finally in Hawthorne the serpent motif is suppressed entirely and the woman, venomous though she is, is also Beatrice, blessed.

These writers' adventurousness in exploring female sexuality is all the more remarkable in view of what has been called the then-current cult of passionlessness, glorifying the appearance of asexuality in women. Through downplaying her sexuality and emphasizing her spirituality, by deception if necessary, she could "exert control in the sexual arena," call the sexual shots and get a better husband besides.[53] The obviously passionate woman was a particularly difficult problem. If, in addition, passion is considered inappropriate for a woman, then the passionate woman is far too much like a man.[54] She, not her lover, is the phallic serpent, combining the fearful elements of both male and female sexuality. If, in addition, it was better to marry than to burn, logically it follows that one should marry a passionless woman to control the burning, not the very symbol of lust, the lamia. But when each of the three heroes fails to give himself totally to the lamia, he is seen in the context of the fiction as a failure.

The sympathetic treatment of the lamia and the conflict experienced by the hero stand out in higher relief when compared with a more conventional treatment of the theme. Samuel Taylor Coleridge's unfinished poem "Christabel" contains many of the elements later seen in Keats, Holmes, and Hawthorne.[55] Had Colderidge finished the poem, some of the elements of plot and characterization may have been developed otherwise, but in the poem as we have it, the conventional negative venomous woman motif is apparent.

"Christabel" is set in a literary version of the medieval world, complete with castles, moats, knights, and a damsel in distress. In fact, it often seems that one reason the lamia motif is so attractive to writers of the Romantic period is the opportunity it offers for self-conscious medievalism. Christabel and her widowed father, the Baron, Sir Leoline, live in an isolated castle. One chill bleak night, a "damsel bright, / Dressed in silken robe of white" appears as Christabel prays near an old oak tree. This lady, Geraldine, has been engaged in some suspicious behavior. At first it seems as if she has been kidnapped and apparently undergone a gang rape, described in the metaphorical fashion romantic poets often employed to sanitize their sex scenes:

> "Five warriors seized me yestermorn,
> Me, even me, a maid forlorn:
> They choked my cries with force and fright,
> And tied me on a palfrey white.
> The palfrey was as fleet as wind,
> And they rode furiously behind.
> They spurred amain, their steeds were white:
> And once we crossed the shade of night.
> As sure as Heaven shall rescue me,
> I have no thought what men they be;
> Nor do I know how long it is
> (For I have lain entranced I wis)
> Since one, the tallest of the five,
> Took me from the palfrey's back,
> A weary woman, scarce alive."

(ll. 81–95)

But actually what is happening is that Geraldine is associating herself with one of the major elements of witchcraft, the "wild ride," ancestor of the Halloween flight on brooms and a staple of witchcraft lore. In the wild ride, "a procession of beings, led by a spirit, roamed through the countryside, reveling, killing, devastating or eating whatever they found in their path."[56] Geraldine has not done any devastating or killing, but she has been on the ride, in the company of a tall leader of demonic mien. Although the ride took place while she claims to have been in a trance, she is not excused; much witchcraft could be done that way.[57] So Geraldine is a *striga*, or witch, and both concepts are connected, as we have seen, with the shape-shifting characteristic of the lamia or serpent-woman. The Baron, however, does not see this, preferring to regard her as a damsel in distress in need of his knightly protection. The shape-shifting motif here shades into simple mis-perception as the Baron adjusts his understanding of Geraldine to his own self-concept.

It appears that Geraldine needs help and a place of refuge. Christabel takes her not only into her castle but into her bed as well. Granted that women sleeping together was a common practice and considered innocent up to the very recent past, still the nighttime experiences of Geraldine and Christabel are unusual in that Christabel wakes up with a strong sense of sin: " 'Sure I have sinned!' said Christabel, / 'Now heaven be praised if all be well!' " (ll. 381–82). Evidently the night was not an innocent one. Homo-sexuality is rarely connected in literature with the venomous woman, but at their trials witches were often accused of participating in orgies featuring indiscriminate sex. The formula "*masculi in masculos, et feminae in femi-nas*" became a standard description of such midnight revels.[58] Heretics were also accused of such behavior, perhaps on the theory that one who deviates at all does so in all possible ways.

On the morn, the Baron vows to take revenge on the raptors of Geraldine because that is the knightly thing to do for damsels but also because he and Geraldine's father are long-lost friends separated by a feud, and this offers a chance of reconciliation. Christabel is hesitant about this commitment; indeed she throws herself at her father's feet and begs him not to involve himself further with Geraldine, but to no avail. She cannot give the father all the information he needs to make a judgment because that would mean disclosure of the previous night's activities. The Baron, however, is warned by the bard, Bracy, who has had a prophetic dream. He dreams that a sweet dove named after Christabel is being strangled by a bright green snake. They symbolism seems obvious enough, especially given the names, but the Baron misinterprets the dream by assuming that the dove is Geraldine, not his daughter, and the snake is her captors, whom he will crush. Again the demon lady changes her significance to suit the desires of the male perceptor.

At this point the poem veers back to the usual pattern of the poison-lady plot. The Baron, influenced by the beauty of the venomous woman, ignores all warnings. She is at the ready to deceive him with the usual array of feminine wiles:

> And Geraldine in maiden wise
> Casting down her large bright eyes,
> With blushing cheek and courtesy fine
> She turned her from Sir Leoline.

(ll. 573–76)

This is how she appears to him, but when Christabel sees the same scene, she sees the serpent-woman:

> A snake's small eye blinks dull and shy;
> And the lady's eyes they shrunk in her head,
> Each shrunk up to a serpent's eye,
> And with somewhat of malice, and more of dread,
> At Christabel she looked askance!—
> One moment—and the sight was fled!
> But Christabel in dizzy trance
> Stumbling on the unsteady ground
> Shuddered aloud, with a hissing sound.

(ll. 583–91)

Now it is Christabel who makes the hissing sound: she has been, and she fears her father will be, contaminated by the deceptively sinful Geraldine. She tries to protect him, but she is infected by Geraldine's venomousness to the extent that to her father, Christabel herself looks like the venomous woman:

> The maid, devoid of guile and sin,
> I know not how, in fearful wise,
> So deeply had she drunken in
> That look, those shrunken serpent eyes,
> That all her features were resigned
> To this sole image in her mind:
> And passively did imitate
> That look of dull and treacherous hate!
> And thus she stood, in dizzy trance,
> Still picturing that look askance
> With forced unconscious sympathy
> Full before her father's view.

(ll. 599–610)

The bewitching powers of Geraldine are such as to disrupt the natural affection between father and daughter. In addition, his infatuation causes him to ignore the prophet/poet, Bracy. He rejects both, assuming that his daughter is just jealous and Bracy misinformed, and he leads Geraldine from the hall, leaving the others and allying himself with her.

There the poem ends, unfinished like so many other works of the English Romantics, and we have no way of knowing what Coleridge would have done with the rest of it. So far, the lady Geraldine conforms to the dominant pattern of venomous woman as deceiver and seductress. But the plot elements of the wild ride and lesbian sexuality are not well integrated. If indeed Coleridge wanted us to see Geraldine as the seducer of Christabel, as well as the Baron, this would have been an unusual, if not illogical, variant on the idea of the venomous woman as symbol of sexual sin. The conflict experienced by the Baron is less pronounced than in the lamia story involving a young protagonist. The Baron is an older man and Christabel's father and thus presumably sexually experienced, so the initiation theme is eliminated. The mentor role is diffused by being divided between two people, Christabel and the bard, Bracy, each younger than the Baron and socially inferior to him, being his daughter and retainer, respectively; therefore their advice can be ignored with little conflict. By contrast, it becomes apparent that the set of characters used by Keats, Holmes, and Hawthorne makes for a more powerful conflict. All three works—Keats's poem *Lamia,* Holmes's novel *Elsie Venner,* and Hawthorne's short story "Rappaccini's Daughter"—focus on a young and sexually inexperienced hero who wishes to satisfy himself emotionally through love but at the same time to conform to society's values as expressed by an older and respected mentor.

This is exactly the situation found in Keats's *Lamia.* His source, Robert Burton's *Anatomy of Melancholy* (1621), gives him his basic plot:

One Menippus Lycius, a young man twenty-five years of age, that going betwixt Cenchreas and Corinth, met such a phantasm in the habit of a fair gentlewoman, which taking him by the hand carried him home to her house, in the suburbs of Corinth.... The young man, a philosopher, otherwise staid and discreet, able to moderate his passions, though not this of love, tarried with her a while to his great content, and at last married her, to whose wedding, amongst other guests, came Apollonius; who, by some probable conjectures, found her out to be a serpent, a lamia, and that all her furniture was, like Tantalus's gold described by Homer, no substance, but mere illusions. When she saw herself descried, she wept, and desired Apollonius to be silent, but he would not be moved, and thereupon she, plate, house, and all that was in it, vanished in an instant: "many thousands took notice of this fact, for it was done in the midst of Greece." (III, 494)

Here are the basic characters—young man, serpent lady, mentor—and the basic themes—reason versus passion, society versus individual. The young man is "staid and discreet, able to moderate his passions," and the mentor figure, voice of reason and of human education, Apollonius, intends to keep him that way. The lamia, on the other hand, lures him to her house in the suburbs, outside the mainstream of (male) life, and causes him to tarry there. He attempts to incorporate his new love into the society he has temporarily forsaken by marrying her. As in all other marriages, this presents the problem of rendering her acceptable to his old companions. This is impossible because his adviser, Apollonius, represents the antithesis of all she stands for. He is reason, and reason must be suspended when loving a lamia. If he insists on knowing her instead of loving her, the supernatural lady will be destroyed.

One major element Keats takes from his source is the basic goodness of the lamia. She has no intention of harming Menippus and weeps when her true identity is discovered. Burton's source is Philostratus's *Life and Times of Apollonius of Tyana* (c. 217), but he seems to have modified the story, since Burton's lamia is less threatening than Philostratus's. In a recent translation of Philostratus, many of the plot elements remain the same, but the lamia is portrayed as more deadly. Apollonius accuses the lamia of using techniques of sexual seduction to facilitate her main goal, cannibalism. He triumphs in causing the lamia to admit "that she was fattening up Menippus with dainties so that she might devour his body, and that she made a practice of feeding on bodies that were young and beautiful, because their blood was untainted."[59] Burton's version suppresses the cannibalism motif and adds the element of the enchantress's own sorrow, both of which increase sympathy for the lamia, a main feature of Keats's poem.[60]

Long, long ago, in a fairy-tale land, the god Hermes steals from Mount Olympus to seek a nymph dwelling on a sacred island. He seeks her in vain; but while doing so, he hears a lamenting voice, which turns out to belong to a "palpitating snake / Bright, and cirque-couchant in a dusky brake" (I, 45–46).[61] Hermes, being a god, should know better, but he strikes a bargain with this creature: He will grant her anything she wants if she will tell him where to find his nymph. This lamia has power to keep the nymph invisible by causing her to "steep / Her hair in weird syrops" (I, 106–7). But she will release the nymph from this spell, to be visible only to Hermes, if he will grant her this request:

> "I was a woman, let me have once more
> A woman's shape, and charming as before.
> I love a youth of Corinth—O the bliss!
> Give me my woman's form, and place me where he is."
>
> (I, 117–20)

Lamia's motives for changing back into a woman are not insidious at all; she was once a woman. It is not clear how the initial transformation from woman to snake occurred or why she can metamorphose Hermes's nymph but not herself—however, we are in the land of faery. Perhaps Keats wants the reader to remember Hera's transformation of Lamia in retaliation for Lamia's affair with Zeus, and suggests a remetamorphosis. One difference, however, is that this Lamia begins as a complete serpent and then becomes a complete woman; she is not the dual creature of myth, woman on top but serpent at bottom. Now this Lamia wants to be restored to her former shape, for a simple reason: she is in love, and wants to be loved in return, an unlikely eventuality if she stays a snake.

And so the shape shifting occurs. Her transformation is described as discharging venom: "Her mouth foam'd, and the grass, therewith besprent, / Wither'd at dew so sweet and virulent" (I, 148–49). The serpent discharging its venom is an image from medieval beast lore used as emblem of the repentant sinner, and so the image indicates that Lamia is rejecting her old life as a serpent. Although metamorphosis creates doubt in others about the real identity of the changed being, to Lamia a total and irrevocable transformation has occurred. As woman, not serpent, she is off to Corinth. Not only is she "a maid / more beautiful than ever twisted braid" (I, 185–86), but she has supernatural powers besides. Again notice the idea that woman's powers are supernatural and mysterious and involve secret knowledge: in spite of being "a virgin purest lipp'd" (I, 189), she is

> in the lore
> Of love deep learned to the red heart's core:
> Not one hour old, yet of sciential brain
> To unperplex bliss from its neighbor pain.
>
> (I, 190–92)

The type of learning Lamia has is not sexual experience or that achieved by Apollonius through reason and hard study but rather the intuitive knowledge often attributed to women. Its feature is to dissociate bliss from pain— that is, to offer perfect happiness uncontaminated by the influence of the "real" world. The "young Corinthian Lycius" is no match for this power. His falling in love at first sight is expressed in the familiar image, the potion of love:

> soon his eyes had drunk her beauty up,
> Leaving no drop in the bewildering cup,
> And still the cup was full.
>
> (I, 251–53)

At first he thinks she is a goddess, and she plays along with this belief to allure him even more, but she finally persuades him that she is a real woman and not supernatural at all. This is still deceptive; a woman who was once a serpent cannot, with her "dubious lineage,"[62] portray herself as an ordinary girl. Although Lycius is joyously in love, the voice of wisdom, personified by his sage, old tutor, Apollonius, "trusty guide / And good instructor" (I, 375–76), warns him of his folly. Lamia, knowing she has something to hide from the light of reason, trembles in the presence of its representative. The voices of human education warn the man off from the destructive allure of the deceptive female. It is too late, though. Lycius is a subject in Lamia's "empery / Of joys" (II, 36–37), and the correct natural order of things is reversed: she has the power.

Lycius wants to marry Lamia, but one of the problems confronting this whirlwind courtship is that he does not know her name. In word magic, to know the name of a being is to know its essence. The power of the supernatural mistress depends on keeping her aura of mystery, to violate which is to destroy her and everything she has brought with her.[63] The rule she imposes is not to learn her name. Once Lycius knows her name, he will be influenced by the intellectual constructs surrounding it—the ideas implicit in Apollonius's warnings—instead of responding to her self, which is separate from her meaning. Therefore she deceives him into planning the marriage ceremony on the basis of this incomplete knowledge (again, as all marriage ceremonies must be planned). She tries to exclude Apollonius, who, as his name after the god Apollo implies, would be able to provide healing remedy, antidote to her venom. Apollonius comes anyway. At the lavish wedding feast, the mere sight of Apollonius causes Lamia's power to wither. He names her; her power is destroyed; the "sweet bride withers" at the "potency" of Apollonius's eyes (II, 290). As soon as Lycius is undeceived, she vanishes, as the supernatural mistress always does when the rules of the game are violated. Apollonius, wisdom and science, is antidote and remedy; his job is to protect Lycius, and he thinks he has. But with the disappearance of Lamia, Lycius dies too, that very night, to be buried in his wedding garment.

What killed Lycius? On one level, he dies as a result of an incorrect response to the idea of the maleficent venomous woman. In an earlier passage, it is implied that the courtship of Lycius and Lamia included sexual consummation:

> side by side
> They were enthroned, in the even tide,
> Upon a couch....
> For the first time, since first he harbour'd in
> That purple-lined palace of sweet sin,
> His spirit pass'd beyond its golden bourn
> Into the noisy world almost forsworn.
>
> (II, 16–18, 30–33)

In other words, entering into the lady's room/couch/body, Lycius has let his vital spirits go out to her and is now in her power. What he has lost, she has gained. If this were a simple chastity allegory, his fate would show the dire results of sin. Her venomousness is contagious through physical contact, so the body of Lycius is as envenomed as hers is, and the only possible remedy is a strong dose of continence. But the situation is more complex since the lamia is not only a simple symbol of sin. The solution depends on whether the antidote is considered homeopathic or allopathic remedy. In homeopathic medicine, like cures like; in allopathic medicine contraries cure. The chastity/lust pairing is an allopathic relationship; so is the reason/passion pairing. But reason cannot save Lycius because the conflict engendered by two such powerful human drives is so violent that it kills the receptacle. A better approach would be the homeopathic one, through which Lycius can survive by gradually incorporating into himself what reason might regard as Lamia's venom but which to him provides healing remedy for body and soul.

A young man's education, and therefore his way of thinking, stresses the rational; he must now, for the sake of his own happiness, try the female way of knowing through empathy, through the emotions. Love disorders the brain and corrupts judgment (called melancholy or "heroical love" in Burton),[64] but this is a tragedy only if one believes that an orderly brain is good. It is no accident that this interpretation of the lamia myth is contemporaneous with the Romantic period and its questioning of rationality.

There is yet another dimension to Lycius's death. The young man relies too heavily on the advice of the mentor because of his own inexperience. As in the case of the allopathic remedy of reason, so in the case of the marriage plan. His decision to marry Lamia is a mistake based on an attempt to incorporate their love into standard social arrangements. When he is with Lamia in her place, her "golden bourn," he is content; nevertheless he persists in defining his world, the "noisy world" outside, as the real world and assumes that she must enter it with him. If he were able to accept the self-definition of a woman, admittedly an unusual one, thus symbolically staying in her place instead of moving her into his place, he would be happy. Lamia represents an ideal—bliss unperplexed from pain—that can only be approximated, not completely achieved, in the real world. This ideal cannot be encompassed by the "conceptual brain."[65] Lycius responds fully and freely to Lamia, and their life approximates perfection until he contrives the inappropriate scheme of allowing society to intrude. This destroys the ideal love. When Lycius insists on marrying, he abandons the dream of a perfect love and, by attempting to make it ordinary, kills it.[66]

A lady who is also a serpent is an excellent symbol of the difficulty of differentiating between good and evil. If the didactic chastity allegory is to be superseded by a more sophisticated analysis of human sexuality, then the element of moral ambiguity must be stressed. As Richard Benvenuto points out, Lamia cannot be judged by the absolute moral standards imposed by society; she is "a merger of contraries" not amenable to discussion under the principles of "conventional morality." To think that man's journey through life can be envisioned as a straight path with clearly marked moral turnoffs is a gross oversimplification. Indeed, Lamia's duality indicates that "man's sins cannot be unknotted from his salvation."[67] It can even be said that in certain circumstances, man must risk sin to be saved. To approach the woman is to risk falling into sexual sin; not to approach her at all is to violate the higher law of charity.

Keats's poem, written in 1819, began the nineteenth-century modification of the interrelated themes of sin, snakes, and sex. Later in the century, first Hawthorne (1844) and then Holmes (1859) published venomous-woman stories. Both Holmes and Hawthorne are linked in a relationship of mutual influence with Melville, who, in *The Confidence-Man* (1857), explores the question of the moral responsibility of the serpent.[68]

While "clinking the social glass" (162), the cosmopolitan and the stranger discuss the coexistence of beauty and evil in creatures.[69] Their conversation is not adversarial; rather, they are discussing the ramifications of the idea of the serpent's guiltlessness. The stranger, regarding the handsome appearance of the cosmopolitan, expresses the opinion that the cosmopolitan must have "a beautiful soul" (162) to correspond with his body. The cosmopolitan agrees: " 'beauty is ... incompatible with ill' " (162). Therefore the serpent, being beautiful, is not evil, indeed has a " 'latent benignity' " (162).

The stranger, not surprised by this assertion, invites empathy with this maligned, not malign, being. He asks the cosmopolitan to imagine what it would be like to " 'change personalities with him ... to feel what it was to be a snake ... your whole beautiful body one iridescent scabbard of death ... to feel yourself exempt from knowledge, and conscience, and revel for a while in the care-free, joyous life of a perfectly instinctive, unscrupulous, and irresponsible creature' " (162). The cosmopolitan replies that he would not like to be a rattlesnake, for that would mean having to suffer isolation because of the significance imposed on the serpent: " 'men would be afraid of me, and then I should be a very lonesome and miserable rattle-snake' " (163). The stranger regards the serpent's rattle, " 'a sound ... like the shaking together of small, dry skulls in a tune of the Waltz of Death' " (163), as Nature's warning:

"When any creature is by its make inimical to other creatures, nature in effect labels that creature, much as an apothecary does a poison. So that whoever is destroyed by a rattle-snake, or other harmful agent, it is his own fault. He should have respected the label. Hence that significant passage in Scripture, 'Who will pity the charmer that is bitten with a serpent?' " (163)

In reply to Scripture's rhetorical question, the cosmopolitan answers, " 'I would pity him' " (163). Scriptural symbolism—tradition—is not the last word on the issue. It is not self-evident that the venomous being should be avoided. The snake charmer's defiance of warnings gives him a special dignity; he deserves empathy, and so does the serpent. Although, as the stranger says, it is " 'presuming' " for " 'man to pity where nature is piti-less,' " the cosmopolitan regards this as " 'casuistry,' " a cerebral approach (163). Intellectually responsive though he is, the stranger is described as having a "passionless air," but the cosmopolitan speaks of " 'compassion,' " through which the " 'heart decides for itself ' " (163).

The stranger restates the issue: " 'Is a rattle-snake accountable?' " (163). The snake may be a traditional symbol of moral evil, may be capable of physical evil, but is it " 'accountable' "? The concept invites rational anal-ysis, moral judgment, the logician's *sic* or *non*. Raising the question this way, the stranger is described as "more a metaphysical merman than a feeling man" (163). Philosophical analysis is not appropriate; being a "feel-ing man" is. The cosmopolitan has the "caution of no inexperienced thinker" (163). He knows how to use thought and logical analysis, but he knows when to suspend them. He will neither affirm nor deny the propo-sition: " 'such accountability is neither to you, nor me, nor the Court of Common Pleas, but to something superior' " (163). Reason or law must be suspended when dealing with rattlesnakes. Morality does not apply. Unlike man, who is bound by moral prohibitions, the snake has " 'an implied permit of unaccountability to murder any creature it takes capricious um-brage at' " (164). Why this should be so is a mystery. Each speaker, ex-hausted with the complexity of the subject, sips wine and changes the subject.

In thinking about this dilemma in connection with *Elsie Venner*, Holmes may well have drawn a comparison between Melville's snake and his own snake-woman. How can a being be beautiful yet evil? The question defies a simple answer. If one could have compassion for that maligned being, greater comprehension would result, but not from the action of reason. It is as impossible for a man to be a woman as for a man to be a snake, and hardly more desirable from the man's viewpoint since to be a woman would mean bearing the weight of the intellectual constructs describing femaleness and, consequently, enduring isolation, loneliness, and misery. Like the rattle of the serpent or the label of the poison, the voices of religion and culture warn men that women are dangerous. If a woman leads a man into ruin, it is no more than he deserves: " 'He should have respected the label.' " And yet if the bitten snake charmer is worth pity, so is the man who risks compassion. To be dispassionate and reasonable is to risk loss of the ex-perience, which can be achieved only when the judgment is suspended, when assent or dissent is rendered irrelevant. This is risky, but the cautious life is ignoble. The accountability of the woman for the evil she seems to rep-resent is for a higher court to judge. It is a mystery.

ELSIE VENNER

Holmes's *Elsie Venner* explores this mystery in his story of an envenomed women and the young man she loves.[70] Unlike Keats, who was writing a poetic romance and consequently could be vague about how Lamia came to be a serpent, both Holmes and Hawthorne were working in the more realistic fictional forms and so were specific about how their heroines became venomous. The old wives' tale of prenatal influences was still taken seriously in Holmes's day and discussed at medical meetings and in medical journals.[71] Holmes, himself a physician, could with some scientific respectability describe his Elsie as having been envenomed in utero because her mother was bitten by a serpent, from which wound the mother dies after Elsie's birth. This influence leaves Elsie with serpentine characteristics and moods: she could "lie ... basking for whole hours in the sunshine"; her strength waxes and wanes with "the juices of all the poison-plants and the blood of all the creatures that feed upon them" (261); she even dresses in serpentine patterns and wears jewelry that resembles the rings on snakes' skin. The necklace she always wears is particularly significant in that it is believed to conceal telltale markings. A serpentine woman, but a real woman, Elsie combines Keats's serpent transformed and Hawthorne's woman envenomed.

Both Holmes and Hawthorne are influenced in the creation of their stories by a very old legend: the poisoned maiden. This story dates back at least to the *Secreta Secretorum* and is connected with Alexander the Great in most versions. According to the legend, a beautiful girl had been "fed upon poison from infancy, 'until she was of the nature of a snake.' " After proving her mettle by poisoning many lovers, she was called upon by the enemies of Alexander as an assassination weapon, the plan being that she should seduce him and poison him too. In varying accounts, certainly her embrace but even her breath, saliva, and perspiration were deadly poisons. The author of the *Secreta Secretorum* claims to have discovered her true nature " 'by tests' " and thus saved Alexander.[72] The same idea of a woman's sexuality used as a weapon is repeated in a work on law and medicine published in Avignon in 1660. According to this account, one King Ladislas (not assisted by the wise philosopher) suffered the unpleasant fate of being *"empoisonné mortellement par son membre viril qui avait absorbé un poison préalablement déposé dans le vagin de sa maîtresse."*[73] As with the Alexander the Great story, the woman is not perpetrator but weapon. Someone else has *"déposé"* the poison; she has not chosen to be the way she is. Both legends raise the question of the moral responsibility of the woman so envenomed, a question both Holmes and Hawthorne addressed.

Combining esoteric pseudoscience with simple misogyny, the story of the poisoned damsel captured the imagination of writers on poison for hundreds of years. Any reader on the subject of poison will find repeated debates on the possibility of being envenomed through physical contact with another person.[74] In such cases the victim is always male and the perpetrator female. Since the way to "truth" in medical writing for centuries was de-

duction from the principles laid down by the great authorities, or by deducing from other treatises deducing from them, once this story got into
the medical lore, it took a long time for it to get out. Medical writers
conveyed the same information for centuries, unscathed by experimentation.
But one writer, Andrea Bacci, saw a new angle to the problem. In his *De
venenis et antidotis* (1586), a new angle of reasoning is added to the story:
"He denies that the maiden fed on poison would have poisoned Alexander
the Great, had he lain with her, because what she ate would have been
transformed into nutrition."[75] It is this crucial change—the idea of transformation by incorporation into the self—that affects the depiction of the
venomous woman in Holmes and Hawthorne. In *Elsie Venner*, it is the
misfortune of the protagonist, Bernard Langdon, that the physician whom
he consults for advice on Elsie seems not to know this theory. Elsie Venner,
venomous though she is, may be antidote as well. The serpent-woman may
be morally superior to the people around her who are defined as normal;
more important, she offers Bernard a chance to participate in that
superiority.

In fact, in *Elsie Venner* the townspeople surrounding Elsie, by whom and
in relation to whom she is judged, are relentlessly normal, even stereotypical.
Rockland is populated by a sensitive but overworked schoolmarm, a pious
and dedicated black servant woman, an equally dedicated but somewhat
uppity Yankee manservant, socially ambitious bourgeoises, Brahmin gentry,
wise, concerned and learned authority figures (fathers, professors, doctors,
and clergymen), and even a black sheep of the family. To this hypertypical
town comes Bernard Langdon, a young medical student interrupting his
education because of his family's diminished fortunes. He is an excellent
student and shows promise as a teacher as well, according to his medical
school professor, who is the narrator of the novel. All the events of the
novel are seen through the consciousness of this professor, who also serves
as adviser to Bernard.

In the typical lamia story, as we have seen, the young man needs a mentor.
As events unfold, it becomes increasingly clear that Bernard has allowed
his professor to guide his response to Elsie. To depend on a former teacher
is not unusual, but at some point this dependence can become harmful, as
even the best-intentioned adviser has his own inadequacies. But Bernard is
not yet at that point of maturity. He needs his old teacher, and so the
question is, What kind of man is this professor? The answer: smug, self-
assured, and opinionated (like many other academics before and since). He
has no name; he is always "the professor"—a typical example of his calling.
His bias is rationalistic, his stance detached and cool. He presumes to judge
persons and events from afar and has no qualms about issuing definite and
authoritative opinions about any subject. Unlike Dr. Kittredge, a practitioner
whose sympathies are exercised by daily patient contact, the narrator is a

stereotyped ivory-tower theoretician who judges people according to ideas found in books. As a medical student and physician himself, Holmes must have known both types.

Teachers who influence the lives of their students beyond the classroom typically have nothing material to gain from the interaction but enjoy the psychological power, and this is the case with the relationship in the novel. Each intrusion into the life of Bernard Langdon is motivated by sincere concern. The professor has high hopes that after "ten brilliant years of spirited, unflagging labor" (20), Bernard can stand at the top of his profession. Therefore Bernard must be cautioned to avoid "love and all that nonsense" (21) and, when the time arrives, to marry with an eye to professional and social advancement. This commonsense life plan, coming as it does from a seemingly wise and unselfish source, unduly influences the young man. Bernard does not see that the plan leaves no room for the fortuitous accident of falling in love.

Another bias the professor passes along to Bernard is again endemic to his calling: the intellectual tradition of rationalism. The professor assumes all problems can be solved if one keeps a cool head, and he reinforces a tendency to emotional detachment in the chilly Bernard. The professor is also an adherent of an elaborate theory of human responsibility, which he communicates to Bernard at a crucial point in Bernard's relationship with Elsie. A theoretician rather than a practitioner, the professor does not hesitate to prescribe at long distance. He has never met Elsie, yet he is positive that his theories apply to her, and like the docile student who would naturally be a favorite of a professor like this, Bernard accepts his mentor's ideas.

Elsie then is set in the novel in contrast with both the ordinariness of the town and the rationality of the professor's theories. The first meetings of Bernard and Elsie occur in situations that stress Elsie's nonconformity. They first meet as teacher and student at the Apollinean Female Institute, where young ladies are brought into conformity with the rules of reason. Then they meet again at a party given by the socially aspiring Sprowles as a showcase for their marriageable Matilda. In each group—fellow students and fellow eligibles—Elsie stands out from the rest of the ordinary girls of Rockland. To the basic situation, then, of young male teacher and nubile female student, alluring enough in itself, is added Elsie's too-drastic difference from the other girls: she is extremely attractive, and she is venomous.

Who is Elsie? What is she? "By what demon is she haunted, by what taint is she blighted, by what curse is she followed, by what destiny is she marked, that her strange beauty has such a terror in it, and that hardly one shall dare to love her, and her eye glitters always, but warms for none?" (175–76). Over the peaceful little town hovers the shadow of Rattlesnake Ledge, where snakes breed. Into the careful, rational life of Bernard Langdon comes Elsie Venner, challenging every presupposition. She is dangerous.

From early childhood her envenoming was threatening: as soon as Elsie cuts teeth, her wet-nurse sickens and dies; as a child, she bit her cousin Dick Venner so that he retains the scars as an adult; at fifteen, she rids herself of an objectionable governess by inducing in her a mysterious illness. Throughout her life, she is perceived as so intractable that Dr. Kittredge advises her father to let her have her way. She wanders off, an odd behavior for a girl anyway and made odder still by her preferred destinations: trees, caves, Rattlesnake Ledge.

In the fictional present, she is seventeen. The problem child has become an even more problematic young woman. What is to be done with a female like Elsie at sexual maturity? She cannot just be married off like any other young girl. She is a maze of contradictions. Snakelike, she is cold: the light in her eyes is like the "lustre of ice" (183), her expression is that of "remoteness, of utter isolation" (184). Yet she is also passionate: her mother was a Spaniard, and this influence (perceived by the xenophobic narrator as venomous in itself) makes for wild blood. Dancing to Spanish music, she whips herself into a frenzy, "undulating with flexuous grace" (147). Clearly she is nothing at all like the other girls.

The good citizens of Rockland chorus their disapproval of Elsie. She is possessed of "ungovernable anger" and "an irritable state of mind and body" (192). She is a "strange, wild-looking girl" (51). She is an "apparition of wild beauty" in her bracelets scaly as "Cleopatra's asp" (99). She may be " 'possessed of devils' " (127). She may have the " 'evil eye' " (212). She " 'would have been burned for a witch in old times' " (212). Like witches, she is a knower of drugs. Dick Venner notices her possession of a white powder; knowing she dislikes him, he "took certain precautions with reference to his diet" and "refused the cup of coffee which Elsie offered him" (361). She has an affinity with the serpentine even in literature. Says Bernard, her teacher, " 'She read a passage from Keats's "Lamia" the other day, in the school-room, in such a way that I declare to you I thought some of the girls would faint or go into fits' " (213–14). Clearly the sexual maturation of such a woman presents a problem. As her father, Dudley Venner, puts it, " 'Who would *dare* to marry Elsie?' " (270).

There are two candidates for that honor, Bernard and also Dick Venner. The conflict between the two (a new element in the lamia story) further adumbrates the reason/passion conflict. As we have seen, Bernard represents the intellectual achievements made possible by taming the passions. As a class, the Brahmins have been remarkably successful in producing intellectuals, but not without paying a price. The trade-off has been a loss of the vigor of the animal nature, a decrease of "vital energy" (8); the Brahmins are slender, pallid, smooth-faced, delicate of feature. In short, they are cerebral and asexual. In contrast, his rival, Elsie's cousin Dick Venner, is, like Elsie herself, a " 'half-breed,' " with "Southern impulses in [his] wild blood" (378), which conflict with and overpower the "cunning and calculating" rationality of his "New-England side" (356). He is given to such symbolic gestures as riding his "half-tamed horse" when the "savage passion of his young blood came over him" (158). He is a bit of an outlaw; he has a dark past; and, because he is Elsie's cousin, there is a subdued incest motif. Dick Venner would seem to be a proper mate for Elsie, but she does not love him. Nor does he love her; although he is drawn to her, stronger still is the lure of her father's money. He is blood, Bernard is brain, and Elsie seems attracted to what she lacks. That, and Dick Venner's elimination fairly early in the novel, leave Bernard as the only candidate for Elsie's venomous hand.

Bernard is simultaneously attracted to and repelled by the danger Elsie represents. Cautious though he is, one of his first excursions on arriving at the town is to Rattlesnake Ledge, attracted by the "excitement," the "gratification in this infinitesimal sense of danger" (55). Beneath the chilly Brahmin exterior lurks normal male passions, upon which Elsie exerts " 'an odd sort of fascination' " (127). At the Sprowles's party, the narrator theorizes that Bernard is attracted to Elsie as Odysseus to Circe and discourses on the "occult influence exercised by certain women" who are "phosphorescent with the luminous vapor of life" (104). Bernard finds her distracting, disturbing, sees her as an "Eve just within the gate of an untried Paradise... on tiptoe to reach the fruit of the tree of knowledge" (105). The Venners's garden triggers "reminiscences of a lost Paradise" (142). Clearly he is on the verge of a sexual initiation. Elsie—Eve, Circe, basilisk, sorceress—represents the mysterious power of sexuality: "this over-womanized woman might well have betwitched him" (105).

Yet Bernard is too much the intellectual simply to respond to Elsie naturally. He must perforce cerebralize her. Ever the attentive student, he sees her as an interesting case. He muses on the concept of fascination as a manifestation of man's affinity for the serpent, his inherited tendency to evil, the "fruit of the curse" (205), original sin. He is able to test this theory when, himself fascinated by a snake on Rattlesnake Ledge, the spell is broken by Elsie's superior power. His medical/theological speculations are furthered when, one morning, a "dark, gypsy-looking woman" brings him a *crotalus*, a breed of snake living in the neighborhood that he desires to investigate. Alarmed, Bernard warns her of their deadliness, but the gypsy-looking woman reassures him of her immunity: " 'rattlers never touches our folks!' " Bernard has never heard of the "possession of a power by certain persons, which enables them to handle these frightful reptiles with perfect impunity" (207). However, he should have. In the New Testament, the followers of Christ are given the power to handle serpents with impunity, and this is a sign of their goodness.[76] Could this mean that if he were good enough, Elsie would not be venomous for him, would perhaps even be beneficial? Rather than apply the implied moral lesson to himself, he muses on the general subject of the serpent and evil.

Again, the subject debated by Melville's stranger and cosmopolitan returns: is the serpent, symbol of evil, itself evil? Bernard cannot take the
question further, but, although he never knows it, Elsie has. In a conversation
between the two ministers, Rev. Dr. Honeywell and Mr. Fairweather, the
latter recounts an incident from Elsie's childhood. Mr. Fairweather had sent
a religious book to Elsie for her edification. From the book she tore out
and kept the frontispiece, a picture of Eve's temptation, and threw the rest
of the book out the window. For Elsie, Eve is the only important figure in
religion. She said that "Eve was a good woman—and she'd have done just
so if she'd been there" (192). Mr. Fairweather sees this as evidence of her
" 'natural obliquity' " (192) and in fact the " 'congenital sinfulness of human nature' " (193). But Elsie's instinctive identification with Eve can be
seen as a rejection of the concept of sinfulness imposed on Eve. Eve sinned
because the serpent deceived her. If she was deceived, then she was victim,
not perpetrator. Like Eve, Elsie has been singled out to be a symbol, to
represent a theory.

In fact everyone around Bernard is devising theories—medical, philosophical, theological. Elsie's father, Dudley Venner, sees her as a victim of
hysteria: she is deadly because she is a woman. He stands helplessly by in
wan hope that Elsie will grow out of her venomous nature. The long-
suffering schoolmarm, Helen Darley, has a theory that makes Elsie no more
free: she blames " 'the force of transmitted tendencies' " (75). Rev. Dr.
Honeywood cites a "visitation of God," which "impairs the intellectual or
the moral perceptions" but renders the person thus afflicted exempt from
"common working standards of right and wrong" (246). All agree that
Elsie's problem is not her fault, but none agree on what should be done
about the fact that Elsie cannot marry. As Old Sophy tells Dr. Kittredge,
Elsie's husband would die. Confused, Bernard consults his old professor.

The questions he asks of his medical/philosophical adviser, his former
professor, bear on the health of body and soul. First, he wants to know if
envenoming is physically possible; if it is, he wants to know whether a
person thus envenomed is morally dangerous as well. He writes: "Is there
any evidence that human beings can be wrought upon by poisons, or otherwise, so that they shall manifest any of the peculiarities belonging to beings
of a lower nature?" (219). The professor replies at great length and with
many citations from academic authorites. And along comes, here in the
nineteenth century in America, the hoary story of Alexander the Great and
his poisoned lady, cited "upon pretty good authority" (222) as medical
evidence by a medical school professor. The search for truth in medical
matters proceeds in a manner virtually unchanged from the Middle Ages;
answers are found not by experimentation or observation but by looking
them up in "old books" (221). In this version of the old story, from Miz-
aldus's *Memorabilia*, Alexander is warned by a mentor, in this case the very
voice of reason: " 'When Aristotle saw her eyes *sparkling and snapping like*

those of serpents, he said, "Look out for yourself, Alexander! this is a
dangerous companion for you!" ' " (222). The professor goes on, citing
more recent instances of the poisoned lady, including the "malignant witch-
woman" in Coleridge's "Christabel" and the "serpent transformed" in
Keats's *Lamia* (225).

Bernard has also raised the related question about the serpent-women
Melville raised in reference to the actual serpent: is the venomous being
responsible for its own venomousness? Can people in this condition be "as
free from moral responsibility as the instincts of the lower animals? Do you
think there may be a *crime* which is not a *sin*?" (220). The professor replies
with a discourse on the "limitations of human responsibility" (226). He
does believe in diminished responsibility; some people are less responsible
for their actions because of predisposing conditions—heredity being one,
reflex or involuntary action another—and both applying to Elsie. The moral
insanity defense in criminal trials, an innovation in Holmes's day, is based
on the postulate that there exist people who are not morally responsible
for their legal crimes. Holmes defended the theory of unconscious and
mechanical mental action that limits human will, a theory Holmes summarized in his Phi Beta Kappa address, "Mechanism in Thought and
Morals."[77] The theory is obviously an early version of the modern "not
guilty by reason of insanity" plea, and like that plea, it is not likely to inspire
confidence in the person so absolved. In practice, according to the professor,
the distinction between sin and crime is irrelevant: "*Treat bad men exactly
as if they were insane*. They are *in-sane*, out of health, morally. Reason,
which is food to sound minds, is not tolerated, still less assimilated" (228).
Although the professor does not know he is advising on Elsie, his message
is the same as that given by the mentor figures to Lycius in *Lamia* and
Giovanni in "Rappaccini's Daughter": avoid the dangerous being.

Bernard Langdon is thus influenced by many theories—theological, medical, philosophical, psychological. Elsie is Eve, the channel through whom
primordial guilt is transmitted. She is Circe, the enchantress whose sexual
potency can distract a man from the goal of his life journey. She is amorality,
irresponsibility, madness. All these ideas stand between Elsie Venner and
Bernard Langdon. The only character in the novel who can respond to Elsie
without the barrier of ideas is the simple servant, Old Sophy. In fact, *Elsie
Venner* is unusual as a lamia story in that there is a woman character to
respond to Elsie. Usually the lamia is alone, a woman in a man's world,
seen through men's perceptions. Here Old Sophy is the only person un-
judgmentally sympathetic (even her father needs to pin a concept, hysteria,
on his daughter). Being black, female, nurturing, and instinctual in a white,
male, and intellectually judgmental world, Sophy's influence is weak. What
self-respecting young man would think of going to such a person for advice?
Instead he follows the voices of reason, and it is their influence that determines his fateful reaction at the novel's climax.

Elsie, distressed, approaches Bernard. He is sympathetic but distant. " 'Tell me what I can do to render your life happier,' " he asks. Elsie replies, " '*Love me*!' " This is the only thing she needs but the one thing he cannot give her. He offers the handshake of friendship, a tepid substitute for the embrace of love. To Bernard, the frigidity seems to emanate from Elsie's hand: "a cold *aura* shot from it along his arm and chilled the blood running through his heart" (243). But the cold really emanates from Bernard's passionless nature; his attribution of it to Elsie is a classic case of projection. He has previously told Dr. Kittredge that he does not love Elsie; if he helps her, it would be " 'in cold blood' " (214). This stance of professional detachment is the reason that, after this crucial encounter, "it was all over for poor Elsie." Deprived of the warmth of love that would have kept her alive, she sickens. The offer of her maidenhood—" 'Love me!' "—and Bernard's rejection are expressed in the imagery of flowers so often connected in literature with the young maiden. Earlier in the novel, Elsie puts a flower in Bernard's copy of the *Aeneid*, at the point of the story that describes Dido's suicide after Aeneas's betrayal. Like Aeneas, Bernard betrays her passionate love. In her final illness, Bernard places a sprig of white ash in a basket of flowers sent to her by her fellow students. Its purple leaves, an antidote to others, are poison to her. Chastity—forcing her to keep the flower of her virginity—is no healthful remedy to Elsie. Bernard's prescription for her, and the flower that represents it, kills her.

In an essay on the motif of poison damsels in folklore and anthropology, N. M. Penzer discusses the relationship of the image of the poison damsel to the tabus surrounding loss of virginity. This correlation is important in understanding the behavior of the heroes in both *Elsie Venner* and "Rappaccini's Daughter." Both Elsie and Beatrice are clearly virgins. Charles and Giovanni are offered the opportunity of deflowering them; both retreat in fear. Although Penzer alludes to neither of these works specifically, he traces the ways in which the poison damsel's poison is considered to be transferred in anthropology and folklore. The first way is by sight, as in fascination by the basilisk. This would render the damsel a threat to all who look upon her, male and female. Obviously neither Beatrice nor Elsie is poisonous in this way. The next possibility is envenoming by breath; this requires closer contact and limits the number of victims to intimates. Elsie is not venomous this way, but apparently Beatrice is, as flowers, lizard, and butterfly die in her aura. Both young girls are feared to be poisonous in sexual intercourse; this is the most common form the legend takes and one that allows for the poison damsel to be used as a weapon, as in the stories of Alexander the Great and the hapless King Ladislas.

Whether Elsie and Beatrice are really poisonous in this way is never known; both die virgins. What is important is not the truth of the allegation about them but the young men's fear of it. Penzer traces the superstition of the poison damsel to the fear of deflowering a virgin. He offers Mandeville's story of the women harboring serpents as evidence. He cites cultural tabus related to a first act of intercourse as caused by the belief that it is a "critical time [when] evil spirits are especially active"; he connects such tabus to the *vagina dentata* motif on the irrational side and to the "fear of venereal contagion" on the rational side.[78] It is not uncommon, then, for a young man to draw back from deflowering a virgin; in some religions and cultures, this reluctance is, of course, an act of virtue. But neither Bernard Langdon nor Giovanni Guasconti is motivated by virtue; they are motivated by fear. To draw back from this quintessentially male experience is to fail to move into full manhood.[79]

The serpent in Elsie is her sexuality. Bernard fails to respond to it out of fear; his failure kills her. In a larger sense, Elsie's sexuality is killed by the attitudes prevailing around her, as expressed by the men around her: her doctor, her father, her potential lover, his professor. Dr. Kittredge points out that serpents have shorter life spans than humans, and perhaps the human in Elsie can outlive the serpent. Dudley Venner regards the prenatal influence as a "blight." His hope had been that "the lower nature which had become engrafted on the higher would die out and leave the real woman's life she inherited to outlive this accidental principle which had so poisoned her childhood and youth" (445). These ideas have a dual significance. If she can be gotten safely through her peak sexual years, she will eventually become less powerful and consequently less threatening. She might outlive her venomous sexuality. But this is a counsel of despair. On the other hand, her sexuality might also be regarded less negatively and stripped of its association with evil. This connection joining sex, snakes, and sin can also be the "accidental principle" that should "die out and leave the real woman's life" of mature sexuality. For this to happen, she needs a man who is not only emotionally responsive but also brave. Bernard is fearful and trapped in his own intellectualism. Even on Elsie's deathbed, he looks at her "with almost scientific closeness of investigation" (446), an attitude of which his medical mentor would surely approve. The lover's gaze, so crucial to the love tradition in literature, is here perverted by the spirit of dispassionate science. "Needing a Heathcliff, she has found only a proper Bostonian."[80] He is too cold and cerebral to bring Elsie to sexual maturity.

At the funeral, before closing Elsie's coffin, Sophy takes off the gold cord Elsie had always worn around her neck. Everyone, even Sophy, thought that Elsie wore this cord to conceal serpentine marks. But "there was no shade nor blemish where the ring of gold had encircled her throat." Sophy attributes this to a miracle—the Lord taking away the mark of evil so Elsie would be fit to join the " 'holy angels' " (451). But his event at the novel's conclusion leaves a drastic ambiguity. Was Elsie really envenomed, or was she merely unusual?

Elsie's life violates several sacred norms. An undercurrent in both

Holmes's novel and Hawthorne's story is the "idealised view of the daughter."[81] Both Elsie and Beatrice Rappaccini are the only children of widowed fathers. The nineteenth-century unmarried woman in her father's house has a special set of responsibilities, summarized in the telling pharase "Angel in the House." She is often raised in the image and likeness of her father (Beatrice being an extreme example of this), to be a companion to him in all ways save sexual. She is supposed to be a gentle, cheerful, smiling " 'sunbeam,' " who can "adorn the household" with "ladylike accomplishments," provide "rest and amusement," attention, affection, and understanding for her father.[82] She should be in no way independent; a "strong-minded girl" who is "self-willed and arrogant, eccentric in dress and disagreeable in manner" is a blight on her father's household.[83] Even in the crucial process of achieving maturity by moving out of her father's house into another man's house, she is supposed to give no trouble. While Beatrice Rappaccini approximates this image, Elsie Venner is a source of lifelong pain and suffering to her father. As a daughter, she is a disaster.

In an ordinary town, too, Elsie's beauty and sensuality are aberrant. Early in the novel, the narrator muses on beauty. While "in the abstract we all love beauty," to be beautiful also "carries an atmosphere of repulsion." Many people are "too poor, too ordinary, too humble, too busy, too proud" (125–26) to pay the price for loving an unusually beautiful person. Most people are, like Bernard, ordinary, and avoid the extraordinary. In the novel, Elsie is regarded as extraordinary by all, but she is seldom depicted as doing anything very unusual. There is little objective correlative to the fictional judgments. This could be a flaw in the narrative technique, but it could also reflect the fact that everything the narrator knows about her is filtered through the perceptions of conventional people.

These ordinary people live happily and bloodlessly ever after: Bernard finishes medical school, sets up a successful practice, and marries a "safe little lass,"[84] the granddaughter of the Rev. Dr. Honeywood (of the famous banking family). Even Dudley Venner remarries, allying himself with the soothing schoolmarm, Helen Darley. For Elsie, who loved someone not up to the challenge of loving her, the eulogy is spoken by Dr. Honeywood: "From the life and the death of this our dear sister we should learn a lesson of patience with our fellow-creatures in their inborn peculiarities, of charity in judging what seems to us wilful faults of character" (458). Judge not, lest you be judged; approach your fellow creatures with charity, all the more when dealing with the unusual person. Because the evidence of Elsie's venomousness is inconclusive, venom becomes, in addition to a symbol of female sexuality, also a symbol of divergence from socially imposed norms.

And so Elsie may not marry. The unusual woman cannot reproduce herself without a courageous male to accept her in all her fearful complexity. For Bernard to respond to Elsie, he would have to ignore the voices of his upbringing that encourage him to quell the stirrings of passion and take the safe and intelligent path through life. Retreating from the challenge, Bernard never completes the psychic work of confronting his own sexual nature. Back in medical school, he reads a paper entitled "Unresolved Nebulae in Vital Science" (481). He has learned nothing from his unresolved relationship with Elsie. For him, there will always be areas of darkness in his understanding of life because he approaches life as a science, not an art. His marriage follows the chastity prescription, taming once and for all the dangerous emotions connected with Elsie. But when one marries so as not to burn, much is lost. In Bernard, all passion is buried. He is like the "terrible Rattlesnake Ledge" itself, which, after the earthquake, "with all its envenomed reptiles, its dark fissures and black caverns, was buried forever beneath a mighty incumbent mass of ruin" (464). Lost forever too is Bernard's opportunity to be extraordinary, like Elsie.

POISON AND THE EXTRAORDINARY

Well-informed medical men like Holmes and his fictional professor might have been influenced in their perception of Elsie as venomous by a long (and very dull) poem, *The Botanic Garden, Part II. Containing the Loves of the Plants: A Poem with Philosophical Notes*, written by Erasmus Darwin and published in 1790.[85] Its purpose was, in Darwin's words, to explain the then-controversial "sexual system of Linneus" (B), which, somewhat vulgarly for the time, classified plants according to the arrangement of stamens, construed as male, and pistils, female. Darwin described the process as a courtship and marriage, the pistils as "virgins" being wooed by varying numbers of "swains," the taller stamens getting more impressive names such as "knights" and "lords," the shorter, less favorably termed "squires" or "menial youths." The poem is written in romantic (not to say flowery) language, the notes in more crassly scientific language. The process of reproduction in the *curcuma*, a plant having five stamens, looks this way to Darwin:

> Woo'd with long care, *curcuma* cold and shy
> Meets her fond husband with averted eye:
> *Four* beardless youths the obdurate beauty move
> With soft attentions of Platonic love.

> (I, ll. 65–69)

Such, however, is not the behavior of poisonous plants. These, to which Darwin devotes himself in Canto III, are given to less modest behavior. Reproduction in the poisonous plants is a steamier matter altogether: no averted eyes or Platonic love here. *Circaea*, or enchanter's nightshade, which is "much celebrated in the mysteries of witchcraft, and for the purpose of raising the devil," which "grows amid . . . mouldering bones and decayed coffins," is described as engaging itself in various witchlike activities in funereal settings featuring screaming bats, tombs, hideous laughter, and trappings of a black mass (98 nn). *Laura*, "the most sudden poison we are acquainted with in this country," is the antithesis of the demure *curcuma*. *Laura* has a "laboring bosom...foam on her lips, and fury in her eyes... wild dishevell'd hair" (III, ll. 41–43). In fact, her behavior launches Darwin into a digression on erotic dreams (a young girl in bed with an allegorical Nightmare). Climbing venomous plants are very bad: they pretend to be the sweet ladies of Cantos I and II, "in the meek garb of modest worth disguised, / The eye averted, and the smile chastised." But in reality they are "Harlot-nymphs" who "spread their dangerous charms, / And round their victim wind their wiry arms" (III, ll. 329–32). The host plant, a horticultural version of Mortdant in *The Faerie Queene*, is seduced and destroyed. Other poisonous plants are similarly described. For Erasmus Darwin, plants with demure and ladylike pistils are ready symbols of acceptable habits in courtship and marriage. Their sexuality is tamed and licit. Plants with unpleasant behaviors are described in terms of witchcraft and illicit (because too powerful) sexuality. In *The Botanic Garden*, only the pistils misbehave; the stamens, for all their being "knights" and "lords," are victims.

In retrospect, Darwin's correlation between poison and the sexually threatening woman clarifies the problems in the hero's relationship with the serpentine woman. Most of these young men are like the "swains" or "beardless youths" in Darwin's garden; they are not like Demetrius in the Plutarch story, unthreatened by the unusual woman and independent of the advice of counselors. The threatened hero is more like the men of the Mandeville legend who let others make the dangerous journey before them.

In the Mélusine story, the hero, Raymond, at first does dare to deal with a powerful woman on her own terms. As a result he shares in her power; he does not become its victim. But the story's divergence from the usual romance that ends in marriage emphasizes the continuing development necessary to maintain the relationship. Usually the romance heroine is the reward for demonstrated prowess; she brings to the hero "stability, virtue, and the end of adventure."[86] Mélusine, however, is problematic after marriage. Again unlike the typical romance heroine, passive, "acted upon rather than acting," Mélusine is continually busy planning Raymond's military moves, building, cultivating, bearing offspring.[87] Raymond cannot relax after having passed one test; he finds that marriage to the serpent-woman is a continual test. While he might feel that he has a right to expect a typical romance heroine, enduring and patient, "not...in any way unusual or more capable than other women,"[88] much less himself, what he has is a woman so unusual that she is supernatural.

This places him in the same situation as Lycius in *Lamia* and Bernard Langdon in *Elsie Venner*. Those older men who represent the status quo are threatened by the younger men's relationship with a serpentine (or supernatural or just unusual) woman. It is as if they believe that every man has the right to an unvenomous flower in his garden, to an ordinary wife, in whom the poison of power is muted. If marriage is supposed to be a remedy for lust, then a dispassionate courtship, followed presumably by an even chillier marriage, seems desirable. The message of the mentors is to avoid an unusual woman. Exclude her from the ordinary life of women, involving marriage and childbearing, lest her influence extend into future generations as Mélusine's does through her numerous progeny. The retreat of the hero ensures that this woman will not reproduce herself; her race will die out.

5

Conclusion: Beatrice Rappaccini

For evil are women, my children; and since they have no power or strength over man, they use wiles by outward attractions, that they may draw him to themselves. And whom they cannot bewitch by outward attractions, him they overcome by craft.... Women are overcome by the spirit of fornication more than men, and in their heart they plot against men; and by means of their adornments they deceive their minds, and by the glance of the eye instil the poison, and then through the accomplished act they take them captive. For a woman cannot force a man openly, but by a harlot's bearing she beguiles him. Flee therefore, fornication, my children, and command your wives and your daughters, that they adorn not their heads and their faces to deceive the mind: because every woman who useth these wiles hath been reserved for eternal punishment. For thus they allured the Watchers who were before the flood.

Testament of Reuben[1]

In 1839 Nathaniel Hawthorne transcribed into his notebook the following passage from Sir Thomas Browne's *Pseudodoxia Epidemica* (1646): " 'A story there passeth of an Indian king that sent unto Alexander a fair woman, fed with aconite and other poisons, with this intent complexionally to destroy him!'—Sir T. Browne."[2] This same Alexander the Great story, which had occupied the attention of writers on poisons for hundreds of years and which Holmes used in his novel sixteen years later, grew into the plot of "Rappaccini's Daughter," the most sophisticated treatment of the venomous woman theme in Western literature.

Hawthorne had long shown an interest in the correspondence between physical and moral evil symbolized by poison. Like medieval and Renaissance medical writers, Hawthorne was attracted by the metaphorical thinking needed to "symbolize moral or spiritual disease by disease of the body." In the note that probably developed into his story "Egotism, or the Bosom

Serpent," the snake that the man swallows is described as a "symbol of a cherished sin." Later that year, after recording Browne's entry but before publishing "Rappaccini's Daughter" in 1844, Hawthorne transcribed this story:

Madame Calderon de la B (in Life in Mexico) speaks of persons who have been inoculated with the venom of rattlesnakes, by pricking them in various places with the tooth. These persons are thus secured forever after against the bite of any venomous reptile. They have the power of calling snakes, and feel great pleasure in playing with and handling them. Their own bite becomes poisonous to people not inoculated in the same manner. Thus a part of the serpent's nature appears to be transfused into them.[3]

Here Hawthorne explores the idea of the antidotal properties of venom itself and the ambiguity surrounding the idea of poison as moral metaphor. In his diary for 1837–1838, he wrote: "A company of persons to drink a certain medicinal preparation, and it to prove a poison or the contrary, according to their different characters."[4] For these people, poison is a relative, not an absolute. Another idea for a story: "To poison a person, or a party of persons, with the sacramental wine"—good and evil merging in the poisonous fluid. In "Rappaccini's Daughter," he uses some significant elements of the conventional theme and apparently adheres closely to the traditional symbolism of woman as seducer. Although he fuses the two images of woman and poison, he omits the image of the serpent, which could have reinforced a more negative characterization. Instead, in creating Beatrice Rappaccini, he explores all the ambiguities he found in the idea of a being whose spirit is innocent but whose flesh is poisonous.

In Holmes's *Elsie Venner*, Bernard Langdon's response to Elsie is limited by his medical adviser's ignorance of one interpretation of the Alexander the Great story, based on Andrea Bacci's homeopathic theory. Bacci said that the envenomed maiden would not, in fact, "have poisoned Alexander the Great, had he lain with her, because what she ate would have been transformed into nutrition."[5] Through Sir Thomas Browne's discussion of the issue, Hawthorne was exposed to this more complex tradition concerning the venomous woman's antidotal properties. Knowingly or not, Browne follows Bacci's theory. Right before the Alexander the Great story in *Pseudodoxia Epidemica*, where Hawthorne must have seen it, Browne cites the cardinal rule of homeopathic medicine: "one contrary hath another, and poison is not without a poison unto itself." Applying this principle to Alexander's maiden, Browne expresses doubt that she could poison others. He reasons by analogy with the animal kingdom. In animals, the interaction of the poison with the organism produces a chemical change. Ingested poisons are "so refracted . . . and subdued as not to make good their first destructive malignities." Not only are such poisons weakened, they become their own contraries: "Animals that can innoxiously digest these poisons, become antidotal unto the poison digested."[6] Thus poisonous flesh becomes homeopathic nourishment, and it is this strand of the tradition that becomes the basis for the complex characterization of Beatrice as a combination of sexual seductress and spiritual savior. Beatrice, like all other people, is a creature of body and soul, each with different characteristics. On the one hand, men have always been warned that women's beauty draws them to physical and spiritual ruin. Yet, paradoxically, could Giovanni perceive and respond to this one unusual woman, to her unique blessedness, he would be saved.

Twentieth-century criticism of "Rappaccini's Daughter" tends to see Giovanni as a flawed hero because of his neurotic fear of adult female sexuality,[7] which causes him to regress to psychological infancy for fear of "being dominated by a woman...and having his personality swallowed up."[8] According to this reading, the story dramatized the classic male fear of entrapment so often found in stories of venomous women. Another contemporary interpretation of Beatrice sees her as one who "suffers from an acute case of inhibition"[9] and a perverted erotic attraction to the venomous plant in her garden, which is deviant not only in being a hybrid but is also described as female and her sister.[10] Like Elsie, she is too strongly and too amorphously sexual to be an appropriate wife. Giovanni is not strong enough to accept Beatrice;[11] and in his fearful withdrawal he is similar to all the other heroes who retreat from the serpent-woman. Post-Freudian interpretations of "Rappaccini's Daughter" mirror twentieth-century preoccupations, but Hawthorne would have been more concerned with exploring the true nature of the virtue of chastity than with analyzing sexual neuroses. In a recent interpretation of *The Scarlet Letter*, "the marriage relationship ...becomes a metaphor for the Paradox of the Fortunate Fall."[12] The same is true in "Rappaccini's Daughter," and the paradox is strengthened by the poison metaphor.

Hawthorne saw chastity as a great virtue. In a notebook entry for July 13, 1837, he describes a Mr. Shaeffer whom he particularly admires because he "preaches obedience to the law of reason and morality; which law he says (and I believe him) that he has so well observed, that, notwithstanding his residence in dissolute countries, he has never yet sinned with a woman."[13] Similarly, in his *American Notebook* entry for September 7, 1838, Hawthorne expresses astonishment at the sympathy of a Mr. Leach for a girl who had once " 'strayed from virtue.' Mr. Leach spoke to me as if one deviation from chastity might not be an altogether insuperable objection to making a girl his wife!"[14] Dr. Rappaccini might have been modeled on a contemporary of Hawthorne who punished for violations of chastity. George Rapp, a Unitarian commune builder in the Midwest in the early 1800s, constructed a symbolic garden controlled by a beautiful girl, Hildegard. The commune was celibate; violations were cause for dismissal. This

Hildegard was forgiven even though she had violated her vows; Rapp's controversial decision led to a schism. On the other hand, male violators were treated more harshly. Rapp was thought to have murdered or at least castrated his son for sexual sins.[15] That people believed this story, whether true or apocryphal, shows the high value placed on chastity in Hawthorne's day. But if Hawthorne knew the story of George Rapp, the irony becomes clear: if perfect chastity is practiced, one's sons are murdered; there are soon no men to be chaste. A *via media* must be found; the flesh and the spirit must be reconciled, and the female is a perfect symbol for both the problem and its solution. Beatrice is absolutely sexual yet totally chaste as well, like Elsie Venner. There must be a way for such women to find a life in which their dual natures can be expressed. The solution lies in the reconciliation of flesh and spirit in a marriage based on the love of a man for both body and spirit. To find such a man is not easy. The same question that Elsie's father asked of his daughter must be asked of Beatrice also: Who will dare to marry her?

As the story opens, Giovanni Guasconti is a young man in a prelapsarian state of sexual innocence. It is "the first time out of his native sphere" (93),[16] his first exposure, alone and away from home, to the new region of sexual experience. The mansion in which he stays is associated with hell. His room, like Giovanni himself, is above the garden of Rappaccini. To associate with Beatrice, he must deliberately descend and consent to his fall. The overt association of Rappaccini's garden with Eden points to the pattern of innocence seduced. The sexual initiation of the innocent young man is the repetition of the Fall in the life of the individual, and Beatrice is the instrument through which the fall takes place.

Yet Beatrice herself is not evil. She is virginal, "redundant with life, health and energy" (97). The paradox of Beatrice's nature is foreshadowed in the characterization of old Lisabetta. The first time Giovanni meets Lisabetta, her language is full of prayers for his salvation, prayers he certainly needs because he is about to be tested. The second time Giovanni meets her, she acts as procuress, arranging the interview between Beatrice and Giovanni in the garden. Lisabetta's behavior points to the characterization of Beatrice. As a woman, Beatrice can touch poison and not die; that is, she can operate in the world of sexuality and not be corrupted. Indeed, she must; her sexuality may be a powerful attraction to the male and chaste resistance to it a great virtue, but perfect chastity for all means the end of the human race. To function as life source, the female must reconcile her physical and spiritual natures. As Dr. Rappaccini urges her, she must exult in her " 'marvellous gifts against which no power, nor strength could avail an enemy.' " Without these, she would be " 'a weak woman, exposed to all evil and capable of none' " (127).[17] Like the true believer in Scripture, she can touch poison and not be harmed.

Giovanni has not yet reached this point of spiritual/physical integration. All he can see is the destructive effects of sexual experience on the male, according to the ancient medical beliefs still current in Hawthorne's day. The lizard's death symbolizes the depletion of the male body in sex; the butterfly perishes as his soul may; the mentor, Dr. Baglioni, warns him about the dangers of the poisoned maiden; Beatrice's fingers burn his flesh in lust; the flowers of his own virginity wilt and die. All these are traditional emblems for the destructive allure of the female. Because of the medical and theological beliefs of the time, the male perceives himself as risking the health of his body and the salvation of his immortal soul when he allows himself to respond to the attraction of the female. "Flower and maiden," the female sex organ and the owner thereof, are "fraught with some strange peril" (98). Yet he cannot resist her: "The instant that he was aware of the possibility of approaching Beatrice, it seemed an absolute necessity of his existence to do so," (109). His rational side knows that he should not be "thrusting himself into an incalculable position" (109). When he descends into the garden, in a section of the story filled with unmistakable sexual metaphors, he is doing so as a conscious yielding to the imperatives of his sexual nature. It is a motion downward, and it is described in terms of entrapment: "Giovanni stepped forth, and forcing himself through the entanglement of a shrub that wreathed its tendrils over the hidden entrance, he stood beneath his own window, in the open area of Dr. Rappaccini's garden" (109). Even without the metaphorical consummation of the kiss, Giovanni has yielded to the poisoned maiden and, according to the old tradition, fallen into sin and death, despite the warnings of an adviser and of his own reason.

But, as Browne reasons, one poison cancels out another; the poisoned creature does not poison others but can be an antidote. Hawthorne does not use the old tradition as the basis of simple allegory. In "Rappaccini's Daughter," the nature of sexual sin is ambiguous. Sexuality perpetuates the human race, yet it is limited by prohibitions and guilt. There is a Manichaean duality in the messages Giovanni receives. Dr. Rappaccini, a god of "evil," creates the body of the female to lure the male to destruction. Dr. Baglioni, a god of "good," warns against her power and supplies an antidote, "a medicine potent... and almost divine in its efficacy" (126): chastity. Giovanni invites Beatrice to " 'quaff' " this medicine, to be " 'purified from evil' " (126). But the matter is not so simple as a choice between the evils of the flesh and the virtues of the spirit. A more complex judgment must be made. If Beatrice is venomous, it is only in the flesh; in the spirit she is pure, blessed. When Giovanni responds to Beatrice only as a physical being, he can see only the "evil" in her. But if he could respond to the totality of Beatrice, to her spirit and not just her flesh, this fuller acceptance would be an antidote against the sin of unchastity, now redefined by Hawthorne as sensuality without spirituality. "Rappaccini's Daughter" is "the most explicit condemnation of unhallowed sex that Hawthorne ever published,"[18] and sex is unhallowed precisely because it remains unconsummated out of fear and misunderstanding. The corruption in Giovanni is his limited response to Beatrice as body only. Because the voices of his tradition warn him of the dangers associated with women's bodies, he does not allow his physical attraction for Beatrice to develop into love for her whole self. As in both *Lamia* and *Elsie Venner*, the young man must come to an understanding of the venomous woman as person rather than as a simple symbol of evil.[19]

When Giovanni causes Beatrice to drink the "antidote," she dies because the antidote is a response to only her physical nature. The true antidote is Beatrice herself. The traditional reconciliation of flesh and spirit is marriage, not just as a remedy for concupiscence but as a legitimate expression of it. Giovanni and Beatrice are free to marry; they are capable of this reconciliation, but Giovanni is afraid. He is all the more fallen in that his attraction for Beatrice cannot generate new life but rather destroys the life source. Love unconsummated for the wrong reasons is itself a violation of chastity in that it is unproductive. Giovanni fails the test of Dr. Rappaccini's experiment. He is not able to reconcile flesh and spirit. He has not truly preserved his chastity, nor has he redeemed its loss by creating a new life with a remarkable woman.

Like Bernard Langdon, Giovanni is held back from the success he could have achieved by the inadequacy of his mentor's traditional message. Dr. Baglioni treats Beatrice as a physical being only. If the true antidote is Beatrice herself, Dr. Baglioni's spurious antidote becomes itself a poison. As an allopathic physician, Dr. Baglioni is "convinced that heroic doses of medication are the only cures."[20] It is as if Dr. Baglioni is a representative of those religious traditions that prescribe heroic doses of chastity as a response to the needs of the flesh. He clearly disapproves of the way Dr. Rappaccini has made his daughter; moral prohibitions against sexuality represent objection to the Creator's modus operandi. This remedy responds only to Beatrice's flesh, and so it kills the flesh. Baglioni's medical error and Giovanni's incomplete perception of Beatrice combine to kill Beatrice. Neither of them can understand that Beatrice is not poisonous but is rather an antidote to the venom she had been fed. Beatrice's pure spirit has transformed the venomous substance into remedy. Giovanni is too immature, and his mentor is too committed to his own allopathic approach, to see that the old correspondence between physical and moral poison has broken down.[21] Not allopathic but homeopathic medicine is appropriate here because ingested poisons become their own remedies, and so, "if like cures like, these two should be able to cure each other by bodily contact."[22]

In addition to Beatrice's physical venomousness, fearful enough in itself, another threatening characteristic allies her with the *venefica* characters of the literary past. Beatrice is, according to Dr. Baglioni, not only " 'young and beautiful' " but also " 'qualified to fill a professor's chair' " (101). Excluded from the ordinary channels of medical education at the University of Padua by her sex, she is apprenticed to her father, much as a medieval woman healer might have been. Although she restricts herself to assisting her father, the mere fact of her having a degree and kind of knowledge unusual for a woman is enough to engender both amazement and hostility in a traditionalist like Dr. Baglioni, attitudes he passes along to his student, Giovanni. Baglioni's prescription of the deadly potion is then an attempt to show that he knows more than his rival Rappaccini; through the potion, as Carol Marie Bensick points out, traditional patriarchal authority is asserted against the power of "the rogue experimentalist and his scientific daughter."[23] Beatrice is intelligent enough to know that the gift of education conferred on her by her father is yet another way of rendering her less marriageable, removing her even further from the possibility of leading a normal woman's life. As in the *venefica* tradition, the combination of intelligence and sexuality in one being is too much for an ordinary young man to handle. Beatrice's learning complicates Giovanni's initiation task even further.

In literature, when a young man goes into a garden, he often finds a seductress there. His test, his moral task, is to distinguish the apparent earthly paradise from the heavenly one. The classic Renaissance garden is "the beautiful-seeming earthly paradise which is in reality a dangerous and deceptive place where man's will is softened, his moral fiber unraveled, and his soul ensnared. It is the garden where insidious luxury and sensual love overcome duty and true devotion."[24] In Hawthorne this old dichotomy breaks down, and ambiguity is substituted. There are elements of the classical garden: Giovanni forgets the purpose of his visit to Italy in his obsession with Beatrice. Beatrice, however, is not the conventional temptress in the garden. The complexity of Giovanni's decision is embodied in Beatrice's dual nature. There is no real split between her "poisonous" body and her "antidotal" spirit. But Giovanni is a student; if even his mentor fails to realize this, how can he? In the Renaissance epic, "the narrator will pass through and break out of this paradise turned dungeon of the mind; but certainly not without anguish and expense, and ... lingering regret."[25] Giovanni gets out of the garden but without resolving the moral issues encountered there. His opportunity for blessedness is lost. His concern has been all for himself, and this is the poison in his nature that Beatrice refers to in her dying words. Concern for the self, failure to risk the self in the act of procreation that would have redeemed him, are the poisons that destroy the life force. Hawthorne has appropriately named his hero after the Italian verb *guastare*, to spoil or destroy, to taint or infect.[26] It is Giovanni, not Beatrice, who is envenomed in both body and spirit. Beatrice has drawn him to an awareness of the venom that was always in his nature. Giovanni's chastity, while apparently a good, is really only fear of risk. Would Giovanni dare, he could, in Dr. Rappaccini's words, stand apart from " 'common men' " as Beatrice does from " 'ordinary women' " (127).

This is the challenge offered to the hero in every venomous woman story. Giovanni's tragedy is like that of all the others: he is too ordinary to comprehend the venomous woman.

POISON AND FEMALE SEXUALITY

Discussing the impact of St. Augustine's thinking on misogynism in Christian theology, Rosemary Ruether says that Augustine makes a distinction "between what woman is, as a rational spirit," and "what she 'symbolizes' in her bodily nature." In the spirit, she is "equivalent to the male"; but in the body, she "stands for the subjection of body to spirit in nature and the debasing carnality that draws the mind down from its heavenly heights." For Augustine, the division between flesh and spirit is more pronounced, it seems, in women than in men. Having distinguished between what woman is and what she means (to men), Augustine fuses being and seeming again: "he also thinks that what she thus symbolizes, in the eyes of male perception, is also what she 'is' in her feminine nature!" He cannot perceive that all of this is "*from the perspective of the male visual impression of her as a body.*"[27]

If so great a theologian made this error, and as a major voice of tradition transmitted it into the mainstream of Christian theology, it is small wonder that fictional heroes do too. Each is offered the opportunity to transcend the physical/spiritual dichotomy by responding totally to one woman. The symbolic significance of her body is a concept as much imposed from without as her venomousness is; none of the women has chosen her relationship with the venomous or with the ideas it symbolizes. If the man can move beyond his initial simple sensory attraction for the woman, past the barrier of the concepts that describe her, to an understanding of her total and complex being, then his fall into sexuality becomes a fortunate one. In "Rappaccini's Daughter" especially, but in the other serpent-woman stories as well, the reader is even invited to question the metaphor of the fall: why must response to these women be construed as a decline? From what heights? In many ways the serpent-women are superior to those around them. Mélusine, Lamia, Elsie, and Beatrice are beautiful and alluring; except for Mélusine, who has been punished by her mother, their serpentine qualities are not their fault. Mélusine is a good wife and mother and wants to continue to live a normal woman's life; Lamia wants to be "a real woman"; Elsie's misfortunes begin prenatally; and Beatrice is the way her father made her. Unlike the murderers, the potion-makers, and the seductresses, these women are not rebels. Although they are not ordinary, they want to live ordinary lives, married lives, with a man willing to take the risk of a relationship with them. Advisers, voices of reason and tradition—Raymond's brother, Apollonius, Dr. Kittredge, the professor, Dr. Baglioni—prescribe the antidote of avoidance: stay away from a woman who is too unusual. Raymond loses his wife and the political power she brought him; Lycius dies; Bernard Langdon finds the obvious alternative, an ordinary woman; Giovanni is left alone, with his future ambiguous. None of them is up to the challenge that the extraordinary woman poses. They are advised to take the safe course, but this too has its dangers because it does not take into account the complexity of the moral situation. These four men cannot merely protect their innocence; they must venture the new experience to move to a higher plane of existence. If they cannot do so, they are fated to remain ordinary. Instead of drawing back in horror, they are given the chance to accept the Mélusines, the Lamias, the Elsies, the Beatrices of the world in all their terrifying complexity. They all fail this test because of their fear.

And well they might fear, says the misogynistic tradition. Ever since Eve, woman brings death; a man cannot trust her or confidently take what she gives him. Fear of a subtle and secret domestic enemy surely constitutes an admission that there are good reasons for such an enemy to want to escape from her powerless position. Even if she does not resort to murder, she may try to manipulate body or feelings with her special knowledge and dangerous fluids. A man must admit that in at least one crucial area, sexuality, she seems to be much more in control not only of her own body but of his as well. This certainly looks like a fall, is so inexplicable that it must be bewitchment, this succumbing to the influence of a being so small and weak. If she metamorphoses, a man must be almost supernaturally flexible to respond to the shifting demands of a complex and challenging, not soothing and docile, being. When her flesh is envenomed, she seems to be the most dangerous of all. Her partner must overcome all the externally imposed symbolisms invented by other men to describe her to him but to which she herself has never assented. He must learn that she is not what his advisers say she means. But this is a difficult task at which men often fail, responding as does Eliot's Prufrock: "And in short, I was afraid."

Notes

PREFACE: SECRET WEAPON

1. *The Sixteen Satires*, trans. Peter Green (New York: Penguin, 1967) 6: 151.
2. (New York: Bantam, 1961). All references to primary sources will appear in parentheses in the text.
3. Peter R. Gwilt and John R. Gwilt, "The Use of Poison in Detective Fiction," *Clues* 1 (1980): 9.
4. As quoted in Miriam Hirsch, *Women and Violence* (New York: Van Nostrand and Reinhold, 1981) 142.
5. *The Criminality of Women* (Philadelphia: U of Pennsylvania P, 1950) 11, as quoted in Hirsch 142; also cf. Ann Jones, *Women Who Kill* (New York: Holt, 1980) 7.
6. xv–xvi.
7. Hirsch 152.
8. (Bonn: Bouvier Verlag Herbert Grundmann, 1977) 7.
9. In *The Short Stories of Ernest Hemingway* (New York: Modern Library, 1938) 102–36.
10. 8.
11. A. T. Hatto, introduction, *Tristan*, by Gottfried von Strassburg, trans. A. T. Hatto (Thirteenth century; New York: Penguin, 1960) 7.
12. According to M. M. McCrea in "Sex and Suicide," *Psychology Today* (July 1984): 12, guns are catching up as women become more comfortable with "male" behavior.

1. INTRODUCTION: ARCHETYPES AND STEREOTYPES

1. *In Defense of Women* (New York: Knopf, 1922) 176.
2. (New York: Random House, 1941).
3. Quoted in Fredson Bowers, "The Audience and the Poisoners of Elizabethan Tragedy," *JEGP* 36 (1937): note 497.
4. Elisabeth G. Gitter, "The Power of Women's Hair in the Victorian Imagination," *PMLA* 99.5 (1984): 936–54.
5. In *The Portable Faulkner*, ed. Malcolm Cowley (New York: Viking, 1967).

6. British Library, MS Royal 17EIV, f. 872, as reproduced in Frances Gies and Joseph Gies, *Women in the Middle Ages* (New York: Barnes, 1978) 171.

7. *Haven in a Heartless World: The Family Besieged* (New York: Basic, 1977).

8. Trans. Robert Fitzgerald (New York: Doubleday Anchor, 1963) x. References are to page numbers.

9. As quoted in Julia O'Faolain and Lauro Martines, *Not in God's Image: Women in History from the Greeks to the Victorians* (New York: Harper, 1973) 7.

10. 62.

11. Sybille Harksen, *Women in the Middle Ages* (New York: Abner Schram, 1975) plate 104; cf. Barbara Ehrenreich and Deirdre English, *Witches, Midwives, and Nurses: A History of Women Healers* (Westbury, N.Y.: Feminist P, 1973) 11.

12. *Against Our Will: Men, Women and Rape* (New York: Bantam, 1976) 5.

13. Nathaniel Hawthorne, "Rappaccini's Daughter," *Mosses from an Old Manse* (1846; Columbus: Ohio State UP, 1974) 91–128.

14. 175–76.

2. MOTHER EVE AND OTHER DEATH-DEALERS

1. Quoted in Marina Warner, *Alone of All Her Sex: The Myth and the Cult of the Virgin Mary* (New York: Vintage, 1983) 59.

2. *The Forerunner of Revenge, Vpon the Duke of Buckingham for the poysoning of the most potent King Iames . . . and the Lord Marquis of Hamilton* (Franckfort, 1626) 10, as quoted in Bowers 497.

3. Ronald Frye, *Milton's Imagery and the Visual Arts* (Princeton: Princeton UP, 1978) plate 198.

4. Frye 103.

5. Frye 104; cf. John K. Bonnel, "The Serpent with a Human Head in Art and Mystery Play," *American Journal of Archaeology* 21 (1917): 265.

6. John A. Phillips, *Eve: The History of an Idea* (San Francisco: Harper, 1984) 39.

7. Moncure David Conway, *Demonology and Demon Lore*, 2 vols. (London: Chatto and Windus, 1879) 2: 100.

8. Phillips 39.

9. Conway 2: 96.

10. George H. Tavard, *Women in Christian Tradition* (Notre Dame: U of Notre Dame P, 1973) 89.

11. As quoted in Katherine Rogers, *The Troublesome Helpmate: A History of Misogyny in Literature* (Seattle: U of Washington P, 1966) 20.

12. Phillips 43.

13. Rogers 71.

14. Trans. Guido A. Guarino (1361; New Brunswick: Rutgers UP, 1963) 2.

15. O'Faolain and Martines 132.

16. O'Faolain and Martines 130.

17. Trans. Horace Gregory (New York: Mentor/NAL, 1958) 9: 247–53.

18. *The Complete Plays of Sophocles*, trans. Richard Claverhouse Jebb, ed. Moses Hadas (New York: Bantam, 1982) 149–80.

19. Madeline Pelner Cosman, *Fabulous Feasts: Medieval Cookery and Ceremony* (New York: Braziller, 1976) 29–30.

20. Lynn Thorndike, *A History of Magic and Experimental Science*, 8 vols. (New York: Macmillan, 1929–1934) 3: 34–35.

21. Charles Singer and E. Ashworth Underwood, *A Short History of Medicine*, 2d edition (New York: Oxford UP, 1962) 60.

22. David Riesman, *The Story of Medicine in the Middle Ages* (New York: Hoeber, 1936) 74.

23. Thorndike 5: 496; cf. Riesman 302–3.

24. Thorndike 1: 25, 61, 441.

25. Thorndike 2: 905, 909.

26. Thorndike 2: 905; V, 60; VI, 223.

27. Wilfred Bonser, "General Medical Practice in Anglo-Saxon England," *Science, Medicine, and History: Essays on the Evolution of Scientific Thought and Medical Practice written in honour of Charles Singer*, ed. E. Ashworth Underwood, 2 vols. (New York: Oxford UP, 1953) 1: 161.

28. Russell Hope Robbins, "Medical Manuscripts in Middle English," *Speculum* 45 (1970): 400.

29. Thorndike 6: 423.

30. Thorndike 7: 503.

31. All quotations from Chaucer are from *The Riverside Chaucer*, Larry D. Benson, based on the second F. N. Robinson edition (Boston: Houghton, 1987).

32. Riesman 67.

33. Thorndike 3: 34.

34. A manuscript account of Bianca's death and source for the play is included in appendix I of the J. R. Mulryne edition of *Women Beware Women* (early 1620s; London: Methuen, 1975) 177.

35. Riesman 178.

36. Thorndike 3: 18–20.

37. F. J. Child, *The English and Scottish Popular Ballads*, 5 vols. (1884; rpt. New York: Dover, 1965) 1: 160 (version D).

38. E. Flatto, " 'Lord Randal,' " *Southern Folklore Quarterly* 34.4 (1970): 332.

39. Cosman 40.

40. Robert Paquin, " 'Le Testament du Garcon Empoisonné': A French 'Lord Randal' in Acadie," *Folklore* 91.2 (1980): 163.

41. Flatto 335.

42. Flatto 334.

43. Joseph E. Grennen, "Chaunticleer's 'Venymous Cathartics,' " *Notes and Queries* 10 (1963): 286–87.

44. Sir Thomas Malory, *Works*, ed. Eugène Vinaver (c. 1450; Oxford: Oxford UP, 1977). Where there are variant spellings for characters' names in various versions of the same story, I have retained a common familiar spelling in my text and have used the original author's spelling in direct quotations.

45. Sadahide Kato, "Alice Arden of Feversham and her Company of Evil," *Poetry and Drama in the Age of Shakespeare*, Renaissance Monographs 9 (Tokyo: Renaissance Institute of Sophia U, 1982) 190.

46. 498–504.

47. *The Tragedy of Master Arden of Faversham*, ed. M. L. Wine (1592; London: Methuen, 1973).

48. Sybil Truchet, "Alice Arden and the Religion of Love," *Caliban* 17 (1980): 39.

49. Alexander Leggatt, " 'Arden of Faversham,' " *Shakespeare Studies* 36 (1983): 124.

50. Eugene P. Walz, " 'Arden of Faversham' as Dramatic Satire," *Massachusetts Studies in English* 4.2 (1973): 25.

51. See appendix II in the Methuen edition, 148–59, esp. 149, for Holinshed's account of the poisoning attempt.

52. Michael T. Marsden, "The Otherworld of 'Arden of Faversham,' " *Southern Folklore Quarterly* 36 (1972): 37.

53. Thorndike 3: 533.

54. Methuen edition, appendix II, 149.

55. 124.

56. Leggatt 131.

57. Walz 24–25.

58. Catherine Belsey, "Alice Arden's Crime," *Renaissance Drama* 8 (1982): 89.

59. O'Faolain and Martines 146.

60. Ben Jonson, *Sejanus*, ed. Jonas Barish (1603; New Haven: Yale UP, 1965). The argument appears on 29 in this edition.

61. Daniel C. Boughner, "Sejanus and Machiavelli," *Studies in English Literature* 1.2 (1961): 81–100.

62. "Face-Painting in Renaissance Tragedy," *Renaissance Drama* 12 (1981): 82–83.

63. Thorndike 5: 459.

64. (London: Edward Marchant, 1616). Drew-Bear's article called my attention to Tuke's treatise, but the reading of it hereafter is my own.

65. All the information on this crime is from William McElwee, *The Murder of Sir Thomas Overbury* (London: Faber and Faber, 1952), and from Beatrice White, *Cast of Ravens: The Strange Case of Sir Thomas Overbury* (London: John Murray, 1965); for thoroughly documented information on the case, see White's book.

66. A. L. Rowse, in *Sex and Society in Shakespeare's Age: Simon Forman the Astrologer* (New York: Scribner's, 1974) exonerates Forman from complicity in the Overbury poisoning (but not necessarily from the love potion episode) on the excellent grounds that Forman died in 1611, two years before Overbury; White concurs (58).

67. White 32–33.

68. McElwee 82.

69. McElwee 93.

70. McElwee 170.

71. 52.

72. Anne Lancashire, "*The Witch*: Stage Flop or Political Mistake?" "*Accompaninge the players*": *Essays Celebrating Thomas Middleton, 1580–1980*, ed. Kenneth Friedenreich (New York: AMS, 1983) 168.

73. J. R. Mulryne, introduction, *Women Beware Women*, by Thomas Middleton (early 1620s; London: Methuen, 1975) xliv–xlv.

74. Mulryne, introduction lxi.

75. Irving Ribner, "Middleton's *Women Beware Women*: Poetic Imagery and the Moral Vision," *Tulane Studies in English* 9 (1959): 22.

76. George Core, "The Canker and the Muse: Imagery in *Women Beware Women*," *Renaissance Papers* (1968): 75.

77. Larry Champion, "Tragic Vision in Middleton's *Women Beware Women*," *English Studies* 57 (1976): 413.

78. Paolo de Certaldo, *Handbook of Good Customs* (c. 1360), as quoted in O'Faolain and Martines 169.

79. *The English Gentlewoman Drawne out to the full Body* (1631) 42, as quoted in Caroline Lockett Cherry, *The Most Unvaluedst Purchase: Women in the Plays of Thomas Middleton*, Jacobean Drama Studies 34 (Salzburg: Institut für Englische Sprache und Literatur, 1973) 9–10.

80. Mulryne, introduction lx.

81. Daniel Dodson, "Middleton's Livia," *Philological Quarterly* 27.4 (1948): 380.

82. Thomas Middleton, *Women Beware Women*, ed. J. R. Mulryne (early 1620s; London: Methuen, 1975).

83. Dorothy Farr, *Thomas Middleton and the Drama of Realism: A Study of Some Representative Plays* (New York: Harper, 1973) 82.

84. Kenneth Muir, "The Role of Livia in *Women Beware Women*," *Poetry and Drama, 1570–1700: Essays in Honor of Harold F. Brooks*, ed. Antony Coleman and Antony Hammond (London: Methuen, 1981) 76.

85. Norman A. Brittin, *Thomas Middleton* (New York: Twayne, 1972) 119.

86. G. R. Hibbard, "The Tragedies of Thomas Middleton and the Decadence of the Drama," *Renaissance and Modern Studies* 1 (1957): 44–45.

87. Verna Ann Foster, "The Deed's Creature: The Tragedy of Bianca in *Women Beware Women*," *JEGP* 78 (1979): 516.

88. Brittin 119.

89. J. R. Mulryne, *Thomas Middleton* (London: Longman Group, 1979) 30.

90. J. B. Batchelor, "The Pattern of *Women Beware Women*," *Yearbook of English Studies* 2 (1972): 82.

91. "Word-Play in *Women Beware Women*," *Review of English Studies* ns 12 (1961): 238.

92. Leonora Leet Brodwin, *Elizabethan Love Tragedies, 1587–1625* (New York: New York UP, 1971) 321.

93. Ricks 239.

94. Stephen Wigler, "Parent and Child: The Pattern of Love in *Women Beware Women*," *"Accompaninge the players": Essays Celebrating Thomas Middleton, 1580–1980*, ed. Kenneth Friedenreich (New York: AMS, 1983) 184.

95. Wigler 183.

96. Robert Ornstein, *The Moral Vision of Jacobean Tragedy* (Madison: U of Wisconsin P, 1960) 193.

97. *Themes and Conventions in Elizabethan Tragedy*, 2d ed. (Cambridge: Cambridge UP, 1980) 223.

98. Bradbrook 221.

99. Barbara Baines, *The Lust Motif in the Plays of Thomas Middleton*, Jacobean Drama Studies 29 (Salzburg: Institut für Englische Sprache und Literatur, 1973) 133.

100. As evidence for an incest motif in the play, Wigler argues that Isabella too has chosen a "paternal surrogate" (194) in Hippolito; but I see no evidence in the play for Hippolito's being as much older than Isabella as the Duke is compared to Bianca. Livia seems to treat him as if he is younger than she.

101. Brodwin 323.

102. Foster 512.

103. Foster 513.

104. Mulryne, introduction lxx.

105. Una Ellis-Fermor, *The Jacobean Drama: An Interpretation* (London: Methuen, 1958) 142.

106. Ornstein 193.

107. Hibbard 44–45.

108. Baines 60.

109. Michael McCanles, "The Moral Dialectic of Middleton's *Women Beware Women*," *"Accompaninge the players": Essays Celebrating Thomas Middleton, 1580–1980,* ed. Kenneth Friedenreich (New York: AMS, 1983) 215.

110. Ellis-Fermor 142.

111. Dorothy Krook, *Elements of Tragedy* (New Haven: Yale UP, 1969) 149.

112. Charles Hallett, "The Psychological Drama of *Women Beware Women*," *Studies in English Literature* 12 (1972): 381.

113. Samuel Schoenbaum, *Middleton's Tragedies: A Critical Study* (New York: Columbia UP, 1955) 115–16.

114. Hibbard 51.

115. Charles Hallett, *Middleton's Cynics: A Study of Middleton's Insight into the Moral Psychology of the Mediocre Mind,* Jacobean Drama Studies 47 (Salzburg: Institut für Englische Sprache und Literatur, 1975) 264.

116. Hallett, *Middleton's Cynics* 11.

117. Mulryne, *Thomas Middleton* 31.

118. Mulryne, introduction lxv.

119. Batchelor 83.

120. John Potter, " 'In Time of Sports': Masques and Masking in Middleton's *Women Beware Women*," *Papers in Language and Literature* 18.4 (1982): 380.

121. Brodwin 331.

122. Brodwin 334; cf. Foster 520.

123. T. B. Tomlinson, *A Study of Elizabethan and Jacobean Tragedy* (Cambridge: Cambridge UP, 1964) 166.

124. *The Art of Thomas Middleton* (Oxford: Clarendon P, 1970) 164.

125. Trans. Earl Jeffrey Richards (New York: Persea, 1982) 189–90.

126. *Mythology* (New York: Mentor/NAL, 1940) 288.

127. (New York: Schocken, 1977).

128. (London: Michael Joseph, 1971) 9.

129. 2.

130. 9.

131. 23.

132. 4.

3. *VENEFICA*: HEALER AND WITCH

1. *Arthurian Romances*, trans. W. W. Comfort (London: Everyman's Library, 1983) 130.

2. 3 vols. (1621; London: Chatto and Windus, 1898) 2: 294.

3. Trans. P. A. Chilton (1558; New York: Penguin, 1984) 507–9.

4. *Concerning Famous Women* 35.

5. *Metamorphoses* 7: 191–97.

6. Euripedes, *Medea and Other Plays*, trans. Philip Vellacott (New York: Penguin, 1963) 54.

7. Muriel J. Hughes, *Women Healers in Medieval Life and Literature* (New York: Books for Libraries P, 1943) 23.

8. Hughes 45–50.

9. *The Pastons: A Family in the Wars of the Roses*, ed. Richard Barber (New York: Penguin, 1984) 107.

10. Andrée Lehmann, *Le Rôle de la femme dans l'histoire de France au moyen âge* (Paris: Berger-Levrault, 1952) 473.

11. Hughes 99; Lehmann 474.

12. Lehmann 472–73.

13. O'Faolain and Martines 165, quoting Charles, duke of Calabria.

14. Hughes 19.

15. Hughes 83.

16. Hughes 52–56.

17. Hughes 9.

18. Hughes 93.

19. Hughes 95.

20. Hughes 86.

21. Thorndike 8: 360.

22. Ovid, *The Art of Love*, in *The Erotic Poems*, trans. Peter Green (New York: Penguin, 1982) book II, ll. 99–103.

23. Thorndike 1: 61, 94.

24. Thorndike 2: 904, 905; 6: 147, 419.

25. Thorndike 2: 605.

26. "Ligature," *The Encyclopedia of Witchcraft and Demonology* by Russell Hope Robbins (New York: Crown, 1959) 305–7; cf. Thorndike 6: 539, 546, 548.

27. Robbins, "Maleficia" 331.

28. Jeffrey Burton Russell, *Witchcraft in the Middle Ages* (Ithaca: Cornell UP, 1972) 280.

29. Trans. and with an introduction by Montague Summer (1484; London: Pushkin P, 1948).

30. Robbins, "Malleus Maleficarum" 337.

31. Ed. and with an introduction by Brinsley Nicholson (1584; London: Rowman and Littlefield, 1973).

32. Nicholson, introduction xxxiii.

33. King James I, *Daemonologie* (1597; New York: Barnes, 1966) 42–49.

34. Thorndike 8: 577.

35. Fernando de Rojas, *Celestina*, trans. James Mabbe (1499; trans. 1631; New York: AMS P, 1967).

36. 3: 549.

37. *The Lais of Marie de France*, trans. and with an introduction and notes by Robert Hanning and Joan Ferrante (1160?–1215?; Durham, NC: Labyrinth P, 1978).

38. Hanning and Ferrante 135.

39. Margot M. Sinka, "Wound Imagery in Gottfried's 'Tristan,' " *South Atlantic Bulletin* 42.2 (1977): 3–10.

40. References to the Tristan story in this section are to the Gottfried/Thomas version, trans. A. T. Hatto (c. 1210; New York: Penguin, 1960).

41. Gerard J. Brault, "Isolt and Guenevere," *The Role of Women in the Middle Ages*, Papers of the Sixth American Conference of the Center for Medieval and Early Renaissance Studies, State University of New York at Binghamton, 6–7 May 1972, ed. Rosemary Thee Morewedge (Albany: State U of New York P, 1975) 50.

42. As quoted in John H. Fisher, "Tristan and Courtly Adultery," *Comparative Literature* 9 (1957): 150.

43. Joan Ferrante, *The Conflict of Love and Honor: The Medieval Tristan Legend in France, Germany and Italy* (The Hague and Paris: Mouton, 1973) 7, 16, 92.

44. *Woman as Image in Medieval Literature, From the Twelfth Century to Dante* (New York: Columbia UP, 1975) 94.

45. All references are to the Comfort translation.

46. Paul R. Lonigan, "The 'Cligés' and the Tristan Legend," *Studi Francesi* 18 (1974): 204–5.

47. J. P. Migne, *Patrologiae Cursus Completus, Series Latina*, 221 vols. (Paris: Garnier et Migne, 1844–1880) 22: 684; translation mine.

48. David J. Shirt, "*Cligés*—A Twelfth-Century Matrimonial Case-Book?" *Forum for Modern Language Studies* 18.1 (1982): 82–83.

49. Joan Ferrante, "The Education of Women in the Middle Ages in Theory, Fact and Fantasy," *Beyond Their Sex: Learned Women of the European Past*, ed. Patricia A. Labalme (New York: New York UP, 1980) 30; and Michelle A. Freeman, *The Poetics of "Translatio Studii" and "Conjointure": Chrétien de Troyes' "Cligés*," French Forum Monographs 12 (Lexington, KY: French Forum, 1979) 123–24.

50. See especially 204, 207.

51. Edmund Ross, *Sir Thomas Malory* (New York: Twayne, 1966) 110.

52. Larry D. Benson, *Malory's "Morte Darthur"* (Cambridge, MA: Harvard UP, 1976) 110.

53. For this insight I am indebted to my colleague Dr. Richard Griffith.

54. P. E. Tucker, "Chivalry in the *Morte*," *Essays on Malory*, ed. J. A. W. Bennett (Oxford: Clarendon P, 1963) 73.

55. Donald G. Schueler, "The Tristram Section of Malory's 'Morte Darthur,' " *Studies in Philology* 65 (1968): 59.

56. Schueler 59.

57. Schueler 60.

58. "Education of Women" 30.

59. Page Ann Du Bois, " 'The Devil's Gateway': Women's Bodies and the Earthly Paradise," *Women's Studies* 7.3 (1980): 47.

60. Joan Larsen Klein, "From Errour to Acrasia," *Huntington Library Quarterly* 41 (1978): 183; cf. Du Bois 47.

61. Charles Baxter, "Spider Lady: Images of Domination in Book II of *The Faerie Queene*," *Paunch* 35 (1974): 71.

62. Trans. Sir John Harington (1516; Bloomington: Indiana UP, 1963).

63. Trans. Edward Fairfax (1575; New York: Capricorn, 1963).

64. *The Complete Poetical Works of Spenser* (Boston: Houghton, 1936).

65. A. Bartlett Giamatti, *The Earthly Paradise and the Renaissance Epic* (Princeton: Princeton UP, 1966) 184.

66. Giamatti 141.

67. Robert M. Durling, "The Bower of Bliss and Armida's Palace," *Comparative Literature* 6 (1954): 342.

68. 252.

69. Baxter 92.

70. Baxter 92.

71. Patricia Parker, "The Progress of Phaedria's Bower: Spenser to Coleridge," *ELH* 40 (1973): 374; cf. Giamatti 187, 197.

72. Du Bois 47–49.

73. Susan Hannah, "Womb(an) Power: or a Faerie Tale of the Good, the Bad, and the Ugly," *RE: Artes Liberales* 5.1 (1978): 27.

74. Du Bois 44; cf. Giamatti 144.

75. Du Bois 48; cf. Giamatti 142.

76. Acrasia's baleful influence is reinforced by the story of Cymochles, who is kept on Phaedria's island by the allure of sensual comfort and sexual satisfaction, plus, in case these do not suffice, a soporific potion with which she anoints his eyes (II, vi).

77. N. S. Brooke, "C. S. Lewis and Spenser: Nature, Art, and the Bower of Bliss," *Essential Articles for the Study of Edmund Spenser*, ed. A. C. Hamilton (Hamden, CT: Archon, 1972) 24.

78. Giamatti 279.

79. Giamatti note 273.

80. Zailig Pollock, "Concupiscence and Intemperance in the Bower of Bliss," *Studies in English Literature* 20 (1980): 53.

81. Brooke 34.

82. "The Education of Women" 30.

83. "Book-Lined Cells: Women and Humanism in the Early Italian Renaissance," *Beyond Their Sex: Learned Women of the European Past*, ed. Patricia A. Labalme (New York: New York UP, 1980) 78. In an interesting sidelight on this matter, Roland Villeneuve, in *Le Poison and les empoisonneurs célèbres* (Paris: Le Palatin, 1960) 10, postulates this same intersection of intelligence and sexuality in historical female poisoners. According to Villeneuve, men are repelled by the use of poison, but women are not; in fact poison is a weapon *presque exclusivement féminine.* Poison is most often employed by *des femmes séduisantes ou très intelligentes,* which makes poison a weapon *d'autant plus redoubtable.*

84. Euripides, *Hippolytus* 1: 780, as quoted in Rogers 32–33.

85. O'Faolain and Martines 183.

86. O'Faolain and Martines xx.

4. WOMAN AND THE SERPENT

1. As quoted in Donald Campbell, *Arabian Medicine and Its Influence on the Middle Ages*, 2 vols. (London: Kegan Paul, 1926) 1: 161.

2. *Annales Premonstratenses*, trans. and quoted in R. W. Southern, *Western Society and the Church in the Middle Ages* (Baltimore: Penguin, 1970) 314; cf.

Penny Schine Gold, *The Lady and the Virgin: Image, Attitude and Experience in Twelfth-Century France* (Chicago: U of Chicago P, 1985) 88.

3. *PL* 14: 47/38 ff.

4. *PL* 14: 126/38.

5. *PL* 3: 182.

6. *PL* 22: 684.

7. George Lyman Kittredge, *Witchcraft in Old and New England* (New York: Atheneum, 1973) 224; cf. Russell note 15.

8. Russell 15, 29.

9. Coleman O. Parsons, "The Refining of Lamia," *Wordsworth Circle* 8 (1977): 190.

10. Russell 118.

11. Parsons 188.

12. Parsons 185.

13. J. A. MacCulloch, *Medieval Faith and Fable* (London: Harrap, 1932) 45.

14. M. Oldfield Howey, *The Encircled Serpent* (London: Rider, 1926) 330–32.

15. Coleman O. Parsons, "Primitive Sense in *Lamia*," *Folklore* 88 (1977): 204.

16. Nai-tung Ting, "The Holy Man and the Snake Woman: A Study of a Lamia Story in Asian and European Literature," *Fabula* 8 (n.d.): 148–50.

17. Howey 126–33.

18. Ting 189.

19. Plutarch, *Lives of the Noble Grecians and Romans*, trans. Sir Thomas North (c. 46–120; trans. 1579; rpt. New York: AMS P, 1967) 5: 372–431.

20. Sir Walter Map, *De Nugis Curialium (Courtier's Trifles)*, ed. and trans. M. R. James, rev. C. N. L. Brooke and R. A. B. Mynors (c. 1181–1182; Oxford: Clarendon P, 1983) 289–313.

21. G. R. Owst, *Literature and Pulpit in Medieval England* (New York: Barnes, 1961) 397.

22. Bartholomaeus Anglicus, *De Proprietatibus Rerum*, trans. John of Trevisa (c. 1250; Westminster: W. de Worde, 1495) 11.

23. Cited in George B. Pace, "The Scorpion in Chaucer's Merchant's Tale," *Modern Language Quarterly* 26 (1965): 372.

24. Pace 373–74.

25. Howey 77.

26. *The Travels of Sir John Mandeville*, trans. C. W. R. D. Moseley (c. 1356–1366; New York: Penguin, 1983) 53–54.

27. Elisabeth G. Gitter, "The Power of Women's Hair in the Victorian Imagination," *PMLA* 99.5 (1984): 936–53.

28. John Alcock, *Animal Behavior* (Sunderland, MA: Sinauer Associates, 1975) reverse of title page.

29. Alcock 177–78.

30. *The Dragons of Eden: Speculations on the Evolution of Human Intelligence* (New York: Ballantine, 1977) note 70.

31. Robert J. Nolan, "An Introduction to the English Version of *Mélusine*, a Medieval Prose Romance," diss., New York U, 1970; *DAI*, 31 (1971): 5370A (NYU).

32. Jean d'Arras, *Mélusine*, ed. A. K. Donald, EETS 68 (c. 1394; London: Kegan Paul, 1895). References to this work will be given by page number.

33. La Coudrette, *The Romans of Partenay, or of Lusignen, otherwise known as the Tale of Mélusine*, ed. W. W. Skeat, EETS 22 (c. 1396; London: Kegan Paul, 1866). References to this work will be given by line number.

34. Claude Lecouteux, *Mélusine et le Chevalier au Cynge* (Paris: Payot, 1982) 17; Nolan 69–86.

35. Nolan.

36. Matthew W. Morris, "A Critical Edition of *Mélusine*, a Fourteenth-Century Poem by Couldrette," *DAI* 38 (1978): 4160A (U of Georgia); Matthew W. Morris, "The 'History' of Lusignan: Myth of Origin," *Language Quarterly* 21.3–4 (1983): 30–32; E. S. Hartland, "The Romance of *Mélusine*," *Folklore* 24 (1913): 187.

37. Jacques Le Goff, "Melusina: Mother and Pioneer," *Time, Work, and Culture in the Middle Ages*, trans. Arthur Goldhammer (Chicago: U of Chicago P, 1980) 207.

38. Phillips 41.

39. Georges Duby, *The Knight, the Lady and the Priest: The Making of Modern Marriage in Medieval France*, trans. Barbara Bray (New York: Pantheon, 1983) 163; Warner 144–45; Michael M. Sheehan, "The Formation and Stability of Marriage in Fourteenth-Century England: Evidence of an Ely Register," *Mediaeval Studies* 33 (1971): 236–40.

40. Duby 215.

41. 217.

42. Phillips 143.

43. E.g., title page of EETS edition; also cf. Lillian M. C. Randall, *Images in the Margins of Gothic Manuscripts* (Berkeley and Los Angeles: U of California P, 1966) plate 249.

44. Lecouteux 48.

45. Duby 133.

46. Le Goff 219.

47. Lecouteux 48.

48. 219.

49. Warner 192–205.

50. 345–49.

51. Lecouteux 19, 180, 185–86; translation mine.

52. Hartland 200.

53. Nancy F. Cott, "Passionlessness: An Interpretation of Victorian Sexual Ideology, 1790–1850," *A Heritage of Her Own: Toward a New Social History of American Women*, ed. Nancy F. Cott and Elizabeth H. Pleck (New York: Simon, 1979) 172.

54. Carl N. Degler, "What Ought to Be and What Was: Women's Sexuality in the Nineteenth Century," *American Historical Review* 79.5 (1974): 1468.

55. Coleridge, "Christabel," *Coleridge: Poetical Works*, ed. Ernest Hartley Coleridge (1834; Oxford: Oxford UP, 1979), 213–36.

56. Russell 18.

57. Russell 235.

58. Russell 95.

59. Philostratus, *Life and Times of Apollonius of Tyana*, trans. Charles P. Eells, Stanford U Publications in Language and Literature 2.1 (c. 217; New York: AMS P, 1967) 106.

60. Miriam Allott, " 'Isabella,' 'The Eve of St. Agnes,' and 'Lamia,' " *John Keats: A Reassessment*, ed. Kenneth Muir (Liverpool: Liverpool UP, 1969) 49.

61. Keats, *Lamia, The Poetical Works and Other Writings of John Keats*, 8 vols., ed. H. Buxton Forman, rev. Maurice Buxton Forman (1820: New York: Phaeton Press, 1939; rpt. 1970) 3: 13–54.

62. Richard Harter Fogle, "Keats's *Lamia* as Dramatic Illusion," *Nineteenth-Century Literary Perspectives: Essays in Honor of Lionel Stevenson*, ed. Clyde deL. Ryals (Durham, NC: Duke UP, 1974) 68.

63. MacCulloch 45.

64. Jane Chambers, "Lamia and Burton's Love Melancholy," *Studies in English Literature* 22.4 (1982): 583–600.

65. Earl Wasserman, *The Finer Tone: Keats' Major Poems* (Baltimore: Johns Hopkins UP, 1953) 168.

66. Barry Gradman, *Metamorphosis in Keats* (New York: New York UP, 1980) 109.

67. " 'The Ballance of Good and Evil' in Keats's Letters and *Lamia*," *JEGP* 71 (1972): 6, 11.

68. Stanton Garner, "*Elsie Venner*: Holmes' Deadly 'Book of Life,' " *Huntington Library Quarterly* 37 (1974): 284.

69. Herman Melville, *The Confidence-Man: His Masquerade*, ed. Hershel Parker (1857; New York: Norton, 1971) 162–64.

70. All quotations are from the 1861 Houghton Mifflin edition; italics within the quotations are Holmes'.

71. Eleanor Tilton, *Amiable Autocrat: A Biography of Dr. Oliver Wendell Holmes* (New York: Schuman, 1947) 257–58.

72. Thorndike 2: 277–78; cf. N. M. Penzer, *Poison-Damsels and Other Essays in Folklore and Anthropology* (London: Sawyer, 1952) 14–18.

73. *Questions de médecine légale*, as quoted in Villeneuve 9.

74. According to Thorndike, Aelian (fl. third century) said Medea could kill "by mere touch" (1: 324); Gilbertus Anglicus (fl. c. 1230–1240) tells of "a girl fed on poison who caused the deaths of kings" (2: 483); other treatises on poison from the fourteenth to the seventeenth centuries continue to debate the matter (3: 238; 5: 551; 6: 420; 7: 205; 8: 577).

75. Thorndike 5: 485.

76. Mark 16: 17–18; Luke 10: 19.

77. Charles Boewe, "Reflex Action in the Novels of Oliver Wendell Holmes," *American Literature* 26 (1954): 313–19.

78. 29–41.

79. Gail Thain Parker discusses the theme of male and female adolescence in *Elsie Venner* in "Sex, Sentiment, and Oliver Wendell Holmes," *Women's Studies* 1 (1972): 47–63; see esp. 52–53.

80. Garner 294.

81. Deborah Gorham, *The Victorian Girl and the Feminine Ideal* (Bloomington: Indiana UP, 1982) 6.

82. Gorham 38.

83. Gorham 104.

84. Garner 297.

85. (London: J. Nichols, 1790; rpt. New York: Garland, 1978); see the discussion

of Darwin's reinterpretation of the Linnaean system in Daniel J. Boorstin, *The Discoverers* (New York: Vintage, 1985) 439.

86. Shirley Marchalonis, "Above Rubies: Popular Views of Medieval Women," *Journal of Popular Culture* 14.1 (1980): 89.

87. Marchalonis 91.

88. Marchalonis 92.

5. CONCLUSION: BEATRICE RAPPACCINI

1. From the *Testament of the Twelve Patriarchs*, as quoted in Bernard B. Prusack, "Woman: Seductive Siren and Source of Sin?" *Religion and Sexism: Images of Women in the Jewish and Christian Tradition*, ed. Rosemary Radford Ruether (New York: Simon, 1974) 93.

2. Entry for January 4, 1839. *The American Notebooks*, ed. Claude M. Simpson (1837–1853; Columbia: Ohio State UP, 1972) 184.

3. *The American Notebooks by Nathaniel Hawthorne*, ed. Randall Stewart (1837–1853; New Haven: Yale UP, 1932) 89, 93, 98; entries for October 27, 1841; January 23, 1842; and June 1, 1842.

4. *Hawthorne's Lost Notebook, 1835–1841* (University Park: Pennsylvania State UP, 1978) 59, 62.

5. Thorndike 5: 485.

6. *Sir Thomas Browne's Works, Including His Life and Correspondence*, ed. Simon Wilkins, 4 vols. (London: William Pickering, Josiah Fletcher Norwich, 1835; rpt. New York: Amsterdam P, 1968) volume II, book vii, chapter xvii, heading 3.

7. Frederick C. Crews, "Giovanni's Garden," *American Quarterly* 16 (1964): 407–8.

8. Richard Brenzo, "Beatrice Rappaccini: A Victim of Male Love and Horror," *American Quarterly* 48 (1976): 157–58.

9. David Lyttle, " 'Giovanni! My Poor Giovanni!' " *Studies in Short Fiction* 9 (1972): 153.

10. Charles Boewe, "Rappaccini's Garden," *American Literature* 30 (1958): 49.

11. F. L. Gwynne, "Hawthorne's 'Rappaccini's Daughter,' " *Nineteenth Century Fiction* 7 (1952): 217–19.

12. James Ellis, "Human Sexuality, the Sacrament of Matrimony, and the Paradox of the Fortunate Fall in *The Scarlet Letter*," *Christianity and Literature* 4 (1980): 53.

13. Stewart 11.

14. Stewart 66–68.

15. Jeannine Dobbs, "Hawthorne's Dr. Rappaccini and Father George Rapp," *American Literature* 43 (1971): 427–30.

16. "Rappaccini's Daughter," *Mosses from an Old Manse* (1846; Columbus: Ohio State UP, 1974) 91–128.

17. In a recent book on the Hawthorne story, Carole Marie Bensick's *La Nouvelle Beatrice: Renaissance and Romance in "Rappaccini's Daughter"* (New Brunswick: Rutgers UP, 1985), the author argues that Beatrice's poison is congenital syphilis inherited from her father, who is treating her with his own empirical remedies. Giovanni's fear is exacerbated by the syphilis outbreak in his home town, Naples,

c. 1495–1500. The thesis, while intriguing, presents several problems. First, Beatrice's effect on flowers, butterfly, and lizard must be downplayed to the point of rendering it a subjective perception of Giovanni. Second, Bensick's major source for the poison-damsel motif, Penzer's article, itself questions the validity of interpreting the damsel's poison as syphilis: "the time the disease takes to show itself is greatly against its use in a story where the effect has to be immediate and causing practically instantaneous death" (68). Finally, it is hard to see how, if syphilis is Dr. Rappaccini's bequest to his daughter, he can describe it as a marvelous gift. Nevertheless, the reader's attention is drawn to this book, which will be of interest to all students of Hawthorne's story.

18. Richard C. Sterne, "Hawthorne Transformed: Octavio Paz's *La hija de Rappaccini*," *Comparative Literature Studies* 13 (1976): 232.

19. Kathleen Gallagher, "The Art of Snake Handling in *Lamia, Elsie Venner*, and 'Rappaccini's Daughter,' " *Studies in American Fiction* 3 (1975): 57.

20. M. D. Uroff, "The Doctors in 'Rappaccini's Daughter,' " *Nineteenth Century Fiction* 27 (1972): 66–67.

21. Gallagher 59; Boewe 39.

22. Uroff 66.

23. 132–33.

24. Giamatti 126.

25. Giamatti 128.

26. Agnes McNeil Donohue, *Hawthorne: Calvin's Ironic Stepchild* (Kent, Ohio: Kent State UP, 1985) 173.

27. "Misogynism and Virginal Feminism in the Fathers of the Church," *Religion and Sexism: Images of Women in the Jewish and Christian Tradition*, ed. Rosemary Radford Ruether (New York: Simon, 1974) 158; italics are Ruether's.

Selected Bibliography

All sources are fully documented in the notes. The following bibliography highlights main primary and secondary sources (the former in readily available modern editions and translations) for the reader's convenience.

PRIMARY SOURCES

Ariosto, Ludovico. *Orlando Furioso*. Ed. Rudolf Gottfried. Trans. Sir John Harington. Bloomington: Indiana UP, 1963.

Boccaccio, Giovanni. *Concerning Famous Women*. Trans. Guido A. Guarino. New Brunswick: Rutgers UP, 1963.

Chaucer, Geoffrey. *The Riverside Chaucer*. Ed. Larry Benson. Boston: Houghton, 1987.

Chrétien de Troyes. *Cligés. Arthurian Romances*. Trans. W. W. Comfort. London: Everyman's Library, 1983.

Christine de Pizan. *The Book of the City of Ladies*. Trans. Earl Jeffrey Richards. New York: Persea, 1982.

d'Arras, Jean. *Mélusine*. Ed. A. K. Donald. EETS no. 68. London: Kegan Paul, 1895.

de Rojas, Fernando. *Celestina*. Trans. James Mabbe. New York: AMS P, 1967.

Euripedes. *Medea and Other Plays*. Trans. Philip Vellacott. New York: Penguin, 1963.

Faulkner, William. "A Rose for Emily." *The Portable Faulkner*. Ed. Malcolm Cowley. New York: Viking, 1967. 433–44.

Hawthorne, Nathaniel. "Rappaccini's Daughter." *Mosses from an Old Manse*. Columbus: Ohio State UP, 1974. 91–128.

Homer. *The Odyssey*. Trans. Robert Fitzgerald. New York: Doubleday/Anchor, 1961.

Jonson, Ben. *Sejanus*. Ed. Jonas Barish. New Haven: Yale UP, 1965.

Juvenal. *The Sixteen Satires*. Trans. Peter Green. New York: Penguin, 1967.

Keats, John. *Lamia. The Poetical Works and Other Writings of John Keats*. Ed. H. Buxton Forman. Rev. Maurice Buxton Forman. 8 vols. New York: Phaeton P, 1938; rpt. 1970. 3: 13–54.

Kesselring, Joseph. *Arsenic and Old Lace*. New York: Random House, 1941.

La Coudrette. *The Romans of Partenay, or of Lusignen, Otherwise Known as the Tale of Mélusine*. Ed. W. W. Skeat. EETS no. 22. London: Kegan Paul, 1866.

"Lord Randal." *The English and Scottish Popular Ballads*. Ed. F. J. Child. 5 vols. New York: Dover, 1965. 1: 160 (version D).

Malory, Sir Thomas. *Works*. Ed. Eugène Vinaver. 2d ed. Oxford. Oxford UP, 1977.

Mandeville, Sir John. *The Travels of Sir John Mandeville*. Trans. C. W. R. D. Moseley. New York: Penguin, 1983.

Marguerite de Navarre. *The Heptameron*. Trans. P. A. Chilton. New York: Penguin, 1984.

Marie de France. *The Lais of Marie de France*. Trans. and with an introduction and notes by Robert Hanning and Joan Ferrante. Durham, NC: Labyrinth P, 1978.

Melville, Herman. *The Confidence-Man: His Masquerade*. Ed. Hershel Parker. New York: Norton, 1971.

Middleton, Thomas. *The Witch. The Works of Thomas Middleton*. Ed. A. H. Bullen. New York: AMS P, 1964. 1.

———. *Women Beware Women*. Ed. J. R. Mulryne. London: Methuen, 1975.

Ovid. *The Erotic Poems*. Trans. Peter Green. New York: Penguin, 1982.

———. *The Metamorphoses*. Trans. Horace Gregory. New York: Mentor/NAL, 1960.

Sophocles. *Trachinian Women. The Complete Plays of Sophocles*. Trans. Sir Richard Claverhouse Jebb. Ed. Moses Hadas. New York: Bantam, 1982.

Spenser, Edmund. *The Faerie Queene. The Complete Poetical Works of Spenser*. Boston: Houghton, 1936.

Strassburg, Gottfried von. *Tristan*. Trans. A. T. Hatto. New York: Penguin, 1960.

Tasso, Torquato. *Jerusalem Delivered*. Trans. Edward Fairfax. New York: Capricorn, 1963.

The Tragedy of Master Arden of Faversham. Ed. M. L. Wine. London: Methuen, 1973.

SECONDARY SOURCES

Baines, Barbara. *The Lust Motif in the Plays of Thomas Middleton*. Jacobean Drama Studies 29. Salzburg: Institut für Englische Sprache und Literatur, 1973.

Belsey, Catherine. "Alice Arden's Crime." *Renaissance Drama* 8 (1982): 83–102.

Bensick, Carole Marie. *La Nouvelle Beatrice: Renaissance and Romance in "Rappaccini's Daughter."* New Brunswick: Rutgers UP, 1985.

Bowers, Fredson. "The Audience and the Poisoners of Elizabethan Tragedy." *JEGP* 36 (1937): 491–504.

Cherry, Caroline Lockett. *The Most Unvaluedst Purchase: Women in the Plays of Thomas Middleton*. Jacobean Drama Studies 34. Salzburg: Institut für Englische Sprache und Literatur, 1973.

Cott, Nancy F. "Passionlessness: An Interpretation of Victorian Sexual Ideology, 1790–1850." *A Heritage of Her Own: Toward a New Social History of American Women*. Ed. Nancy F. Cott and Elizabeth H. Pleck. New York: Simon, 1979. 162–81.

Drew-Bear, Annette. "Face-Painting in Renaissance Tragedy." *Renaissance Drama* 12 (1981): 71–93.

DuBois, Page Ann. " 'The Devil's Gateway': Women's Bodies and the Earthly Paradise." *Women's Studies* 7.3 (1980): 43–58.

Duby, Georges. *The Knight, the Lady and the Priest: The Making of Modern Marriage in Medieval France*. Trans. Barbara Bray. New York: Pantheon, 1983.

Ehrenreich, Barbara, and Deirdre English. *Witches, Midwives, and Nurses: A History of Women Healers*. Westbury, NY: Feminist P, 1973.

Ferrante, Joan. *The Conflict of Love and Honor: The Medieval Tristan Legend in France, Germany, and Italy*. The Hague and Paris: Mouton, 1973.

———. "The Education of Women in the Middle Ages in Theory, Fact, and Fantasy." *Beyond Their Sex: Learned Women of the European Past*. Ed. Patricia A. Labalme. New York: New York UP, 1980. 9–42.

———. *Woman as Image in Medieval Literature, from the Twelfth Century to Dante*. New York: Columbia UP, 1975.

Garner, Stanton. "*Elsie Venner*: Holmes' Deadly 'Book of Life.' " *Huntington Library Quarterly* 37 (1974): 283–98.

Giamatti, A. Bartlett. *The Earthly Paradise and the Renaissance Epic*. Princeton: Princeton UP, 1966.

Gies, Frances, and Joseph Gies. *Women in the Middle Ages*. New York: Barnes, 1978.

Gitter, Elisabeth. "The Power of Women's Hair in the Victorian Imagination." *PMLA* 99.5 (1984): 936–54.

Gold, Penny Schine. *The Lady and the Virgin: Image and Attitude in Twelfth-Century France*. Chicago: U of Chicago P, 1985.

Gorham, Deborah. *The Victorian Girl and the Feminine Ideal*. Bloomington: Indiana UP, 1982.

Harksen, Sybille. *Women in the Middle Ages*. New York: Schram, 1975.

Hartman, Mary S. *Victorian Murderesses*. New York: Schocken, 1977.

Hirsch, Miriam. *Women and Violence*. New York: Van Nostrand/Reinhold, 1981.

Hughes, Muriel. *Women Healers in Medieval Life and Literature*. New York: Books for Libraries P, 1943.

Jones, Ann. *Women Who Kill*. New York: Holt, 1980.

King, Margaret L. "Book-Lined Cells: Women and Humanism in the Early Italian Renaissance." *Beyond Their Sex: Learned Women of the European Past*. Ed. Patricia A. Labalme. New York: New York UP, 1980. 66–90.

Kittredge, George Lyman. *Witchcraft in Old and New England*. New York: Atheneum, 1973.

Leggatt, Alexander. " 'Arden of Faversham.' " *Shakespeare Studies* 36 (1983): 121–33.

Le Goff, Jacques. "Melusina: Mother and Pioneer." *Time, Work, and Culture in the Middle Ages*. Trans. Arthur Goldhammer. Chicago: U of Chicago P, 1980. 205–22.

Lonigan, Paul R. "The 'Cligés' and the Tristan Legend." *Studi Francesi* 18 (1974): 201–12.

McElwee, William. *The Murder of Sir Thomas Overbury*. London: Faber, 1952.

Marchalonis, Shirley. "Above Rubies: Popular Views of Medieval Women." *Journal of Popular Culture* 14.1 (1980): 87–93.

O'Faolain, Julia, and Lauro Martines. *Not in God's Image: Women in History from the Greeks to the Victorians*. New York: Harper, 1973.

Parker, Gail Thain. "Sex, Sentiment, and Oliver Wendell Holmes." *Women's Studies* 1 (1972): 47–63.

Parker, Patricia. "The Progress of Phaedria's Bower: Spenser to Coleridge." *ELH* 40 (1973): 372–97.

Parsons, Coleman O. "Primitive Sense in *Lamia*." *Folklore* 88 (1977): 203–10.

———. "The Refining of Lamia." *Wordsworth Circle* 8 (1977): 183–92.

Penzer, N. M. *Poison-Damsels and Other Essays in Folklore and Anthropology.* London: Sawyer, 1952.

Phillips, John A. *Eve: The History of an Idea.* San Francisco: Harper, 1984.

Prusack, Bernard M. "Woman: Seductive Siren and Source of Sin?" *Religion and Sexism: Images of Women in the Jewish and Christian Tradition.* Ed. Rosemary Radford Ruether. New York: Simon, 1974. 89–116.

Ribner, Irving. "Middleton's *Women Beware Women*: Poetic Imagery and the Moral Vision." *Tulane Studies in English* 9 (1959): 19–33.

Rogers, Katherine M. *The Troublesome Helpmate: A History of Misogyny in Literature.* Seattle: U of Washington P, 1966.

Ruether, Rosemary Radford. "Misogynism and Virginal Feminism in the Fathers of the Church." *Religion and Sexism: Images of Women in the Jewish and Christian Tradition.* New York: Simon, 1974. 150–83.

Russell, Jeffrey Burton. *Witchcraft in the Middle Ages.* Ithaca: Cornell UP, 1972.

Sheehan, Michael M. "The Formation and Stability of Marriage in Fourteenth-Century England: Evidence of an Ely Register." *Medieval Studies* 33 (1971): 228–63.

Shirt, David J. "*Cligés*—A Twelfth-Century Matrimonial Case-Book?" *Forum for Modern Language Studies* 18.1 (1982): 75–89.

Truchet, Sibyl. "Alice Arden and the Religion of Love." *Caliban* 17 (1980): 39–44.

Warner, Marina. *Alone of All Her Sex: The Myth and the Cult of the Virgin Mary.* New York: Vintage, 1983.

White, Beatrice. *Cast of Ravens: The Strange Case of Sir Thomas Overbury.* London: Murray, 1965.

Wilson, Patrick. *Murderess: A Study of the Women Executed in Britain since 1843.* London: Michael Joseph, 1971.

Index

Addison, Thomas, 22
Against Our Will (Brownmiller), 12
Aging, women and, 86–87
Alcock, John, *Animal Behavior*, 98–99
Alexander the Great, 120–21, 125–26,
  133, 134
Allopathic medicine, 117, 138
  See also Homeopathic medicine
Ambrose, St., 90
Anatomy of Melancholy (Burton), 59,
  67, 113, 114, 117
Ancrene Riwle, 95, 96
Andreas Capellanus, 72
Animal Behavior (Alcock), 98–99
Animals, venomous
  and homeopathic medicine, 22–23,
    134–35
  moral significance of, 21, 89–90,
    100
  and women, 89–90, 94–95, 96–97
  See also Basilisk; Dog; Dragon; Eel;
    Lamia; Lizard; Scorpion; Serpent;
    Spider
Antidotes, 22–23, 29, 137–39
Aphrodisiac. *See Venefica*; Witchcraft
Arachne, xiv, 55–56, 84
Arden of Faversham, 26–32, 37, 57–
  58
  adultery and poisoning in, 26–27,
    31–32
  oath breaking in, 29–30
  poison as woman's weapon in, 27–
    29
  poison in wine in, 29

poison lore in, 26–27, 28–30, 50
Ariosto, Ludovico, *Orlando Furioso*,
  79–81
  entrapment in, 80–81
  shape shifting in, 80–81
  witchcraft in, 80–81
Aristotle, 125
Arnaldus of Villanova, *Breviarum
  Practicae*, 89
Arsenic and Old Lace (Kesselring), 1–
  4, 10
Asp. *See* Serpent
Augustine, St., 16, 90, 140
Avicenna, *Canon Medicinae*, 2, 21, 22,
  29

Bacci, Andrea, *De Venenis et Antido-
  tis*, 121, 134
Bacon, Roger, *De Erroribus Medico-
  rum*, 25
Baldung-Grün, Hans
  "The Bewitched Groom and the
    Witch's Curse," 65
  "The Love-Spell," 11
Barfield, Velma Margie, xii
Bartholomaeus Anglicus, 95
Basilisk
  and fascination, 92
  and malevolent influence, 28, 50, 94
  and sex, 94, 124
Belsey, Catherine, 32
Bensick, Carol Marie, 139
Benvenuto, Richard, 117

About the Author

MARGARET HALLISSY is a Professor of English at Long Island University. She has published articles in such journals as *Studies in the Novel*, *Studies in Short Fiction*, and *Renascence*.